THE GORBACHEV GENERATION

ISSUES IN SOVIET FOREIGN POLICY

THE GORBACHEV GENERATION

ISSUES IN SOVIET FOREIGN POLICY

Edited by
Jane Shapiro Zacek

A PWPA Book

PARAGON HOUSE
New York

Published in the United States by
Professors World Peace Academy
GPO 1311
New York, New York 10116

Distributed by
Paragon House Publishers
90 Fifth Avenue
New York, New York 10011

A Professors World Peace Academy Book

The Professors World Peace Academy (PWPA) is an international association of professors, scholars, and academics from diverse backgrounds
devoted to issues concerning world peace. PWPA sustains a program of
conferences and publications on topics in peace studies, area and cultural studies, national and international development, education,
economics, and international relations.

Library of Congress Cataloging-in-Publication Data

The Gorbachev generation: issues in soviet foreign policy.

    "A PWPA Book"
    Includes Index.
    1. Soviet Union—Foreign relations – 1975 -
2. Soviet Union – Politics and government – 1982 -
3. Gorbachev, Mikhail Sergeevich, 1931 -
I. Zacek, Jane Shapiro.
DK289.G68 1988   327.47   87-21415
ISBN 0-943852-40-4
ISBN 0-943852-41-2 (pbk.)

Printed in the United States of America

Table of Contents

PREFACE

The Gorbachev Generation: Issues in Soviet Foreign Policy, is designed to review important foreign policy issues and policy choices facing the new leadership in the Soviet Union. Leonid Brezhnev, General Secretary of the Communist Party of the Soviet Union (CPSU) and Chairman of the Presidium of the Supreme Soviet, died in November 1982. During the following 28 months, two additional men occupied both of these positions: Yuri Andropov, from November 1982 to February 1984; and Konstantin Chernenko, from February 1984 until March 1985. Both were elderly and ill, and it was clear that the succession would not be completed until a younger leader was confirmed in office. Mikhail Gorbachev, then 54, was named General Secretary in March 1985. The Supreme Soviet position remained empty until July of that year, when longtime Foreign Minister Andrei Gromyko was named to fill it, thereby relinquishing his position in the Foreign Ministry. As Gorbachev seeks to consolidate his authority, it is an appropriate time for western students of Soviet affairs to consider the major issues that the General Secretary must attend to. While the volume does not attempt to raise all the important foreign policy issues facing current Soviet leaders, it does raise many of the major ones.

It is important for students of Soviet politics, from those in undergraduate classrooms to those preparing policy recommendations for American officials directly involved in Soviet-American relations, to identify those issues and consider how the Soviets might act (or choose not to act) on them. No other existing volume examines issues facing the Gorbachev leadership and suggests possible Soviet responses. For this reason, the book is timely, important, and useful. It is also written with the interests of the general public in mind, and has avoided the jargon and minute detail of books designed for specialists. Consequently, the volume should enjoy a large and varied readership.

All of the chapters were especially prepared for this volume and all authors were invited to a review conference, organized and sponsored by Professors World Peace Academy in Portland, Maine in September 1986. This volume is the result of a collaborative effort of scholars knowledgeable and concerned about Soviet affairs. Kim Carney, William Fletcher, Šumit Ganguly, Darrell Hammer, James Hansen, Roger Kanet, John Karch, Ilpyong Kim, Donald Klein, Susan Linz, Harlow Robinson, Thomas Robinson, Alvin Rubinstein, Rolf Theen, Ivan Volgyes, and David Williams participated in the conference. They thoughtfully and carefully critiqued each potential chapter. (A number of chapters will appear in the companion volume on domestic politics.) The chapters were subsequently revised in accordance with the comments and suggestions and completed in mid-1987. Gorbachev has moved rapidly to adopt and implement a variety of important policies. Consequently, much has happened since these chapters were completed, and no volume on Soviet affairs can hope to include the latest policy and personnel shifts. Nonetheless, each chapter is a solid contribution toward understanding contemporary Soviet policies and strategies in the area under consideration.

We are grateful to Professors World Peace Academy for its continuing support of this project, especially Gordon Anderson, Secretary General of PWPA-USA, Publications Director Nancy Farlow and her successor, Marilyn Morris, and Barbara Kubo, without whom the Portland conference would not have been the success it was. We are also grateful to Ken Stuart, editor-in-chief of Paragon House Publishers, who believed this was an important project.

Finally, I am grateful to my family, who cheerfully tolerated the long hours involved in putting this volume together. Their understanding and encouragement helped move the project along to completion.

J.S.Z.

MAJOR FOREIGN POLICY ISSUES AND CHALLENGES FACING THE GORBACHEV LEADERSHIP

Jane Shapiro Zacek

In the period when a new leader in the Soviet Union seeks to consolidate his political power through both successful policy implementation and personnel changes, he typically (and sensibly) concentrates on pressing domestic problems rather than on foreign policy issues. In this context, while it is important to adopt measures that will ease international tensions and try to correct egregious errors of the previous leadership, the main focus is likely to remain on the domestic situation. However, domestic policy cannot and should not be separated from foreign policy. There is need for limited involvement abroad and for improved relations with major foreign powers in order to concentrate on domestic needs; if those needs are related to better functioning of the economy, then enhanced possibilities for foreign trade and investment through an improved international climate will be beneficial. Similarly, a more aggressive (but not necessarily more militaristic) foreign policy will result when the domestic situation is in less need of attention (unless the leadership calculates that it needs a major foreign policy "breakthrough" or "success" in order to bolster domestic support).

This volume examines a number of important foreign policy issues and challenges that the Gorbachev leadership faces now. Thus far, that leadership has acted predictably in seeking to reduce tensions with a number of states (for its own direct advantage) and to limit its support of potentially revolutionary situations abroad. At the same time, the Soviets have emphasized their role as a major power in Asia and the Pacific, while not relinquishing that same role in Europe. The new leadership has not been passive in international relations but, during the past two years, with the exception of continued support for terrorist elements in the Middle East and participation in the protracted war in Afghanistan, it has limited its direct involvement. At the same time, Gorbachev has differentiated his foreign policy initiatives from those of his two immediate predecessors, who generally continued the Brezhnev policies, and permitted a holdover of foreign policy personnel. Indeed, Foreign Minister Andrei Gromyko not only retained his position but enhanced it and appears to have played an even more important role after 1982 than he did while Brezhnev was alive. Additionally, Brezhnev's foreign policy advisers continued as advisers to both Yuri Andropov and Konstantin Chernenko, but were replaced after Gorbachev came to power, as was Gromyko himself. Input from foreign policy specialists in the relevant ministries, CPSU Central Committee (CC) departments, and prestigious academic institutes of the Soviet Academy of Sciences has continued and perhaps been expanded under Gorbachev. However, the CPSU Politburo still determines foreign policy directions. (In this regard, a number of western specialists have pointed out that while the Foreign Minister and the Chairman of the Committee on State Security (KGB) are full members of the Politburo, the Minister of Defense remains a candidate or nonvoting member. Since 1973, and occasionally prior to that, all three had been voting members.)

John J. Karch's opening essay, "Soviet Foreign Policy in the 1980s," provides an overview of the main issues currently facing the Gorbachev leadership. As Karch sees it, the Soviets will need to handle important challenges in their relationships with several East European countries, with the US (especially in arms control negotiations), with the People's Republic of China (PRC) and, more broadly, with the Third World.

Many of the East European Communist Party (CP) leaders are elderly (East Germany's Erich Honecker and Bulgaria's Todor Zhivkov were both born in 1912) and have held their positions of authority for decades. Their successors are likely to come to power within the next few years. As in the past, the Soviet leadership will ensure that the new leaders maintain basic loyalty to Moscow as well as continued CP rule within their own states. The Soviets will, therefore, keep a close eye on how the successions proceed. The situation in Poland, with General Jaruzelski still at the helm, is far from resolved, and it remains to be seen whether the Gorbachev administration will offer new and constructive ideas on how to contain the continuing unrest satisfactorily.

Soviet-US relations have improved substantially since the early years of the Reagan administration. The first two Reagan-Gorbachev summit meetings (Geneva in 1985, Reykjavik in 1986) did not produce substantive agreements on arms control or arms reductions. Negotiations accelerated during 1987, and an important breakthrough in nuclear arms reductions occurred

3

in late 1987: on December 8, in Washington, Reagan and Gorbachev signed a treaty on the elimination of intermediate range and shorter-range missiles, called the INF Treaty. As of this writing, the Treaty has been submitted to the US Senate for ratification. The importance of the Treaty is that it calls for the elimination of nuclear weapons rather than limiting their growth, as the SALT (Strategic Arms Limitations Talks) agreements did during the 1970s. (SALT I was ratified by the Senate and went into effect, while SALT II was withdrawn by President Carter, without ratification.) A fourth summit meeting between Reagan and Gorbachev was scheduled for late May 1988 in Moscow.

By late 1986, the Gorbachev leadership had decided to try to find a way out of the impasse in Afghanistan. First came the announcement of a withdrawal of Soviet troops from the area. Soon thereafter came the Afghan CP leader's call for a cease-fire and reconciliation of the disparate political factions within the country. By March 1988, Moscow and Washington had agreed to the terms of a Soviet withdrawal, scheduled to begin in May 1988. There is no doubt that the Soviets were anxious to extricate themselves from an unpopular and costly conflict, although whether they will retain essential influence over the country and communist party control within it remains to be seen.

Since Nikita Khrushchev's ouster in October 1964, each Soviet leader has attempted to improve relations with the People's Republic of China on the state level. Relations between the two communist parties continue to be poor and are likely to remain so. Some progress, however, has been made. The volume of Sino-Soviet trade has expanded, the Sino-Soviet border has remained quiet, and the Soviets have talked of reducing the number of troops stationed near that long border. In Gorbachev's July 1986 speech at Vladivostok, in which he called for a greater Soviet role in the Pacific, he seemed to suggest a willingness to reconcile differences with other powers in the region, especially China and Japan. With a volatile political situation in China, Gorbachev and his advisers may believe that it is easier to negotiate with Deng Xiaoping now than it will be with his successors.

In this period of Gorbachev's continuing consolidation of his political authority and attention toward critical foreign policy issues and areas, less attention is likely to be focused on the Third World in general, although targets of opportunity will doubtless not be forfeited intentionally.

Finally, with the appointment of new top-level foreign policy advisers and the selection of a foreign minister without previous foreign policy experience, Gorbachev signalled that he intends to play a major role in the formulation and direction of foreign policy. Current strategy seems designed to produce a renewed detente with the West, particularly with the US, as well as a rapprochement with the leading powers in Asia.

Rolf H.W. Theen's chapter, "Domestic Factors in the Making of Soviet Foreign Policy," reviews elements that contribute to the Soviet leadership's assessment of state and party interests in the world arena and the possibility of influencing events favorably. Among these are: geography (the sheer size of the largest country on earth, its span across Europe and Asia, its long land borders with countries from Finland to Iran to North Korea, and its consequent vulnerability due to lack of natural barriers); demography (a multinational state of almost 300 million, with many nationalities living across international boundaries, labor shortages in the industrialized regions of the country and surpluses in other regions, and little success thus far in redressing the balance); domestic economic weakness in contrast with military strength; and ideology (difficult to determine its influence but dangerous for Western observers and policy makers to ignore).

Theen also inquires into the making of foreign policy: what are the relevant institutions, how do they relate to one another, how do the various CPSU Central Committee departments involved with foreign, defense, and national security policy relate to one another, how do various CPSU Central Committee departments involved with foreign, defense, and national security policy relate to the Ministry of Foreign Affairs, the Ministry of Defense, and the KGB? What are the roles of various research institutes? Of Gorbachev's personally selected foreign policy advisers? While it is impossible to know with certainty the answers to these important and related questions, consideration of them is central toward understanding how Soviet foreign policies are determined.

Thomas W. Robinson's contribution, "Triple Detente? The Strategic Triangle in the Late Twentieth Century," surveys current relations among the US, the USSR, and the PRC and inevitably discusses some of the themes of the preceding two chapters. Soviet relations with the other two members of the triangle remain critical, and high on the foreign policy agenda.

Robinson starts from the premise that relations among all three states have improved during the 1980s, especially Sino-Soviet and Soviet-American relations. (Sino-American relations had improved markedly during the 1970s, but have declined in recent years.) Further, improved bilateral relations need (and should) not be viewed as occurring at the expense of the third member of the triangle, which had been the case earlier.

During the 1980s, each of the three countries has paid greater attention to the domestic economic and social problems inherited from previous regimes. In the United States, the "Reagan revolution" was characterized by substantial tax cuts, initial high unemployment and recession, a large military buildup, an enormous and expanding national debt, reduced federal government spending, and a reordering of federal spending priorities. Deng Xiaoping's "four modernizations" in the PRC put agriculture first and national defense last on the agenda, opened China to unprecedented expansion in foreign trade, foreign investment, and development, while reducing the restrictions imposed by a centrally planned economy and permitting a limited market-oriented pricing structure. Gorbachev's initial efforts to address the stagnant Soviet economy include managerial rejuvenation, substantial investment, decentralized economic decision-making, and greater worker involvement in getting the job done and getting it done well. Gorbachev also needs to counteract mass apathy and translate it into active support for building the communist society. Enlisting foreign policies to support domestic needs seems to characterize the current situation in all three countries, perhaps less in the US than in the others; increased attention to the national debt problem has had a decided effect on US foreign trade policies, however, and will have an impact on Congress's review of the defense budget, particularly if it appears that the Soviets have decided to limit their defense spending in light of domestic needs.

Domestic needs have improved bilateral relations for each of the three members of the strategic triangle, which all three recognize. Further, improved relations are likely to have a substantial impact on other regions of the world where Sino-Soviet-American relations intersect. Arrangements for mutual noninterference, especially in Soviet-American relations (i.e., Eastern Europe and Central America) and caution in those regions where a flare-up could pull states into direct confrontation (i.e., the Middle East and Southwest Asia) are likely to occur. Sino-Soviet relations are more complicated, for the Soviets are not likely to give up their foothold in Vietnam or to reduce their efforts at influence within the Third World in favor of the PRC.

In addition to examining the strategic triangle and relations among its three members, Robinson suggests the importance of external forces that operate on the triangle, particularly Japan and Western Europe, economic giants but not military ones (especially Japan), middle powers (including India, Brazil, Indonesia), and international troublemakers such as Libya and Cuba.

Trond Gilberg reviews Soviet policy toward Western Europe, an area of major but not paramount importance to Moscow (the Soviet-American relationship continues to dominate). Western

Europe is important historically (Marxist ideology is West European-based, the new Soviet state expected communist revolutions in the West to provide essential support, and Russia—and the Soviet Union—have in modern times been invaded more from the West than from any other direction) and economically (by providing needed goods, especially technology, as well as markets and investment). A continuing Soviet policy toward Western Europe has been to treat the region separately from the US, in order to reduce and limit American influence in Europe, especially militarily and economically. Andropov's unsuccessful attempt to rouse Western European public opinion into insisting that their respective governments refuse to permit the US intermediate range ballistic missiles on their soil is but one in a long line of Soviet efforts to decouple Western Europe from the US. Gorbachev has also attempted to fan West European opposition to Reagan's Strategic Defense Initiative (SDI) and enlist it as support for his own campaign to convince the US to slow down (if not end) pursuit of that policy, believed especially threatening to the Soviets.

Gilberg details Soviet bilateral relations with a number of specific Western European states, including the FRG, the Scandinavian countries, Greece, and Iceland. The current Soviet leadership is continuing a well-established policy of differentiating among European states as well as developing an increasingly sophisticated understanding of internal political conditions in states in which they are particularly interested.

Still, Moscow has not substantially improved relations with Western Europe thus far, although this may change, depending not only on policy decisions in Moscow and European capitals but in Washington as well. Unpopular US policies and actions (such as in Central America) play directly into Soviet hands, especially the skilled and sophisticated ones currently in control in the Kremlin.

Moving eastward, Ivan Volgyes explores the current Soviet-East European relationship from the East European vantage point. He argues that it doesn't make sense to consider East Europe as a bloc with common interests and agendas with the USSR, any more than it does to consider West Europe in that way. In dealing with the Soviets, East Europeans emphasize the uniqueness of their internal conditions and their relationship with the USSR. The Soviets are interested primarily in controlling ideological diversity, ensuring that the East European CPs remain firmly in control of their respective political, social, and economic systems, guaranteeing that the military alliance (Warsaw Treaty Organization—WTO) remains intact, and that the economic ties, both multilateral (through the Council of Mutual Economic Assistance—CMEA) and bilateral (trade and investment) are strengthened.

For most East European states, economic relations with the USSR are critical. East Europeans are dissatisfied with many costs imposed upon them, including additional military spending mandated through the WTO (increasing the East European burden although not reducing the Soviets'), the high cost of fuel supplied by Moscow to a generally fuel-deficient region (despite the precipitous decline in fuel prices on the world market), and established prices for goods that must be delivered to the Soviets (sometimes lower than the prices on the world market). From the Soviet point of view, East Europe is an economic liability, with Soviet subsidies necessary (and provided) at critical points (Czechoslovakia after 1968, Poland in 1976 and again after 1980).

Further, as noted earlier, most East European leaders are of the Brezhnev rather than the Gorbachev generation. Most have served in office for a long time; those who have come to power recently are scarcely newcomers in experience or outlook (Albania's Ramiz Alia has long been on the national political scene in a country known for political intrigue and infighting, and Czechoslovakia's Milos Jakes, longtime Central Committee member, headed the Party's Central Control and Auditing Commission, which was responsible for expelling from the Party members deemed "untrustworthy" after the Prague Spring and Soviet-led invasion of 1968). Most of the leaders are concerned the Soviets may seek to reestablish greater authority, particularly with their successors. For the past several years, during the rapid succession of Soviet leaders, East Europe may have enjoyed more autonomy than has typically been permitted, and may continue to do so while Gorbachev consolidates his political authority and focuses on crucial domestic and foreign policy issues facing the USSR. This situation, however, is unlikely to last indefinitely. East European states need to proceed carefully while implementing domestic reforms and building trade and economic relations with Western Europe and the US. Precipitous moves and pronouncements may push the Soviets into insisting upon greater conformity than they have in recent years.

While Soviet interests in Eastern Europe are well-defined and permanent, their interests in the Third World are more general and unspecific. As Daniel R. Kempton and Roger E. Kanet see it, Soviet aims in Africa include reducing both the Western and Chinese influence and presence on that continent, enlisting African support for the Soviet position on various international issues, spreading Marxism-Leninism, and encouraging the establishment and maintenance of friendly regimes. There are several more specific objectives as well: obtaining access to military bases and facilities, and acquiring needed hard currency from arms sales (although prices are often set artificially low in order to gain influence or undercut Western sales). Generally, Soviet policies in Africa seemed more successful in the 1970s than in the 1980s. Efforts to create and sustain one-party Marxist or Marxist-style regimes on the continent produced favorable results, for a time, in the 1960s, as these countries extricated themselves from colonial rule and sought viable political structures. As Soviet-style regimes collapsed, were substantially modified, or turned anti-Soviet in orientation, Moscow sought better relations with non-Marxist regimes sharing mutual interests, such as anti-American sentiment because of US support for Israel, general antagonism toward the West because of the legacy of colonialism, or establishment and maintenance of one-party rule as a means of moving the country toward modernization. Soviet military and economic support of revolutionary movements in Mozambique, Angola, and elsewhere proved generally successful. In supporting such revolutionary efforts, the Soviets have tried (not always successfully) not to antagonize regimes in neighboring pro-Soviet states. (By supporting the revolutionary movement in Ethiopia, for example, the Soviets inevitably forfeited support from neighbor-state Somalia because of continued hostility between the two African states.)

The Soviets (and Cubans) have stationed substantial numbers of advisers and technicians in Africa, which are costly to the host states. In fact, several (Ethiopia, Angola) have insisted on reducing the number of advisers to more manageable proportions. The Soviets are less willing now to provide massive economic and military assistance than they were in the 1970s when chances of establishing durable allies on the continent seemed more promising. In view of pressing domestic concerns, the Soviets need to select carefully those regimes they decide to support financially. Currently, there appear to be only a limited number, and Soviet military and economic aid is likely to be substantially less than the recipient countries expect or need.

Soviet efforts to build support in the Middle East, from Turkey to Afghanistan, have had their share of successes and failures. Alvin Z. Rubinstein suggests that Soviet-Middle East policy is characterized by substantial military capability and commitment, active involvement in Middle East events, willingness to use military force to support client-states, and recognition of the promising and potentially friendly environment in which to pursue particular interests.

While the Soviets seek benefits from anti-Israeli, anti-American, and anti-Western orientation in many of the states in the region, they recognize the need for a long-term view, rather than insisting upon immediate gains. The Iranian revolution, for example, that overthrew the Shah and established a fundamentalist Islamic regime, hostile to the West and the US in particular, has not been pro-Soviet, but the Soviets may well believe that over time better relations are likely to develop. Having failed to build a staunch ally in Egypt (at considerable financial cost), since the mid-1970s the Soviets have sought support from the most dissatisfied elements in the area, especially Syria, Libya, and the PLO, and have discouraged any significant settlement between Israel and its Arab neighbors.

In the Persian Gulf, the Soviets have obtained access to important naval and air facilities in South Yemen, although efforts to establish diplomatic relations with Saudi Arabia (a continuing Soviet goal) have not yet proved successful. In general, in this region the Soviets are hampered by widespread fear of and opposition to communist rule as well as the belief that Moscow is anti-Islam and therefore dangerous.

According to Rubinstein, such concerns seem minimal in Libya, the country in Moslem North Africa most closely aligned with Moscow. In the past decade, the Soviets have sold more than $15 billion worth of military goods to Libya, and a large number of Soviet and East European technical and security forces have been stationed in that country. Still, the Soviets recognize the unpredictable and potentially dangerous behavior of Muammar Qaddafi and do not want to be drawn into a conflict on his behalf, especially against the US.

Apart from Afghanistan, the current Soviet leadership does not appear to have focused on the Middle East and has not expressed views on how to handle the problems and relationships inherited from the Brezhnev period. By accelerating the provision of military supplies to Syria, Libya and South Yemen during 1985-86, the Soviets are not signalling a policy reassessment in the area and do not seem interested in finding a satisfactory political solution to continuing unrest and violence. By coming to a resolution of the Afghan conflict, though, they may be able to improve relations with other countries in the region, particularly Pakistan; Soviet-Pakistani relations have declined precipitously, while Soviet-Indian relations improved markedly during Indira Gandhi's tenure in office.

Turning to South Asia, Šumit Ganguly assesses the nature of the Soviet-Indian relationship, which he considers paramount in the region. The Soviets have capitalized on India's distrust of both the PRC and the US compounded by American willingness to support Pakistan at India's expense. The Soviets have supplied economic and military aid to New Delhi, especially when the West was not willing to do so, and has continued to support Indian positions (on Bangladesh and Kashmir) at the UN and in other international gatherings. For its part, the Soviet Union needs India to balance and contain Chinese influence in Asia, especially in south and southwest Asia. The rapid improvement of Sino-American relations in the mid and late 1970s reinforced this need.

Within the past several years, India has begun to open its economy to increased foreign investment. Initiated by Prime Minister Indira Gandhi, her son and successor Rajiv Gandhi has made this a major policy objective, encouraging foreign investment by US technology firms in particular, in order to expand India's technological base. The Soviets are not able to supply the kind, quantity, and quality of high technology goods as has the West. Still, continued US support for Pakistan is likely to limit the improvement of US-Indian relations. The Soviet withdrawal from Afghanistan is likely to result in reduced US military aid to Pakistan, which might prompt India to seek a more balanced position between the Soviet Union and the United States.

Moving from south to east Asia, an arena of continued potential and sometimes real Sino-Soviet rivalry is Korea, North Korea in particular. Ilpyong J. Kim argues that recent events, especially the marked improvement in relations between North Korea and the USSR, have not resulted in a decline in North Korean-

Chinese relations. Rather, North Korean-Soviet developments should be viewed within the context of Sino-Soviet-North Korean relations, all of which have improved during the past several years. In this regard, 1982 may be considered something of a watershed, the year that included China's adoption of an "independent foreign policy" (neither obviously pro-American or pro-Soviet, as proclaimed at the Party's XII Congress), and the death of Brezhnev, which paved the way for improved Sino-Soviet and Soviet-North Korean relations. Kim recounts briefly the nature of North Korean relations with both the USSR and the PRC prior to the current period, and suggests reasons for improved relations between Moscow and Pyongyang. He also points out the care that the North Koreans have taken to consult continuously with leaders in Beijing, in order to forestall Chinese fears that more cordial Soviet-North Korean relations are achieved only at China's direct expense. High-level meetings were held between Korean and Chinese leaders before and after each Korean-Soviet meeting.

North Korean leader Kim Il Sung, despite his efforts, was not invited to visit the USSR during Brezhnev's eighteen years in power. Since Brezhnev's death, he has paid two visits, which have served his country well, both economically and politically. The most recent visit, in October 1986, resulted in substantial Soviet economic assistance, including cancellation of a $700 million credit that North Korea was in no position to finance, let alone begin to repay, and possible military assistance, in response to US-Japanese-South Korean security arrangements. Perhaps equally important from Kim's point of view was Soviet acquiescence to the arranged succession in Pyongyang: Kim's son Kim Jong Il is scheduled to formally succeed his father as leader of the CP and the state. For their part, the Soviets gained overflight and naval base rights in Korea, as well as Kim's well-publicized support for the Soviets' intention to play a greater role in the Pacific. Gorbachev has also suggested that the Soviets will actively participate in seeking a solution to the Korean reunification problem, a position that North Korea has heartily welcomed. Whether the Soviets will in fact become more involved in that process than they have in the past remains to be seen.

As the Soviet Union turns its attention more toward the Far East and the Pacific than it had during the Brezhnev-Andropov-Chernenko periods, it will actively seek better accommodation with the PRC (which appears more within its grasp now than at any previous time since the late 1950s) and perhaps with Japan as well. Whether the Soviets are ready to confront the divisive issues hampering better relations with Japan is not yet clear. A Soviet-Japanese rapprochement would serve both states well. The Soviets, as exemplified in their recently stated decision to implement wide-scale computerization, need Japanese technology. The Japanese need markets, and the USSR would be a vast and made-to-order one, especially for information technology. The Japanese also need natural resources, especially fuels, which are abundantly available in Siberia for exploitation and export. While there were some efforts to reach agreement on substantial Japanese investment in Siberian resources (with repayment mostly in raw materials) after the Middle East oil crisis of the early 1970s, these efforts were not sustained and did not develop into long-term, mutually beneficial arrangements. Should another international oil crisis develop, with OPEC nations carefully limiting production and driving up prices, renewed Japanese interest in Soviet fuel resources could result.

Donald W. Klein analyzes current Soviet-Japanese relations from political, military, and economic perspectives. Providing some historical background, he recounts the longstanding mutual dislike and mistrust between the two states, which resulted from the Russo-Japanese War, won by Japan. Another contributing factor was World War II, in which the Soviets entered the Far Eastern theater only a few weeks before the war was concluded, but took almost one million Japanese soldiers prisoner and occupied a number of small islands from which they have consistently refused to withdraw during the ensuing forty years—despite a Treaty of Neutrality concluded between the two countries that was formally in effect until 1946.

Further, Japan is frequently influenced by the US reaction to Soviet foreign policy initiatives (e.g., the invasion of Afghanistan, the Soviet-inspired declaration of martial law and accompanying crackdown on mass dissatisfaction in Poland). Tokyo's continued security link with Washington does not encourage closer relations with Moscow, and that link is likely to remain firm for the foreseeable future. If the Soviets want to cool Japanese relations with the US, they have not developed policies to do so. Japan's improved relations with the PRC have also had a bearing on Soviet-Japanese relations as well. While clearly displeased, the Soviets have not figured out how to limit that relationship in ways that would be advantageous to them.

But the major difficulty between the two states, Klein writes, continues to be the Northern Territories, the four Japanese islands that the Soviets occupied at the end of World War II and have refused to vacate since. As a consequence, no peace treaty formally ending that war has ever been signed between the two states, and both sides remain adamant on the issue of the islands. Aside from what the Soviets may consider the islands' strategic value, their general unwillingness to withdraw from territory gained as a result of World War II is well known. They did agree to end military occupation of Austria and withdraw from several ports and naval bases in Finland in the mid-1950s, but it is widely believed that they continue to link withdrawal from the Northern Territories with inevitable East European insistence that they return territory annexed during the war from Poland, Czechoslovakia, and Romania. (This despite the 1975 Helsinki Accords that recognize the post-World War II international boundaries in Europe as "final.") There is also a Chinese claim to territory that the Russian Empire seized in the nineteenth century; a pull-back from the islands could rekindle Chinese insistence of a review of the current Sino-Soviet border and return of "historic" Chinese territory.

While Gorbachev's apparently more reasonable approach to many foreign policy issues (at least compared to his predecessors) might suggest a review of the islands issue, his call for a greater Soviet presence in the Pacific, together with the recent and continuing expansion of the Pacific Fleet and the Vladivostok naval base facilities mitigates against withdrawal soon. Indeed, recently negotiated naval base rights in Vietnam and North Korea add to Soviet military strength in east Asia. All told, it appears unlikely that Soviet relations with Japan will change substantially in the near term.

In contrast, Soviet relations with Latin America have undergone substantial change in the past decade, and probably the Gorbachev regime will want to take advantage of anti-American sentiment there in negotiating advantageously with the United States. Apart from Cuba and the short-lived Allende government of Chile in the early 1970s, Latin America has not provided fertile soil for Soviet influence until the past few years. The situation in El Salvador and, more importantly, in Nicaragua, has rekindled Soviet interest. Whether the Soviets can make lasting inroads into the region will depend on a variety of factors, including the extent to which they will want to risk getting involved in a distant conflict, perhaps incurring direct confrontation with the US, how much it will cost, and whether they would prefer to apply their energies and resources elsewhere.

Morris Rothenberg, with the assistance of Robert K. Evanson, assesses Soviet policy in this region, the United States' "backyard." Ensuring CP rule in Cuba and using Cuba to support anti-American revolutionary efforts (not to mention using Cuban military troops and advisers in Africa) remains a stable element of Soviet foreign policy. The cost of maintaining a pro-Soviet regime in Cuba has been considerable, but Moscow has been willing to pay and will continue to do so, in order to maintain a permanent presence in the western hemisphere. Of course,

the relationship may change after Castro, but there are no indications that he is likely, either for health or political reasons,
to leave the scene soon.

Currently, most promising from the Soviet point of view is
the situation in Nicaragua, where the Sandinista government
has demonstrated interest in developing economic relations with
the Soviets and receiving military assistance. Moscow remains
cautious in supplying military advisers, preferring Cuba to send
them. The Cubans are interested in shoring up the Sandinista
regime as well as promoting Castro-style revolutions in Central
America in general. Soviet involvement in El Salvador has been
more limited and is likely to remain so, as there seems a greater
likelihood that the US would get more directly involved in that
country than it has in Nicaragua.

Generally, Moscow has sought to enhance its diplomatic and
economic role throughout Latin America, thereby countering
to some extent the dominant US presence. The policy of expanding trade with a number of Latin American states, especially
Brazil and Argentina, which was adopted during the 1970s, is
being continued and promoted. With a few exceptions, the possibility of a pro-Soviet socialist revolution occurring seems
unlikely; the Soviets apparently believe it is advantageous to
develop better relations with existing governments than to try
to foment revolution where the potential seems too elusive. (Argentina, for example, became a major grain supplier to the USSR
in 1980, after the Carter administration imposed a boycott on
US agricultural sales to the USSR.) While Latin America is
lower on the Soviets' foreign policy agenda than other regions
of the globe, Moscow has by no means counted it out and may
be expected to continue diplomatic, economic, and cultural efforts, as well as provide cautious support for potentially
revolutionary situations. The challenge is to provide support
without provoking a direct confrontation with Washington.

Having examined current and likely future Soviet policies
toward a number of important regions around the globe, it is

useful to inquire into Soviet policy efforts from a different dimension: Moscow's attempt to project power and influence through military and foreign intelligence efforts. James Hansen explores Soviet efforts to influence events internationally and thereby lay claim to superpower status. The current size and diversity of Soviet the armed forces, including both conventional and strategic nuclear forces, render it a military superpower second to none worldwide. This status was achieved during the 1970s and there is no likelihood short of economic collapse or loss of political control that the Soviet regime will give it up. In addition to the spectacular nuclear arms buildup, the Soviet navy has undergone rapid and impressive expansion, as has its merchant fleet; both play a global role in extending Soviet peacetime influence.

In military operations, Soviet special forces (under the direction of military intelligence or the secret police) assume particular importance. Better trained and equipped than the regular armed forces, they are called upon for special missions, such as the invasion of Czechoslovakia in 1968 and the occupation of Afghanistan in 1979. Worldwide, Soviet intelligence operations provide another means of ensuring superpower status. The Soviets support more intelligence operatives abroad than any other single country and maintain more centralized control through the KGB over international intelligence functions than any other country. This fact, coupled with its domestic responsibilities, demonstrates the central role that the KGB holds in the Soviet system. The military intelligence arm of the Ministry of Defense, presumably also reporting to the relevant CPSU Central Committee departments and sharing information with the KGB, plays a lesser but still important role in intelligence gathering.

In order to maintain the security of the Soviet state and to continue to project power abroad (if not to ensure communist-style revolutions, then at least to develop and maintain influence in regions and states important to Moscow), the leadership will need to decide whether it is able and willing to sustain the level of military spending that has characterized the past several decades. In light of critical domestic needs, but with constant military/security pressure to maintain parity (or rough equivalence) if not surpass the United States militarily, Gorbachev and his associates will need to respond carefully to this urgent issue, perhaps the single most important challenge the leadership faces today.

ONE

SOVIET FOREIGN POLICY IN THE 1980s

John J. Karch

KEY ISSUES FACING GORBACHEV

As of late 1987, the Brezhnev-Andropov-Chernenko legacy of major foreign policy issues facing General Secretary Mikhail Gorbachev may be summarized as follows:

- East European desire for greater freedom from the Soviet Union for national development and increased relations with the West;
- uneven relations with the United States;
- increasing military strength and political cohesion of NATO, US missiles in Europe, and the US Strategic Defense Initiative (SDI);
- continued US-Soviet and multilateral arms control negotiations;

- support for and involvement in "national liberation" movements and aid to Third World countries;
- continuing Soviet imbroglio in Afghanistan;
- unsatisfactory relations with China; and
- a world increasingly competitive and interdependent.

The Soviet Union controls Eastern Europe but internal challenges have erupted periodically. Otherwise loyal regimes have
deviated from the Kremlin's orthodoxy and are attracted by
beneficial relations with capitalist economies. Nationalistic tendencies—in Hungary and Czechoslovakia earlier, and Poland
most recently—pose ideological, political, military, and economic
problems for Moscow.

The Soviet invasion of Afghanistan shattered "detente" and
heightened East-West tensions, as did Moscow's earlier deployment of the SS-20s which led to greater Western cohesiveness,
military preparedness, and ultimately the deployment of US missiles in Europe. Massive NATO-Warsaw Pact forces faced each
other menacingly in Central Europe. Nuclear and conventional arms negotiations seemed deadlocked, and, to Moscow, US
development of SDI threatened to critically alter the East-West
military balance. However, major hurdles for an INF Treaty
were removed by September 1987.

In the vast Third World, the Soviet Union had been heavily
involved in sponsoring and supporting wars of national independence. While scoring successes in helping create
Marxist-Leninist regimes, establishing forward military bases,
and developing beneficial relations, Moscow became overly extended and heavily burdened as domestic economic and social
problems worsened. Its continuing military operations in Afghanistan were universally condemned. In addition, recent
developments in China, particularly Beijing's improved relations
with the United States and Japan, increased anxieties for the new
leadership.

The foreign policy goals of the Gorbachev leadership are not fundamentally different from those of his predecessors. However, there is a perceptible change in style and emphasis—"a new approach," as it is claimed—stemming from a more realistic, pragmatic appraisal both of Soviet capabilities and the international situation. Gorbachev's initial period of leadership was devoted to consolidation and reassessment. Extensive personnel changes were made in the foreign policy making apparatus, including replacement of long time Foreign Minister Andrei Gromyko, and priority considerations were altered due to the serious domestic economic problems that logically affect foreign policy strategies. There would be no lessening of control over Eastern Europe; in fact, a tightening was quickly indicated. Any change in the internal fabric of East European countries was perceived by Moscow as a threat to the "socialist commonwealth" and a diminution of Soviet power.

Gorbachev espoused the policy of "detente" with the West which had proved beneficial in the 1970s and, cognizant of deteriorating East-West relations and the erosion of Soviet prestige and credibility, he sought to project the Soviet Union as a responsible, active superpower seeking peace. The General Secretary embarked on a program that seemed designed to reduce US power and Washington's role and influence among West Europeans, employing a sophisticated and energetic public affairs style unprecedented within the Soviet leadership. Particular importance was given to arms control and to US-Soviet discussions. Despite major differences, Gorbachev appeared determined to engage the US in negotiations and high-level meetings, overcoming even confrontations engendered by espionage and diplomatic expulsions.

To what degree substance will match rhetoric in Gorbachev's call for "new political thinking" is another matter. The difficulty of reconciling declarations with realities is nowhere more obvious than in Moscow's involvement in the Third World which casts doubt on Gorbachev's credibility. The lure of expansion is undeniable but Moscow will probably eschew—at least in the near term—new interventions of the magnitude of Afghanistan and concentrate on more predictable targets of opportunity. In arms control, his negotiators, and Soviet propagandists, have intensified their campaign against the United States, especially SDI, placing the onus for lack of agreements on Washington.

FOUNDATIONS OF SOVIET FOREIGN POLICY

Marxism-Leninism forms the immutable scientific and theoretical foundation for Soviet foreign policy. Guided and controlled by the Communist Party of the Soviet Union (CPSU) the many-faceted and multipolar Soviet foreign policy has clearly defined aims:

- to secure favorable international conditions for the construction of socialism and communism;
- to strengthen the unity and cohesion of socialist countries;[1]
- to support national liberation movements; and
- to defend the principle of peaceful coexistence among states with varied social systems.

Soviet foreign policy is designed to be "an active factor of class struggle," an instrument for "the revolutionary transformation of society."[2] It is marked by flexibility and adaptability, seizing opportunities and applying a variety of tactics in aggressive furtherance of its revolutionary aims. Communist leaders claim it to be "creative" and "active," seeking to discern weaknesses in the capitalist world and taking initiatives to exploit any cracks in the "enemy camp."

In the historical struggle with capitalism, the CPSU since Lenin has pursued a foreign policy based on "peaceful coexistence." With declarations of "strengthening peace" and "easing international tension" the CPSU leaders have never hidden the true nature of peaceful coexistence. According to Boris N. Ponomarev, candidate Politburo member until 1986, "This very principle is nothing but the highest form of the class struggle between two antagonistic systems—socialism and capitalism."[3]

Longtime Politburo ideologue Mikhail Suslov explained some years ago that "Peaceful coexistence refers only to inter-governmental and economic relations; it cannot apply to the ideological struggle between two systems. Armed struggle can be avoided. Ideological struggle is unavoidable." During the period when "detente" was lauded in the West, General Secretary Leonid Brezhnev, whose leadership spanned the period of "detente" through three US presidents, stated that "Peaceful coexistence does not extend to the struggle of ideologies—this must be stressed most categorically." On the contrary, he declared, peaceful coexistence creates "optimum conditions for the development of the struggle."[4]

The evidence is overwhelming as to the nature of Marxism-Leninism pursuing an aggressive revolutionary policy, not necessarily through an overt military war, but utilizing all instruments, including war. These embrace diplomacy, military power, foreign trade and assistance, front organizations, foreign propaganda, active measures, and espionage.[5] Mikhail S. Gorbachev's philosophy on international relations was summed up at the twenty-seventh Party Congress, February 25, 1986:[6]

> . . .there is no alternative to cooperation and interaction between all states. Thus, objective conditions—and I stress objective—have evolved in which the confrontation between capitalism and socialism can take place only and exclusively in the form of peaceful competition and peaceful rivalry. For us, peaceful coexistence is a political course to which the USSR intends to continue rigorous adherence.

Soviet foreign policy strategy is the province of the Politburo, and the new General Secretary immediately became heavily involved in foreign policy. The locus of foreign policy decisions shifted from the Foreign Ministry, where it had increasingly become the domain of Foreign Minister Andrei Gromyko, to the

CP apparatus. To remove a potentially formidable opponent to Gorbachev, who was inexperienced in foreign affairs, Gromyko was appointed Chairman of the Presidium of the Supreme Soviet soon after Gorbachev became CPSU General Secretary. Astonishingly, Eduard Shevardnadze, also inexperienced in foreign affairs, became the new Foreign Minister. Shevardnadze had been First Secretary of the Georgian CP and candidate member of the Politburo; now he became a full member.

Other ministries, committees, and institutes have foreign affairs responsibilities, including the Committee for State Security (KGB). Of particular significance is the Central Committee (CC) on which Gorbachev may depend in preference to the Foreign Ministry. Among the CC Secretariat appointments announced at the conclusion of the twenty-seventh Party Congress were the former Ambassadors to the United States, Anatoly Dobrynin, and to Canada, Boris Yakovlev. Ponomarev was retired. Gorbachev gave US-Soviet relations priority attention and Dobrynin's appointment indicated their continued importance.

Soviet perception of international relations is based on the "systemic" assessment of the "correlation of forces" in the world, a broader concept of comparison than balance of forces. Basic factors determining the shifting correlation of forces are economic, military, political, and international movements. Political factors include an assessment of the degree of popular support. International factors concern the degree of coordination beyond national borders. The interaction of states, especially the United States and the Soviet Union, is crucial and, in ascertaining comparative strengths, will, and determination in the struggle between capitalism and communism, are vital. During detente Brezhnev observed that the correlation of forces changed in favor of "the forces of peace and progress" —that is, of communism.

THE WARSAW PACT AND THE BREZHNEV DOCTRINE

The Warsaw Treaty Organization (WTO), established May 14, 1955, constitutes the most effective instrument of Soviet military control over Eastern Europe, and "Soviet forces deployed in Eastern Europe, together with other Warsaw Pact forces, constitute the major military threat to the Western allies." The Pact's forces are "far in excess of that required to defend its territory" and are organized for "offensive operations."[7] The Commander-in-Chief of the WTO Forces is a Soviet officer, since 1977 Marshal Viktor G. Kulikov, who is simultaneously First Deputy Minister of Defense. Ranking Soviet officers serve as senior Pact commanders as well as Moscow's representatives at Defense Ministries of member states. The USSR provides approximately two-thirds of the Pact's conventional forces and a substantial portion of the most modern weapons systems. However, its nuclear weapons in East Germany and Czechoslovakia would be dismantled under the INF treaty.

The twenty-year Pact, comprising all East European states except Albania and Yugoslavia, was automatically extended for ten years in 1975. In 1985 the Treaty was renewed unchanged for twenty years, with a ten-year extension option. At the twenty-seventh Party Congress Gorbachev confirmed the renewal to be of "great significance." The Treaty provides for sovereignty, independence, and noninterference in internal affairs, but Soviet aggressive policies toward Eastern Europe reduced this provision to fiction. In November 1956, Soviet troops crushed the Hungarian Revolution, and twelve years later Soviet-led WTO forces occupied Czechoslovakia in lightning fashion to destroy that country's "Prague Spring." In justification of the intervention in Czechoslovakia in 1968, Moscow declared the internal developments in that "fraternal" country to be a "threat" to the "socialist system existing in Czechoslovakia."[8]

Soviet policy, subsequently known as the "Brezhnev Doctrine,"[9] was unveiled a month after the invasion. Rejecting an "abstract classless approach" toward sovereignty and self-determination, *Pravda* declared that "every communist party is responsible not only to its own people but *to every socialist country and to the whole communist movement also*" (italics added).[10] On November 12, 1968, Brezhnev unabashedly claimed respect for sovereignty of all countries and noninterference in their affairs. However, he warned, "there are common laws governing socialist construction" and any deviation or the possibility of restoring capitalism would be "cut short by military aid."[11]

The next serious test was Poland in 1980 with the dramatic appearance of Solidarity, with its mass appeal and demands for liberalization. The Kremlin's control was exercised indirectly, through the establishment of martial law in December 1981 and the employment of Polish security forces to combat Solidarity. This action "brutally violated" the Helsinki Final Act. [12] Gorbachev characterized the Polish crisis as a "struggle for the very existence of socialism in Poland" and as "threatening to dismantle the socialist system,"[13] a clear warning to Eastern Europe.

Indications of the Soviet unyielding position under Gorbachev's leadership became evident early, in a hard-hitting *Pravda* article which denounced "national communism," "revisionism," and "anti-Sovietism," and called for "unity," "solidarity," and "fidelity to Marxism-Leninism."[14] In October 1985 the WTO Political Consultative Committee (PCC), meeting in Sofia, reflected bloc cohesion in support of Soviet foreign policies but in a style unprecedented in secretive bloc conferences. The intent appeared to be an effort to influence world public opinion for Gorbachev's meeting with President Ronald Reagan the following month in Geneva.[15]

COUNCIL FOR MUTUAL ECONOMIC ASSISTANCE

The Kremlin's control over Eastern Europe is exercised also through economic arrangements, bilaterally and through the Council for Mutual Economic Assistance (CMEA), established in January 1949.[16] Over half of Soviet trade is with the CMEA countries, and East European economies are dependent upon Soviet fuels and raw materials. In recent years Moscow has increased substantially the price of oil deliveries to East European countries. The current (1986-1990) Five-Year Plans emphasize science and technology. At the extraordinary forty-first CMEA Session (December 17-18, 1985) in Moscow, the Council adopted a fifteen-year "Comprehensive Program for Scientific and Technical Progress." The initiative was Moscow's and Gorbachev declared that the CPSU "regards the implementation of the program as a political task of paramount importance."[17]

In 1985 CMEA established "a truly revolutionary task" to double productivity by the year 2000 in order to compete effectively with capitalist countries. However, it was precisely with the capitalist countries that certain East Europeans, Hungary the most prominent, favored expansion of relations. Gorbachev's position appeared more orthodox than reformists had hoped, as Moscow was exerting greater pressure on East Europe for more intensive integration and linkage within CMEA than previously.

While EEC-CMEA institutional relations were expected to improve, individual East European state association with the community was likely to be severely limited as Gorbachev demanded solutions through "socialism." In sum, the East European dependence on Soviet raw materials, especially energy, economic "socialist" integration, and stringent limitations on reforms, all enhanced the Kremlin's control of the East European economies, and a dramatic change in Soviet-East European relations was no longer expected in the near term.

29

SOVIET RELATIONS WITH WESTERN EUROPE AND THE UNITED STATES

The West, especially the United States, has been of paramount importance to Soviet foreign policy. The West is the adversary— ideologically, politically, economically, strategically, propagandistically—with which the Soviet Union must contend in its effort to achieve its proclaimed dominant position in the world. During the Brezhnev era, the Soviet Union pursued policies that awakened the West to Soviet intentions. Moscow's invasion of Afghanistan finally doomed detente as the Kremlin developed its military power far beyond legitimate defense re- quirements and its use became a serious source of East-West tension. Soviet intimidation and repugnant behavior increased tension that could trigger a military confrontation escalating into a nuclear exchange. Moscow sought to justify its performance by invoking the ideological-historical perspective of "capitalist encirclement," heightened US military capability, "dis- criminatory" US trade policies, and the intensity of the new anti-communism.

However, Soviet aggressiveness sparked a reassessment of Western policies. Washington especially undertook defense preparedness and applied countermeasures, including restric- tions on technology transfer and credit. As a result Gorbachev faced a Western Alliance militarily better prepared than in pre- vious decades and many western leaders apprehensive about Soviet intentions. Indeed, a reassertive Western Europe, together with a renascent United States, presented new challenges to the Soviets.

According to Bialer and Afferica, the United States under President Reagan, with public and Congressional support, ac- quired "an image of the virtual invincibility of American power." These experts submit that strength and the will to exercise it are respected by the Kremlin and that "To undermine and destroy that image is a major goal of Soviet foreign policy." They suggest this objective is to be accomplished through arms control proposals, support of regional conflicts to expose US weaknesses, and "the renewal of detente," the latter a long-term calculation to "weaken the awesome and relentless shadow of American power over Soviet destiny...."[18] Another objective in returning to a policy of detente, which attracted a segment of Europeans, is to weaken the Western Alliance by fomenting discord between the United States and its European allies.

The West was not indifferent to the potential for lessening tension and peaceful engagement offered by the Gorbachev leadership. US-Soviet confrontation became tempered by an increase in personal dialogue and institutional contacts. Discussions described as "constructive" were held with the General Secretary in Moscow by Vice President George Bush and Secretary of State George Shultz in March 1985, and by President Reagan at the Geneva Summit, November 19-21, 1985. At the Summit Reagan emphasized US concern over Soviet continuing intervention, directly in Afghanistan and through proxies in other areas. He proposed intensified joint efforts to halt the "dangerous" conflicts and called for Soviet compliance with the Helsinki Final Act. Their Statement called for resolving humanitarian cases in a cooperative spirit.

The two leaders agreed that, despite the fundamental differences between their two systems, they had a responsibility to compete peacefully and to strengthen peace. They agreed to make a "fresh start," promising to continue their dialogue through the useful summit vehicle in the United States in 1986 and the Soviet Union the following year. The most immediate tangible improvement appeared in US-Soviet bilateral relations, with Shultz and Shevardnadze signing a new exchange agreement resuming the official academic, cultural, and scientific-technical programs. Previous exchange agreements began in 1959 and flowered during the 1960s and 1970s, but were not renewed following the Soviet invasion of Afghanistan.

The twenty-seventh Party Congress confirmed Gorbachev's

involvement in foreign policy matters and, under his leadership, the United States and Europe will continue to be priority areas. He sought to improve relations with Western Europe even before becoming General Secretary. During Chernenko's tenure, he visited London, then personally invited Italy's Prime Minister Bettino Craxi to Moscow in May 1985. He went to France in October, the first Western country that he visited as General Secretary. Those who visualized a major change because of Gorbachev's impressive public affairs demeanor were jolted by his harshly critical tone against the West generally and United States "imperialism" particularly. Despite Gorbachev's indictment of the United States, however, he displayed a measure of realism in stressing the necessity of coexisting with Washington—as a "command of history." Gorbachev identified detente, arms control, and continuation of the Helsinki process as major foreign policy concerns. The need for peace and a "return to detente" had been repeatedly proclaimed and the new Party Program, adopted at the Congress, invoked its imprimatur to "peaceful coexistence."

However, the Geneva talks on nuclear weapons reductions were stalled and there was no visible change in Soviet policies on human rights domestically or in involvement in regional conflicts abroad. These problems contributed to a delay in the next Reagan-Gorbachev summit. The strains escalated into a confrontation with the KGB over the entrapment of Nicholas Daniloff, an American correspondent in Moscow, who was accused of espionage and imprisoned August 30, 1986. The US had earlier arrested Gennadi Zakharov, a Soviet scientist employed by the United Nations in New York, for espionage, and ordered twenty-five Soviet United Nations staff members, also accused of spying, to leave.

US-Soviet determination to move forward, particularly on arms control, overcame the diplomatic stalemate. The Daniloff case was resolved on September 30 with his and Zakharov's expulsions, clearing the way for the October 11-12 Reykjavik "mini-summit." The leaders made bilateral progress, discussed regional questions, and resolved certain human rights issues, but disagreed on arms control and were unable to establish a date for the US summit. Exactly what was agreed upon regarding disarmament became a contentious issue. Possibly this situation arose out of unrealistic expectations, seemingly inadequate preparations, and mutual misperceptions.

US-Soviet strains and confrontations can be expected to continue, given the differences in values, goals, and policies of the two systems.

THE THIRD WORLD AND SOVIET INTERVENTION

Soviet interests in the Third World are of long duration and its objectives are ideological, geostrategic, political, and economic. Moscow seeks to extend its influence directly or through surrogates, and to establish a military presence, including access to ports and airfields in strategically located areas.

During the period of "detente" the Soviet Union behaved confidently and aggressively in "supporting the struggle of peoples for national liberation and social progress" (Article 28 of the 1977 Soviet Constitution), providing military as well as civilian aid and advisers, supporting surrogate military forces, providing training for and supplying arms to Third World regimes and groups. Soviet cumulative economic aid during 1954-84 totaled about $14 billion while military assistance amounted to $75 billion.[19] Moscow became the preeminent supplier of arms transfers to the Third World by the early 1980s—nearly $55 billion during 1980-85.[20] According to the US Joint Chiefs of Staff, since 1955 nearly 80,000 military personnel from less-developed countries have received training in the Soviet Union and Eastern Europe. In 1985, 19,000 Soviet military advisers and technicians were in thirty countries "where they played a central role in organizing, training, and influencing client armed forces." Its expansionist objectives were being realized but, clearly, the Soviet Union had become the most disruptive power in the international arena and its intrusions were not without repercussions.

Soviet aid has been politically motivated, designed to develop dependencies. Over the years Moscow and its WTO allies dispatched thousands of "advisers" —especially to North Africa and the Middle East—who earned badly needed hard currency. They invested heavily in training numerous Third World students in the Soviet Union and Eastern Europe, calculated to develop pro-Soviet elites throughout the developing world.

The Soviet terms of repayment have been comparatively favorable, especially to Marxist-Leninist clients. Only about ten percent were grants, the rest generally ten-year low-interest credits tied to purchases of Soviet goods and services paid in hard currency or strategic goods.

AFGHANISTAN

The Soviet invasion of Afghanistan in 1979, with 85,000 troops, doomed the ratification by the Senate of SALT II and awakened President Jimmy Carter and other US and foreign officials to the realities and limitations of detente and to Soviet goals.[21] The United States voiced strong disapproval of the Soviet occupation. President Carter took punitive measures—imposition of a grain embargo, restriction of exports of machinery and technology, nonparticipation of US athletes at the 1980 Olympics in Moscow, and reduction of the bilateral exchanges program. Washington assisted the Afghan resistance. The Deputy Secretary of State declared that "We resolutely support that struggle for freedom and independence by the Afghan people."[22]

Despite international condemnation, Moscow increased its military operations to 120,000 occupation troops, installed a subservient regime, and established control over the country. It continued its devastation of Afghanistan and increasingly came to treat occupied areas as Soviet territory. Moscow maintained that its withdrawal is a bilateral question between the Soviet

Union and the Kabul regime, a specious contention, and charged the United States and other countries with unwarranted interference. In 1986, Gorbachev announced the withdrawal of 10,000 troops, and in 1987 further reductions seemed possible.

REFLECTION AND REASSESSMENT

Partly as a response to United States resurgence in world affairs, a serious reassessment of Soviet Third World policies began following Brezhnev's demise. There were gains. The addition of such client states (albeit with varying relationships to the USSR) as Angola, Ethiopia, Mozambique, Syria, Libya, South Yemen, and Vietnam had occurred. The invasion of Afghanistan extended a Soviet military presence toward Pakistan and the Persian Gulf. Cuba provided a strategically important foothold in Central America. Soviet ships and aircraft had use of facilities in Africa, the Middle East, and Southeast Asia. India generally supported Soviet foreign policies. Marxism-Leninism appeared on the march.

Were the costs and risks worth it? Failures led to loss of prestige as former client regimes collapsed or turned toward the West for help, and several were tottering. Moreover, aggressive Soviet policies, especially in Afghanistan, had a deleterious effect on East-West and US-Soviet relations, including arms control efforts. "Socialism" proved not viable in the new Marxist-Leninist states whose regimes, lacking popular support, required enormous military and economic support for their survival. Indeed, the regimes were faced with militarily active opposition, and most were obliged to increase their military efforts (with Soviet support) to avert defeat. In Afghanistan the Muhajedin were strengthened by closer political alignment and increased foreign support. Moreover, Soviet aggressive incursions invited strong reactions and condemnation from nonaligned states who had generally reflected pro-Soviet policies.

Under Gorbachev's leadership, Soviet foreign policy toward the Third World seemed to continue and in some cases to accelerate aggression toward conflict areas. However, in view of domestic economic difficulties, WTO military requirements, competition from Third World as well as developed countries, increasing demands from recipients, and questionable loyalties of clients, consolidation, at least in the short term, seemed desirable.

To what extent Gorbachev's and other formal declarations were rhetorical, designed for public consumption and foreign propaganda, must await tangible implementation of Soviet programs. There must be skepticism of any radical change of Soviet objectives in view of ideological convictions, strategic concepts, tactics, commitments to client states, and a desire to maintain revolutionary zeal. Thus, the Third World is likely to continue to be a battleground of wills between communism and capitalism.

SOVIET RELATIONS WITH CHINA AND JAPAN

Gorbachev's leadership assigns the Far East and the Western Pacific increased significance. China and Japan are of special importance, as is the US role, with Moscow perceiving an alignment against the Soviet Union.

The improvement of relations with China became one of Gorbachev's major immediate objectives. Departing from previously unsuccessful efforts to establish a dialogue, he dispatched Deputy Foreign Minister Mikhail Kapitsa, a China expert, to Beijing in December 1985 and the following year assigned an approachable and skillful Ambassador to China—Oleg Troyanovsky. At the Party Congress the General Secretary reviewed developments with China in a positive fashion, despite Beijing's refusal to send a delegation and the seriousness of their bilateral problems. These include doctrinal differences; for example, Gorbachev labeled Chinese modernization policy as "deviationist." However, in a major policy address at Vladivostok on July 28, 1986, Gorbachev indicated flexibility on the protracted border dispute, and Chinese leader Deng Xiaoping was invited to visit Moscow.

The Sino-Soviet talks, which had begun anew in November 1982, faced seemingly insurmountable problems considering Chinese demands for removal first of three major "obstacles": Soviet military withdrawal from Afghanistan, Vietnam's withdrawal from Cambodia, and Moscow's military pullback from the Sino-Soviet border, including troops stationed in Mongolia. These are thorny issues but Gorbachev's concern with the increasing US and Japanese influence in China may be an overriding factor. While prospects for real Soviet withdrawal from Afghanistan and Hanoi's from Cambodia appeared possible, the prospects of military reductions from Mongolia and the border areas seemed more promising.

China and the USSR have signed a five-year trade agreement, and agreed to political consultations, and a more active scientific, technical, and cultural program than in previous years. Here Sino-Soviet relations are improving. Given their ideological foundations and a new-found pragmatism, the possibility of a future Sino-Soviet rapprochement cannot be dismissed. Gorbachev's initial activism toward China was largely one of style, but ultimately substance will be required to remove or ameliorate the obstacles to a major improvement in relations.

Unlike the other World War II allies, the Soviet Union has not concluded a peace treaty with Japan, largely because of the Etorofu, Kunashiri, Shikotan, and the Habomai islands off the coast of Hokkaido which Moscow has occupied since World War II. Moscow has sought to justify its occupation on historical grounds, on the Yalta Agreement of February 11, 1945, the Potsdam Declaration of July 26, 1945, and the September 1951 peace conference held in San Francisco. Tokyo, on the other hand, has maintained the islands to be Japanese "Northern Territories." The 1956 Soviet-Japanese negotiations, held in Moscow, resulted in a Joint Declaration providing for restoration of diplomatic relations. However, no further progress was made because of the islands. For Moscow, there are no "unresolved territorial issues" with Japan and it considers Japanese claims, and US support of them, as "unjust" attempts at "revision" to "distort" World War II and postwar international agreements. Moreover, Moscow claims that the 1960 US-Japanese Treaty "violated" the Soviet-Japanese 1956 Declaration.[23]

Despite this serious territorial dispute, Gorbachev is conscious of Japanese economic power, its improving relations with China, and its increasingly independent proclivities. Japan continues to be a potentially significant partner in Moscow's development of Eastern Siberia. Gorbachev moved rapidly to underline the Soviet intention of improving relations with Japan by dispatching his new Foreign Minister to Tokyo in January 1986. Prime Minister Yasuhiro Nakasone was expected to reciprocate; he expressed hope for an early visit to Japan by the General Secretary.

The importance of such symbolic exchanges should not be underestimated. Gromyko had declined to visit Japan, a posture that reflected negatively on Soviet foreign policy and on Gromyko himself. Past Soviet aggressiveness and insults have contributed to strong anti-Russianism in Japan. Gorbachev's approach reflected a change in style that promised positive results. As with China, Moscow's bilateral activities with Japan have their greatest possibilities for success in trade and cultural-scientific exchanges. To achieve long-term success, however, Gorbachev will find it necessary to go beyond style in facing the issue of the Northern Territories.

THE SOVIET UNION AND ARMS CONTROL

The possibility of nuclear war, and its prevention, has been the major factor in US-Soviet relations. The Soviet messianic impulse for expansionism is challenged by its major adversary with a powerful arsenal of weapons—military, especially nuclear, political, economic, and moral—for a credible deterrent, especially in concert with its NATO allies. The security of the United States and Western Europe is interdependent. NATO is a defensive alliance, its military posture based on "adequate defense to deter aggression," and its strategy "flexible response."[24] These are elements of great import to Soviet leaders, contributing to their declarations for reductions and freezes, and for participation in negotiations.

United States efforts at arms control date from the dawn of the atomic age, beginning with the 1946 "Baruch Plan," making numerous proposals to control nuclear and conventional weapons. During the US monopoly of atomic arms, the Soviet Union conducted intense research on nuclear weapons to acquire military superiority, to be prepared for and to "win" wars, including a nuclear war.[25] The Soviet leaders have a fundamentally different perception of arms control, and of diplomacy and negotiations, from their Western counterparts. For them arms control is part of the "ideological struggle" and an element in determining the international correlation of forces.

As for negotiations, a Congressional study observed that the "Soviet theory of diplomacy is rooted in the Marxist-Leninist interpretation of international relations" and that "negotiation is an instrument of Soviet diplomacy... used to achieve the goals and purposes of the Soviet Union."[26] According to one highly experienced US negotiator, Soviet negotiating decisions are made at the highest level—the Politburo or the Defense Council. In the absence of such a high-level decision "the United States will find itself negotiating with itself."[27] The US objective in arms control negotiations, according to the US Joint Chiefs of Staff, is "... to protect US and allied security interests, build global stability, and promote favorable international relationships."[28]

Over the years the Soviet Union has been motivated by propaganda, including its "peace" offensives, in making general declarations and sweeping proposals intended to have worldwide appeal but which were deficient in specifics and verification. Another objective has been to weaken the Western Alliance by attempting to divide the United States and its NATO allies.

In 1977 the Soviet Union initiated the deployment of its

mobile Intermediate-Range Ballistic Missiles (SS-20s), each with three accurate nuclear warheads and, with a range of 5,000 kilometers, capable of destroying targets in Western Europe, Asia, and the Middle East. By the end of the decade the Soviet Union achieved parity in strategic nuclear arms, superiority in medium-range nuclear forces (INF), and the WTO already had a quantitative preponderance in conventional forces. To correct this imbalance, especially the unprecedented buildup of SS-20s, America's concerned NATO allies adopted on December 12, 1979 a "dual-track" approach: (1) Deployment in Western Europe of 572 US ground-launched cruise missiles and Pershing II ballistic missiles; and (2) US negotiations with the Soviet Union for the mutual reduction of INF.

In 1981 the US, supported by NATO, made a radical proposal: NATO would nullify its deployment if the Soviet Union would eliminate its SS-20s. If accepted, all INF missiles would have been eliminated. However, Moscow rejected this initiative but agreed to US-Soviet INF negotiations, which began in Geneva on November 30, 1981, and to Strategic Arms Reduction Talks (START) on June 29, 1982, also in Geneva.[29] The two sides were far apart in their positions, Moscow claiming that "rough parity" existed, and Washington asserting, with convincing evidence, that the Soviet Union had a decided superiority of INF weapons.[30] The various initiatives, including the publicity-catching "walk-in-the-woods" of the top negotiators and the President's "zero-zero" option, were unable to resolve their differences.

The Soviet objective at the Geneva negotiations and through its propaganda campaign was clear—to prevent the deployment of the 572 missiles on the European continent. If successful, NATO's credibility and unity would be critically undermined and Moscow would achieve a devastating nuclear advantage. According to one thorough analysis, "The Soviet campaign against that NATO decision may well be its most intense and well orchestrated [propaganda] effort since the founding of NATO."[31]

That effort went beyond propaganda and included "active measures" as well as mass demonstrations. This prodigious attempt ultimately failed when deployment began on schedule in November 1983. Repercussions were immediate as the Soviet delegation walked out of the INF talks, later from START, and threatened to do the same at the Mutual and Balanced Force Reductions (MBFR) negotiations in Vienna.

Moscow had hoped for the President's defeat in the 1984 election. With Reagan's decisive victory, however, the Kremlin decided upon a more realistic approach toward the United States. Meeting January 7-8, 1985 in Geneva, Shultz and Gromyko agreed to "new" US-Soviet negotiations in Geneva: (1) Defense and Space, (2) START, and (3) INF. Negotiations began March 12, and although the general objective was not in dispute, differences of substance and application, reflecting each side's priorities, were obvious. Essentially, the United States sought to reduce offensive nuclear weapons and Moscow to prevent the SDI program.

Immediately, the Soviet Union began to conduct a major campaign against SDI, to influence public opinion and governments, especially in Western Europe. However, while attacking SDI, the Soviet Union was developing "an extensive, multifaceted operational strategic defensive network which dwarfs that of the United States as well as an active research and development program... against ballistic missiles."[32]

Under Gorbachev, arms control assumed primary importance in US-Soviet relations. He became directly involved in making proposals, including a unilateral moratorium on nuclear testing. At the Summit the leaders agreed to give impetus to the stalemated Geneva negotiations, especially to the principle of fifty percent reductions in "offensive" nuclear weapons, but they were unable to reach an understanding on SDI. The President reiterated his position that SDI is a research program, compatible with the ABM Treaty, and not an offensive threat to the Soviet Union.

On January 15, 1986 Gorbachev announced a comprehensive nuclear arms proposal, with a three-phase timetable, to eliminate by the year 2000 all nuclear arms. Viewed by Washington as "designed primarily for its political and propaganda impact," the initiative demanded a ban on the so-called "space-strike weapons" as a prerequisite to negotiate reductions of strategic offensive weapons. However, the initiative contained "constructive" elements on INF and "positive" references on verification. The President's response was a phased US-Soviet elimination of INF weapons and "the principle of 50 percent reductions in START together with the SDI research program."[33] Gorbachev not only criticized the US response but conditioned the 1986 Summit on progress in arms control.

Subsequently arms control positions were exchanged in confidential letters by the leaders, discussed by high-level officials, and negotiated in Geneva. US-Soviet differences were being narrowed but essentially stalemated. This led to the Gorbachev-initiated preliminary "mini-summit" in Reykjavik October 11-12, 1986. While no formal comprehensive agreement was reached, the President and the General Secretary managed progress in several areas—on INF, strategic offensive weapons, and a phased test ban. Critical was Gorbachev's demand for SDI research to be confined to the laboratory. This was rejected by Reagan who considered strategic defense "insurance" for US and Western security. The leaders did not set a date for their US Summit and left unclear the question of "package" accord—that is, linking all arms areas to space defense—a departure from the previous Soviet position. Following the meeting both governments dispatched emissaries to brief foreign governments. Admittedly based on the American practice, this was a new tactic in Soviet diplomacy.

For differing reasons, nuclear arms have been considered vital to the United States—as a deterrent—and the Soviet Union as well as America's allies. Arms control and disarmament issues are complex and, in the West, politically delicate, a fact well understood in Moscow. Consequently, expectations of quick solutions are unrealistic. Long, hard negotiations, requiring patience and painstaking preparations, are necessary for mutually acceptable nuclear agreements with effective verification measures.

The most promising area, if linkage were not applied, appeared in the elimination of medium-range missiles in Europe on which the leaders agreed at Reykjavik. The most serious difference was over SDI, not surprising given the sides' objectives—Moscow's to eliminate and Washington's to develop. This and other issues, including a precise definition of "laboratory" research, were to be pursued in Geneva. Not insignificant was the expressed intention by both countries, encouraged by their allies, to continue these important negotiations.

The September 1987 Shultz-Shevardnadze meeting removed the major obstacles facing the INF negotiations, paving the way for a treaty on intermediate-range nuclear forces.

International relations are at a historic stage where bilateral and multilateral negotiations will be a continuing phenomenon as the transition from offensive to defensive weapons systems nears.

MULTILATERAL NEGOTIATIONS

The Soviet Union has been an active participant in multilateral negotiations. Of these, a discussion of MBFR and the Helsinki Process follows.

Conducted by twelve NATO and seven Warsaw Pact members, the unique Mutual and Balanced Force Reductions (MBFR) negotiations on conventional forces in Central Europe have been in progress in Vienna since 1973.[34] The general objective, according to the "mandate" of the Final Communique, is "to contribute to a more stable relationship and to the strengthening of peace and security in Europe." The sides have agreed to reduce their military manpower in Central Europe to parity for each alliance at 900,000 combined ground and air force personnel, including 700,000 ground troops, and provide for verification measures.

The negotiations have been plagued by two major problems: "data" and verification. There is also disagreement over armaments. NATO believes, with credible evidence, that the East has troop superiority—well over 200,000 more troops in the area than it admits; the WTO claims that an approximate parity exists. In an effort to break the deadlock, the West in 1984 took an unprecedented step by altering its requirement on initial force levels but demanding more stringent verification measures. The East rejected the proposal and tabled its "Basic Provisions" in February 1985 which was deficient in several areas, including verification. In December 1985 the West made a "major" proposal, in effect accepting the East's Basic Provisions and providing for US-Soviet reductions but demanding enhanced associated measures. The initial optimism in the West, based on Gorbachev's declarations, including references to on-site inspection, proved unfounded. On February 20, 1986 the East proposed another draft, extending its 1985 proposal, but it too was a "deep disappointment" to the West, especially its provisions on verification. Subsequently the Eastern attitude turned to a rejection of the Western proposals and its position on some issues—for example, exit/entry points—retrogressed.[35]

THE HELSINKI PROCESS

The Final Act of the Conference on Security and Cooperation in Europe (CSCE), signed in 1975 in Helsinki, provides for follow-up meetings to review its implementation and to consider improvement, and for specialized sessions.

Unlike its attitude toward MBFR, Moscow campaigned for a European security conference, where it achieved enormous success with recognition of post-World War II boundaries in the Final Act. At CSCE's various conferences, Moscow, together with its allies, participates actively, receiving worldwide media coverage. While vulnerable to accusations of violations, especially in human rights and the free flow of information, the Kremlin calculated that on balance participation in the Helsinki Process was advantageous. The Conference on Confidence and Security-Building Measures and Disarmament in Europe (CDE) met in Stockholm during January 1984 and again in September 1986 to negotiate measures (CSBMs) designed to reduce the risk of surprise attack and the chances of war by miscalculations.

According to the US, "At the beginning of the Conference, the East took a very polemical approach and advanced... declaratory measures." This contrasted with the NATO proposal which addressed concrete, militarily significant and verifiable CSBMs. Under Gorbachev the Soviet attitude became more positive [36] and at the Summit Reagan and Gorbachev committed themselves to reaching an agreement at CDE. In October 1985 in Paris the General Secretary agreed to exchange annual military exercise schedules, and in his January 15, 1986 proposals he included on-site inspection, both positive signs.

The most controversial issues at the Stockholm conference were verification, especially on-site inspection, and advance notification of military activities. Both NATO and WTO, with assistance from the neutrals, compromised on strongly held positions, an indication of commitment to reach an agreement, the first one involving conventional military forces since World War II. The accord, effective January 1, 1987, was unprecedented in several key areas: it entails binding, rather than voluntary, compliance; it encompasses all Europe—from the Atlantic to the Urals; and it provides for on-site inspection on demand. Signatories are obliged to advise all others two years in advance of military exercises involving 75,000 or more troops, and one year for exercises exceeding 40,000. By November 15 yearly each participant is required to distribute a calendar of out-of-garrison military formations for the following year numbering more than 13,000 troops or 300 battle tanks. Signatories must be invited to observe all military exercises of more than 17,000 troops by the host state. Mandatory, too, is a provision for each state to accept up to three verification challenges annually with inspectors in the area of operations within 36 hours. This and other issues were examined by the third CSCE review conference beginning November 4, 1986 in Vienna.

VERIFICATION

Verification has been a difficult problem in negotiations. Soviet secrecy, bordering on paranoia, has been a major factor, and their violations of arms control agreements have contributed to US and allied demands for "effective" measures and calls for reversal of Soviet behavior. To the United States "effective verification" is of "critical importance" in confidently assessing compliance with provisions of arms control agreements.[37]

There is a conceptual difference between the US and the Soviet Union on verification. Moscow considers general and limited provisions adequate, while the US and its allies favor concrete and comprehensive regimes. The Soviet Union has a unilateral advantage with monitoring in and access to information in open Western societies. Soviet secretiveness, extended to WTO countries, makes it infinitely more difficult for Western monitoring and acquisition of information in those countries. Consequently, national technical means (NTMs) essentially suffice for the Soviet Union, but not for the Western allies, who require a more comprehensive verification package to ensure confidence and strengthen stability.

Due partly perhaps to US insistence, there has been a recent change in the Soviet position on verification, including on-site inspection, with Gorbachev and other officials making numerous references to the subject. More important, Moscow agreed in 1985 to permit limited inspection of its facilities through the International Atomic Energy Agency and in 1986 accepted the Stockholm provision cited above. The latter is especially significant for the Geneva and MBFR negotiations.

SOVIET NONCOMPLIANCE

Noncompliance with treaty obligations, which is of "vital concern" to the United States and its allies, impacts on East-West relations and arms control negotiations. The US considers as a "serious matter" Soviet violations of, among others, the Geneva Protocol on Chemical Weapons, the Biological Weapons Convention, the Helsinki Final Act, and provisions of SALT II. Washington pressed Moscow for "corrective actions" and seeks to incorporate effective verification and compliance provisions into arms control agreements. With continuing Soviet noncompliance and military buildup, Reagan on May 27, 1986 announced that future US decisions on strategic force structure would be based "on the nature and magnitude of the threat posed by Soviet strategic forces." He specifically cited Soviet SALT II Treaty violations, including deployment of SS-25s, a forbidden ICBM.[38] This meant that the US may decide to exceed SALT II limits. Moscow had leveled countercharges against the US—that SDI, deployment of cruise missiles, and Trident II were treaty violations[39]—and now denounced the President's decision, Gorbachev being particularly caustic in his attack.

While there was no evidence of a Kremlin behavioral change in noncompliance, Western vocal concern with Soviet violations, NATO's military strength, and increased effectiveness of verification, may inhibit Soviet proclivities to commit violations and encourage a more responsible attitude toward agreements to which it is a signatory.

CONCLUSIONS AND PROSPECTS

Soviet foreign policy is the prerogative of the Politburo, which is guided by Marxist-Leninist ideology, a revolutionary doctrine, and headed by the General Secretary. Soviet power extends far beyond its borders, and its objective is to achieve further conquests leading toward global domination. The constancy in ideological foundations should neither be overlooked nor confused with changeable tactics or current policies. The perceived strength of Soviet adversaries, especially the United States, assessed through correlation of forces, contributes to establishing policies.

Moscow's control over Eastern Europe has been quickly and explicitly reaffirmed. Soviet involvement in the Third World will continue but new overt interventions will depend both on Western posture and Soviet domestic imperatives. More effective overtures have been made to China and Japan, but the United States and Western Europe are Gorbachev's top priority. While he verbally attacks the West, especially the United States, he eschews military confrontation with them.

Gorbachev's predecessors failed to halt the deployment of US missiles in Europe and Gorbachev has thus far failed to restrict SDI. None succeeded in driving a wedge between the United States and its European allies, an objective Gorbachev, as did every other Soviet leader, hopes to attain. In the face of this militarily strong adversary, a politically coordinated West and a militarily prepared NATO are essential for maximum credibility.

Observers agree that Gorbachev has been invested with Politburo-approved authority, has established firm control, and that his image has been enhanced by his performance at the Geneva Summit. He appeared confident, intelligent, energetic, tough, conscious of public opinion, and distrustful of the West. Not unexpectedly, he is loyal to Marxist-Leninist tenets and an advocate of its objectives. The conduct of foreign policy under his direction will continue to be vigorous and productive, and any expectation of dramatic changes in either conceptualization or fundamental direction would be unrealistic.

NOTES

1. "Socialist countries" and similar misused terminology is used by Moscow and its allies to denote communist-controlled countries.
2. Kratky slovar-spravochnik politinformatora i agitatora (Moscow: 1973), p. 220, in Raymond S. Sleeper, ed., *A Lexicon of Marxist-Leninist Semantics* (Alexandria, Virginia: Western Goals, 1983), pp. 114, 220. For a more extensive discussion of the ideological factor in Soviet foreign policy and of foreign policy processes, see Chapter 2 below.
3. *Pravda*, August 12, 1960, in *Lexicon*, 209.
4. M.A. Suslov, "Speech," February 2, 1962, in *Lexicon*, 84. L.I. Brezhnev, *The CPSU in the Struggle for Unity of all Revolutionary and Peace Forces* (Moscow, 1975), p. 100. L.I. Brezhnev. 1976. "For Peace, Security, Cooperation and Social Progress in Europe." *Information Bulletin* (Prague) 12:8.
5. Richard F. Staar, *USSR Foreign Policies after Detente* (Stanford: Hoover Institution Press, 1985), pp. 63-142. See also Richard H. Shulz and Roy Godson, *Dezinformatsia* (Washington: Pergamon-Brassey's, 1984); and John J. Karch, "Soviet Propaganda Themes," in Richard F. Staar, ed., *1985 Yearbook on International Communist Affairs* (Stanford: Hoover Institution Press, 1985), pp. 391-398.
6. *Pravda*, February 26, 1986.
7. Joint Chiefs of Staff, *United States Military Posture for FY 1987*, p.37. See also Richard F. Staar, *Communist Regimes of Eastern Europe*, 4th ed. (Stanford: Hoover Institution Press, 1982), pp. 271-296; John Erickson, "The Warsaw Pact," in Milorad M. Drachkovitch, ed. *East Central Europe: Yesterday, Today, Tomorrow* (Stanford: Hoover Institution Press, 1982), pp. 143-171.

8. TASS, August 21, 1968 and *Pravda*, August 22, 1968.
9. See R. Judson Mitchell, *Ideology of a Superpower* (Stanford: Hoover Institution Press, 1982), pp. 26-37.
10. Sergei Kovalev, *Pravda*, September 26, 1968.
11. Speech before the Fifth Polish Party Congress, November 12, 1968.
12. Dante B. Fascell, "Helsinki, Gdansk, Madrid," *The Washington Quarterly* (Fall 1984): 172-173. Congressman Fascell was Chairman of the US Commission on Security and Cooperation in Europe.
13. In a speech before the Polish Party Congress, June 20, 1986, *Pravda*, July 1, 1986.
14. O. Vladimirov, *Pravda*, June 21, 1985.
15. For a review of WTO developments during 1985 see John J. Karch, "Warsaw Treaty Organization," in *1986 Yearbook on International Communist Affairs* (Stanford: Hoover Institution Press, 1986), pp. 391-396.
16. John J. Karch, "Council for Mutual Economic Assistance," in *1986 Yearbook*, pp. 385-390. See also Staar, *Eastern Europe*, 300-322; and Werner Gumpel, "East Central Europe and International Economics," in Drachkovitch, pp. 107-124.
17. TASS, December 17, 1985.
18. Seweryn Bialer and Joan Afferica, "The Genesis of Gorbachev's World," *Foreign Affairs*. 64 (1986):631.
19. Department of State, *USSR Background Notes*, October 1985, p. 14.
20. *Military Posture*, pp. 85.
21. Jimmy Carter, *Keeping Faith: Memoirs of a President* (New York: Bantam Books, 1982), pp. 471-472. See also Anthony Arnold, *Afghanistan: The Soviet Invasion in Perspective* (Stanford: Hoover Institution Press, 1981); and Zalmay Khalilzad, "Moscow's Afghan War," *Problems of Communism* 35 (January-February 1986):1-20.
22. John C. Whitehead, "National Security: In Defense of

Something of Value," Department of State, *Current Policy* No. 833, May 9, 1986.

23. Alexander Yakovlev, main ed., *The Yalta Conference 1945: Lessons of History* (Moscow: Novosti, 1985), pp. 81-93.

24. *North Atlantic Treaty Organization: Facts and Figures* (Brussels: NATO Information Service, 1984), pp. 137-140; *NATO and the Warsaw Pact: Force Comparisons* (Brussels: NATO Information Service, 1984), p. 1; *Military Posture*, 2-3.

25. William T. Lee and Richard F. Staar, *Soviet Military Policy Since World War II* (Stanford: Hoover Institution Press, 1986), pp. 2, 171; *Soviet Military Power*, 11-12. See also Uri Ra'anan, "Soviet Strategic Doctrine and the Soviet-American Global Contest," in *The Annals* 475: 8-17.

26. US House of Representatives, *Soviet Diplomacy and Negotiating Behavior: Emerging New Context for US Diplomacy* (Washington: Government Printing Office, 1979), p. 7. This meticulous study was prepared by Dr. Joseph G. Whelan, Senior Specialist in International Affairs, Congressional Research Service, Library of Congress.

27. Paul H. Nitze, "Negotiating with the Soviets," Department of State, *Current Policy* No. 587, June 1, 1984, p.1.

28. *Military Posture*, pp. 77.

29. *Negotiating with Soviets*, pp. 2.

30. *Force Comparisons*, 1982, pp. 24-32.

31. Arms Control and Disarmament Agency, *Soviet Propaganda Campaign against NATO*, October 1983, p. 1. See also Karch, "Soviet Propaganda," and *Dezinformatsia*.

32. Department of Defense and Department of State, *Soviet Strategic Defense Programs*, October 1985, p. 5. See also *Soviet Military Power*, 1986, pp. 41-57.

33. Paul H. Nitze, "Negotiating on Nuclear and Space Arms," Department of State, *Current Policy*, No. 807, March 13, 1986, p. 3.

34. Department of State, "Arms Control: Mutual and Balanced Force Reductions," *Gist*, May 1986; *MBFR—An Overview*, Vienna, December 1985; Ambassador Robert Blackwill, US Representative at MBFR, Statement before House Armed Services Committee, December 12, 1985; *Security and Arms Control*, pp. 44-51; and *MBFR Press Transcripts*, Vienna, weekly.
35. Karch, "Warsaw Pact," pp. 394-396; *MBFR Press Transcript*, February 20, 1986 and September 26, 1986.
36. Robert L. Barry, "The Stockholm Conference and East-West Relations, Department of State, *Current Policy* No. 793, February 4, 1986, p. 2. Ambassador Barry was head of the US Delegation to CDE.
37. Nitze, *Negotiating*, p. 4. See also Department of State, *Security and Arms Control: The Search for a More Stable Peace.* (Washington: Government Printing Office, September 1984), pp. 51-57.
38. Message transmitting the President's Report to Congress on Soviet Noncompliance with Arms Control Agreement, January 25, 1984; see also subsequent Presidential Reports to Congress, and Arms Control and Disarmament Agency, *Soviet Noncompliance*, February 1, 1986; and "President's Statement on Interim Restraint," Department of State, *Special Report* No. 147, May 27, 1986, with Fact Sheet.
39. For example, Novosti, *Who Is Violating International Agreements?* Moscow, 1984.

SUGGESTED READINGS

Bialer, Seweryn. *The Soviet Paradox: External Expansion, Internal Decline*. New York: Alfred A. Knopf, 1986.

Brzezinski, Zbigniew. *Game Plan: How to Conduct the US-Soviet Contest*. New York: Atlantic Monthly Press, 1986.

Holloway, David, and Jane M.O. Sharp, eds. *The Warsaw Pact: Alliance in Transition?* Ithaca: Cornell University Press, 1984.

Kanet, Roger E. *Soviet Foreign Policy in the 1980s.* New York: Praeger, 1982.

Keliher, John G. *The Negotiations on Mutual and Balanced Force Reductions: The Search for Arms Control in Europe.* New York: Pergamon Press, n.d.

Laird, Robbin F., and Dale R. Herspring. *The Soviet Union and Strategic Arms.* Boulder, Colorado: Westview Press, 1984.

Nogee, Joseph L., and Robert H. Donaldson. *Soviet Foreign Policy Since World War II.* 2d ed. New York: Pergamon Press, 1984.

Pipes, Richard. *Survival is Not Enough.* New York: Simon & Schuster, 1984.

Rubinstein, Alvin Z. *Soviet Foreign Policy Since World War II.* Cambridge, Mass.: Winthrop, 1981.

Ulam, Adam. *Dangerous Relations: The Soviet Union in World Politics, 1970-1982.* New York: Oxford University Press, 1983.

TWO

DOMESTIC FACTORS IN THE MAKING OF SOVIET FOREIGN POLICY

Rolf H.W. Theen

There is not a single question of any importance which could at present be solved without the Soviet Union or against its will...

Andrei Gromyko

Even though this statement by the former long-time Soviet foreign minister (1957-1985) and subsequent president of the USSR at the twenty-fourth CPSU Congress in 1971 contains an element of exaggeration and boastfulness, it reflects the enormous growth of Soviet power in recent decades. Within a relatively short time after the Russian Revolution of 1917, the Soviet Union not only succeeded in breaking out of diplomatic isolation, but gained great power status within the community of nations to a degree never achieved by its predecessor, the Russian Empire, in its long history. Gromyko's statement is also a correct assessment of the fact that by the 1970s the Soviet Union clearly had become a global or world power, i.e., a state capable of projecting its power on a worldwide scale. Today the Soviet Union's influence is felt not only in Eastern and Western Europe, the Balkans, the Far East and the Middle East—the traditional spheres of Russian influence—but also in South Asia, Africa, Latin America, and even in an area as close to the United States as the Caribbean. If the USSR acquired lasting great power status in the aftermath of World War II and emerged as one of the two superpowers within a few decades after the most devastating war in history, fought to a large extent on its own soil, this development is due not only to the decline of the traditional great powers of Europe and the fact that Europe effectively ceased to be the center or "hub" of international affairs, but also to the consolidation of the Soviet regime during the Great Patriotic War, as World War II is called in the Soviet Union, and to the transformation of traditional Russia into a modern industrial state and military power.

The foreign policy of any great power is a complex derivative and amalgam of a number of factors, including considerations of geopolitical setting, history and tradition, exigencies of domestic politics, economics, ideology, elite perceptions, ambitions, and military power. Not only does the "mix" of these and other factors change over time, but it develops against the background and within the context of an ever-changing international environment. The foreign policy of the Soviet Union is no exception. Although qualitatively different from the foreign policy of its Tsarist predecessor in many respects, the foreign policy of the USSR also contains important elements of continuity linking the present with the past. Thus, for example, while Soviet policy has become global in reach and scope, it has also remained imperial in character. The Marxist-Leninist vision of the new *homo Sovieticus* notwithstanding, the modern Soviet Union, like Tsarist Russia, remains essentially a multinational empire. In spite of Brezhnev's claim in 1972, during the celebration of the fiftieth anniversary of the formation of the USSR, that the "historical nationality problem" had been definitively solved under the Soviet regime, the "national question" continues to complicate the Soviet Union's domestic political agenda and to impose significant constraints on its foreign policy.[1]

This chapter deals with some of the important domestic factors that help to explain the nature of Soviet foreign policy. A comprehensive discussion of this subject is not possible within the confines of a single chapter. Our discussion will therefore focus on a selection of domestic factors that have been important in the shaping of Soviet foreign policy—more specifically, geography, demography, ideology, economic strength, military power, and the institutions and process of Soviet foreign policy.

GEOGRAPHY

Like Imperial Russia, the Soviet regime faces a regional political environment that is extraordinarily complex—certainly much more complex than that of the United States. The immediate political "neighborhood" of the USSR includes a dozen nations with which it has common land frontiers—Norway and Finland in the northwest; Poland, Czechoslovakia, Hungary, and Romania in the West; Turkey, Iran, Afghanistan, China and Mongolia in the south; and North Korea in the southeast. Thus, along the world's longest land frontier (12,815 miles) the Soviet Union's immediate neighbors range from neutral Finland and political and military allies (Poland, Czechoslovakia, Hungary, and Romania) to NATO countries (Norway and Turkey), communist competitors (China), Third World countries (Iran), and "independent" North Korea, as well as Mongolia, which—though technically independent—is aligned with the Soviet Union and heavily dependent on it for military, economic, and cultural assistance. In addition to this bewildering array of extensive land frontiers, the geographical-political position of the Soviet Union is complicated by direct sea contact with a number of countries: Finland, Sweden, Norway, Denmark, West and East Germany, and Poland in the Baltic Sea; Romania, Bulgaria, and Turkey in the Black Sea; Iran in the Caspian Sea; Japan and North Korea in the Sea of Japan; and the United States in the Bering Sea. In the larger political environment of the USSR, it is primarily the People's Republic of China, the highly industrialized nations of Western Europe, the United States, and Japan which pose a challenge to Soviet power—similar to a century ago when the technologically superior states of Europe threatened autocratic Russia under the tsars.

In terms of size, another important geographical dimension from the standpoint of foreign policy, the Soviet Union is in a category all by itself. More than twice the size of the United States or China, its two most important political rivals, the USSR is by far the largest country in the world. Occupying 8,649,489 square miles, it straddles two continents, Europe and Asia, stretching across eleven times zones for a distance of nearly 6,000 miles. It takes approximately ten days and nights of constant travel by train to cover this enormous expanse from west to east.

The large physical size of the country has been both a blessing and a curse. When invaded from the West (by Napoleon in 1812 and by Hitler in 1941, for example), the vastness of Russia's territory proved to be a definite military asset, allowing the country to employ a defense-in-depth strategy—a strategy that involved limited engagement of the enemy at the front, subsequent retreat in an eastward direction, regrouping for renewed attack, constantly stretching the enemy's supply lines and complicating his logistics. However, when fighting Japan in 1904-1905 in areas far removed from its own center of population and industry, Russia found its own supply lines overextended and was defeated by its relatively tiny adversary.

From an economic standpoint, the vast size of the Soviet Union, on balance, has been more of a liability than an asset.

While extremely well endowed with natural resources—according to Soviet estimates, the USSR controls nearly 60 percent of the world's coal and oil reserves, 41 percent of its iron ore, 25 percent of its timberland, 83 percent of its manganese, 54 percent of its potassium salts, and close to one-third of its phosphates[2]—the greater part of this mineral wealth is located east of the Urals, far from the country's industrial base and population centers. As a result, industrial exploitation of these resources is greatly complicated by the requirement of an efficient far-flung and necessarily costly transportation system—with important consequences for the Soviet national economy. Moreover, given the present state of Soviet technology, a large portion of the natural resources found in Siberia is effectively inaccessible. Even when these resources eventually do become accessible, their exploitation will be difficult and expensive—due to the adverse climate and the great distances involved. Generally speaking, therefore, the Soviet Union is faced with rising fuel and raw material costs as the natural resources in the western parts of the country are depleted and the center of its extractive industries shifts eastward.

Certainly, at present there is a striking mismatch between the location of the Soviet Union's industrial base and population centers on the one hand, and its fuel and raw material resources on the other. Thus, for example, while more than two-thirds of the Soviet Union's industry and population are located in European Russia and the Urals, at least four-fifths of the energy resources are found in Siberia.[3] There is a similar mismatch between the location of natural resources and the actual economic development of the country. While approximately 90 percent of the Soviet Union's fuel reserves are located in the Asiatic part of the country, more than 80 percent of its power production comes from European Russia.[4]

Paradoxically, combined with its vast physical size, the topography of the Soviet Union—to briefly touch on another geographical dimension of importance for the understanding of

Soviet foreign policy—makes the country both hard to conquer and hard to defend. Although the Mongols, invading from the east, succeeded in conquering and dominating Russia from the thirteenth to the fifteenth centuries, the Poles, the Swedes, the Turks, the French under Napoleon, and the Germans, twice in this century, failed in their attempt to invade and occupy Russia or the Soviet Union. They found it relatively easy to invade Russia from the West, encountering no natural barriers of any significance. But to occupy and control Russia proved beyond their capacity. Only in the north, partially in the south, and in the southeast are the Soviet Union's borders well protected— by the frozen expanse of the Arctic Ocean and by some of the world's highest mountains. By contrast, the borders in the east, the southwest, and especially the west offer virtually no natural barriers to invasion.

Of particular concern to both Russian and Soviet rulers has been the vulnerable western border—especially the area between the Baltic Sea in the north and the Carpathian Mountains in the south, where the East European plain extends into the western territories of the USSR—the Baltic States, Belorussia, and the Ukraine. It is precisely from the West that Russia has suffered numerous invasions over the centuries—a fact that has shaped the country's concern with the need to secure defensible borders in the west and, if possible, friendly neighbors along this vital frontier.

Soviet concern about the exposed position of Leningrad, the second largest city and most important seaport of the USSR (then only fifteen miles from the Soviet-Finnish border!) led to the Soviet attack on Finland in the Winter War of 1939-1940 and the harsh treatment of that hapless country, which was forced to cede the entire Karelian isthmus to the USSR. As a result, the Soviet-Finnish border was pushed back approximately 100 miles from Leningrad. Similarly, Soviet territorial acquisitions in the west, in the south, and in the far east reflect the understandable concern with the establishment of more secure and defensible borders. At the same time, the scale of Soviet territorial expansion is seldom realized: as a result of World War II, the Soviet Union added 265,000 square miles of territory—an area large enough to contain Norway, Poland, and Costa Rica, or nearly all of Texas—making the Soviet Union almost as large as the Russian Empire at its zenith in 1904.

The historical experience of Russia and the Soviet Union with a hostile international environment and frequent invasions, as well as the ever-present specter of the possibility of having to fight a war on several fronts simultaneously, has meant that, both in the past and in the present, a large share of the country's wealth and resources has been spent for national defense. As the result of the need to support a large army and an ever-growing state apparatus with limited resources, the people have not fared very well in terms of their standard of living. The more or less continuous process of "state building" in Russian and Soviet history has led—in the words of Robert C. Tucker—to a "swollen state" and a "spent society."[5]

In addition to the vast physical size and the topography of the Soviet Union, its extreme northern location constitutes yet another important dimension of geography—with important economic and foreign policy implications. Nearly all of the territory of the Soviet Union is located north of the 45 parallel or latitude. Leningrad, the Soviet Union's second most important city, is on the same latitude as southern Alaska. Moscow, the capital of the USSR, is located further north than Edmonton, Alberta, the northernmost city of any importance in Canada. Only the southern Ukraine, the Caucasus, and Soviet Central Asia are comparable to the (northern!) United States in terms of latitude. Thus, for example, Odessa, the Soviet Union's most important port on the Black Sea, in the southern Ukraine, is comparable to Seattle; Baku, the capital of Azerbaijan, in the Caucasus, is comparable to Salt Lake City; and Tashkent, the capital of Uzbekistan, in Soviet Central Asia, is comparable to Chicago.

One of the consequences of the extreme northern location of the USSR is its extremely harsh and inhospitable continental climate. The severe climate has been Russia's ally against foreign invaders—as Napoleon and Hitler found out when their initially successful armies were ultimately defeated by "General Winter." On the other hand, the extreme northern location of the USSR explains the relative scarcity of productive farmland in the largest country on earth. Only 10-15 percent of the Soviet Union's 8.6 million square miles of territory is arable land. Moreover, there is a lack of rainfall in those areas that do have good and even excellent soil. Finally, the agricultural problems of the Soviet Union are further compounded by a very short growing season.

While there have been periods when Russia was a net grain exporter—during 1909-1913 the Russian Empire was the world's largest exporter of grain—the country has historically had a major food supply problem. Per capita food production has traditionally been low. The scarcity of food, due—at least in part—to the geographic location of the country, has meant a constant battle for survival for the people. In recent years, the agricultural problem of the Soviet Union has become so severe that it has had to import large quantities of food, especially grain and meat, becoming the largest importer of grain in history. In 1982 the Soviet leadership recognized the severity of the food problem by the adoption of a national Food Program. Although it would be a serious error to blame the malaise of Soviet agriculture entirely or even predominantly on the combination of poor soil, inadequate rainfall, and short growing season, i.e., on the vicissitudes of nature and geography, there is little question that the northern location and the adverse climate play a significant role in the difficulties experienced by Soviet agriculture. In terms of foreign policy, the inability of the Soviet Union to produce an adequate food supply for its 280,000,000 citizens has resulted in an unwanted dependence on imports from foreign countries, including its chief rival, the United States.

Another consequence of the Soviet Union's extreme northern location has been the lack of warm-water ports and the consequent lack of maritime activity, both commercial and naval. Almost the entire Soviet coast is ice-locked during the winter months; even Odessa and Vladivostok, Russia's great ports in the southwest and southeast, have trouble with ice. Paradoxically, Murmansk, although within the Arctic Circle, is completely ice-free—due to the Gulf Stream—as are the ports in the Baltic Sea, acquired by the Soviet Union as the result of World War II. In any event, the interaction between man and the sea, which is so striking and important in the history of the countries of Western Europe, is almost entirely lacking in Russia's past. Only very recently, during the Soviet era, has Russia become a first-rate naval power. Again, it is geography that explains the paradox that, until recently, the country with the longest coastline in the world did not develop a strong maritime tradition.[6] The lack of year-round usable ports also explains Russia's historic preoccupation with the Turkish Straits and its drive for warm-water ports—an economic necessity given its involvement in trade with Europe.

DEMOGRAPHY

One of the determinants of a nation's power is its population. With a population of 277.5 million in 1985,[7] the USSR has the third largest population in the world after China (1985 estimate: 1.043 billion) and India (1985 estimate: 768.1 million). As in the past, there is no country in Europe that can even begin to match the population of the USSR in numbers. Thus, at first glance it would seem the Soviet Union is well endowed with human resources. But a large population, like the large size of a country, is not necessarily a blessing per se. A country like India, for example, must continually invest scarce national resources in agricultural production to ensure an adequate food supply for its constantly growing population. As we have seen, the Soviet Union too is faced with an acute food supply problem. In recent years, the agricultural sector of the Soviet economy has swallowed as much as 27 percent of the national investment budget—without showing any appreciable results.

In assessing a country's population, a great deal depends on its particular demographic configuration and characteristics. Not only is the overall size of the population important, but also important is the degree of its homogeneity or heterogeneity, the extent of its urbanization, its level of general education and technical training, its natural rate of increase, its geographical and age distribution. In spite of rapidly rising levels of education, the Soviet Union today is faced with a serious shortage of skilled manpower, as well as a general labor shortage—a problem that is, at least to some extent, caused and compounded by the inefficient allocation of human resources. The labor shortage currently experienced by the Soviet Union, however, also reflects basic and long-term demographic facts and trends. First of all, in spite of the fact that the USSR has the third largest population of any state in the world, its population is not as large as it should be. Between 1913 and 1970, for example, the population of the Russian Empire and subsequently the Soviet Union registered an increase of only 70 million in 57 years—from 170.8 million to 241.7 million. By comparison, despite its much smaller base, the population of the United States grew from 97 million to 204.5 million during the same period, i.e., by more than 100 million. Even during the past 15 years, from 1970 to 1985, population growth in the USSR, considering its much larger base, has not kept pace with that of the United States.[8] In 1913, the population of Russia was 43 percent larger than that of the United States; in 1939, on the eve of World War II, it was 45 percent larger than that of the United States. But in 1970 the population of the USSR was only 15 percent larger than that of the United States, and in 1985 the difference was a mere 13.9 percent. If population growth projections prove to be correct, the difference in the size of the population between the two superpowers will further narrow by the year 2000—in spite of the

fact that the natural rate of increase of the Soviet population
(1.0 percent) is currently higher than that of the United States
(0.9 percent).

Reflected in these statistics, above all, are the staggering
population losses suffered, especially during the Soviet period,
by the people living in what is now Soviet territory. In 40 years,
from 1917 to 1957, the Soviet Union lost, according to different estimates, between 48 and 56 million people. According
to an estimate by Murray Feshbach, the leading American
authority on the population of the Soviet Union, by 1973 the
Soviet population should have been 375,000,000 to 450 million instead of 250 million—assuming that the 1917 population
living in the area now occupied by the Soviet Union had increased at the rate of 1.5 or 1.75 percent a year—a normal rate
of growth for a rural country at that time. Seen from this perspective, by 1973 the Soviet Union, although the third most populous
state in the world, had a population deficit of some 120 to 200
million people.[9]

The severe population losses during World War II, especially
among the relatively young age groups and most of all among
young males,[10] have not only significantly reduced the birth rate,
but have also had a lasting effect on the ratio of males and females
in the Soviet Union. According to the last census (1979), there
were still 17.3 million more females than males in the USSR.
Although other factors, such as urbanization and industrialization, are also involved, there is little question that the abnormal
age and sex configuration of the Soviet population is a major
factor contributing to the low population growth of the Soviet
Union and the resulting labor shortage.

The labor shortage—the result of the combination of population losses in the past, increasing mortality rates among men of
working age, and decreasing fertility—has profound implications for the Soviet economy and the supply of manpower for
the military. In the 1980s and beyond, the Soviet leadership can
no longer, as in the past, rely on the availability of new workers

for new jobs. During the 1980s, the net increase in the population of men and women of working age (16-59 for men; 16-54 for women) will only be 6 million—compared to 24 million in the 1970s. Expressed differently, while the labor force grew at an annual rate of 1.77 percent between 1970 and 1979, its growth is projected to drop to 0.44 percent between the January 1979 census and that of January 1990, and to 0.61 percent per year in the 1990s.

The labor shortage will be particularly serious in the RSFSR, which alone accounts for 60 percent of Soviet industrial output, and the Ukraine—two key republics, where the population of working age will actually decline in number during the years 1980-1995. In Belorussia, another important republic located in the western, industrialized part of the USSR, the increase in the population of working age in these three five-year plan periods will be a mere 5-30 percent of what it was during 1975-1980. Only in Central Asia is the population picture, as far as manpower supply is concerned, relatively bright—a fact, however, which presents the Soviet leadership with another set of problems, as we shall see. Because of significantly higher birth rates, this region will see about the same increase in the working age population as during the second half of the 1970s. According to the projections available at present, approximately 20 percent of the working-age population of the USSR will be located in Soviet Central Asia (Kirgizia, Tajikistan, Turkmenistan, and Uzbekistan) and Kazakhstan—regions of the USSR which as yet lack the requisite industrial development to make productive use of this manpower—by the year 2000.[11]

Aside from the already existing and growing mismatch between the location of the country's industrial base (mainly in the Western portions of the USSR and especially the RSFSR) and the location of available manpower (in Soviet Central Asia), the Soviet Union will have to cope with a decrease in the nationwide net gain in the working population from the peak gain of 2.7 million in the 1970s to just 300,000 a year in the mid-1980s.

No particular elaboration is needed to point out that this population crisis also significantly affects the military. Suffice it to say that during the 1980s the Soviet Union will be confronted with an annual reduction of nearly half a million men of draft age (18- and 19-year-olds). Not only will the Soviet Union have difficulty in supplying the Red Army with the necessary manpower to maintain it at its level of strength in recent years (4.8 million men), but in the coming decades more and more recruits will come from the non-Russian, especially the Central Asian, republics. Whereas the RSFSR supplied 56.3 percent of the potential conscripts for the Red Army in 1970, its share will drop to 44 percent by the year 2000.[12] This dramatic shift in the ethnic composition of the Soviet Union's armed forces, due to long-term demographic and therefore essentially uncontrollable trends, may have a significant adverse effect on the efficiency of the Soviet armed forces because Russian is the sole language of communication in the Red Army, and the recruits from the non-Slavic republics in Soviet Central Asia are notorious for their poor command of the Russian language. The Soviet leaders will also have to reckon with the possibility of rising tensions within the ranks of the armed forces—a possibility that has been frankly acknowledged by high-ranking Soviet military leaders.[13]

Space limitations preclude a full and comprehensive discussion of the multiple dimensions of the Soviet population problem. Suffice it to say that, in addition to the problems already discussed, the Soviet Union will have to cope with the socioeconomic and political consequences of a substantial overall decline and sharp regional differentials in fertility, the effects of an aging population, especially in the RSFSR, the most industrialized part of the Soviet Union, where the people of retirement age will account for 22 percent of the total population by the year 2000, and rising mortality rates, especially among the Slavs and males of working age. Perhaps most significant, from a political standpoint, will be the dramatic change in the nationality composition of the Soviet population. The Russians, the dominant nationality in the USSR, will lose their absolute majority status. Their share of the total population will decline from 52.4 percent in 1979 to under 47 percent by the year 2000. Similarly, the Slavic component of the population will decline from 72 percent in 1979 to 65 percent by the year 2000. By contrast, the nationalities of Soviet Central Asia will register a dramatic growth in their population—from 43.8 million in 1979 to as much as 64 million by the year 2000—a 40 percent increase! In view of the seriousness and the multifaceted nature of the population problem, it does not come as a surprise that the demographic situation of the Soviet Union has been singled out for attention by the top Soviet leadership, beginning with the twenty-fifth CPSU Congress in 1976 and concrete follow-up measures at the twenty-sixth CPSU Congress in 1981.[14] These measures included a variety of support programs for families with children, newlyweds, young people and, above all, women. Premier Nikolai Tikhonov, then chairman of the USSR Council of Ministers, announced the appropriation of more than 9 billion rubles (US $12.2 billion) to support state aid to families with children, including lump sum payments ($67.50 for first births, $135.00 for second and third births), increased monthly child allowances, increased aid to unmarried mothers, partially paid maternity leaves, and improved working conditions for women.

ECONOMIC STRENGTH AND MILITARY POWER

Factors of geography, such as the more or less strategic location of a country in the world, the presence or absence of natural resources, and the potential of a country for agriculture, industry, trade, and commerce, as well as demographic factors, such as the size, general education and technical training of the population, are important in the determination of a nation's capabilities. The ability of a nation to conduct foreign policy, however, is influenced even more directly by the level of economic development and military power attained by a nation compared to its actual or potential adversaries.

Soviet political leaders have been acutely aware of the political implications of economic weakness and backwardness. Stalin, in particular, was convinced that Soviet Russia had no future unless it succeeded in overcoming its backwardness relative to the leading countries of Europe and the United States. He interpreted the history of "old" Russia, that is pre-1917 Russia, as "the history of defeats due to backwardness" —military, cultural, governmental, industrial, and agricultural.[15] According to Stalin, the "jungle law of capitalism" knew no mercy for the backward and weak. Therefore, the foremost task of the "new" Russia was "to put an end to this backwardness in the shortest possible time." In 1931 Stalin put the issue graphically in a speech to economic managers: "We are 50-100 years behind the advanced countries. We must cover this distance in ten years. Either we do this or they will crush us."[16]

Stalin firmly believed that power in international politics is a function of military power, which in turn derives from economic, especially industrial, strength. Accordingly, he launched his country on a course of industrialization at breakneck speed. Stalin's task was a formidable one. While the economic development of Russia was well underway at the turn of the century—in 1900, for example, Russia was the world's largest oil producer and registered more rapid industrial growth than England or Germany—in terms of overall industrial development, the Russian Empire ranked only in tenth place, behind Spain and Italy, in 1910. World War I and the Civil War resulted in enormous destruction and economic losses. In 1928, when Stalin embarked upon his rapid industrialization drive, the Soviet Union had just managed to regain its prewar level of production. In spite of the impressive growth statistics, in absolute terms and by the standards of the industrialized world, the Soviet Union was still comparatively backward and underdeveloped.

It was this absolute difference in the level of development that Stalin sought to overcome through a series of five-year plans, to be carried out with "genuine Bolshevik speed." Proceeding with great determination and a good deal of ruthlessness, he succeeded in expanding and modernizing Soviet industry and collectivizing agriculture—all within the space of two five-year plans. Between 1928 and 1940, the Soviet gross national product increased at an average annual rate of approximately 12 percent.[17] Using 1913 as the base year, the index of Soviet industrial output increased from 132 in 1928 to 852 in 1940. In more specific terms, between 1928 and 1940, Soviet production of steel and coal more than quadrupled, oil production increased nearly threefold, cement production tripled, and the output of electric power increased nearly tenfold.[18]

A large part of the industrial capacity built up under Stalin, especially in the Ukraine, Belorussia, and the western regions of the RSFSR (European Russia), was destroyed during World War II. Moreover, in addition to the 20 million lives lost during the war, the Soviet Union also suffered enormous losses of livestock, farm machinery, transportation equipment, housing, and many other economic assets. In short, the losses inflicted by the war on the Soviet civilian economy, its infrastructure, the Soviet population, and Soviet industrial and agricultural production were staggering. It took another concerted effort on the part of the Soviet leadership and the Soviet people to restore the production capacities of basic industries to prewar levels—a task that was largely accomplished by 1950. In a sense, the Soviet Union had its own kind of "economic miracle" during the difficult years of postwar reconstruction. Nevertheless, the effects of the losses and dislocations caused by World War II are felt in the Soviet economy to this day.

During the postwar period, the Soviet Union has continued to enhance its capabilities by expanding its economic and military power. Stalin's ambitious economic objectives, set in 1946 to be achieved by 1960, were more than fulfilled. Whereas in 1950

Soviet GNP amounted to only 34 percent of that of the United States, by 1960 it accounted for 45 percent, and by 1983 for 55 percent of the US gross national product. In the past two decades, however, Soviet growth rates have steadily declined. In 1984 and 1985, for example, Soviet national income registered its lowest growth since the end of World War II—2.4 and 3.1 percent respectively. The pronouncements of Soviet leaders, from Brezhnev to Gorbachev, make it quite clear that the issue of economic growth is a top priority on the nation's political agenda.

The problems that have surfaced in the Soviet economy in recent years are complex and multifaceted. Not only has the overall growth rate of the Soviet economy declined substantially, but there has also been a sharp decrease in the growth of such basic inputs as investment, the labor force, and the output of the extractive industries. According to Academician Abel Aganbegian, chairman of the Commission for the Study of Productive Forces under the Presidium of the USSR Academy of Sciences, the Soviet labor force expanded at the rate of 6 percent in the 1970s, but at only 3 percent in the first half of the 1980s; the output of the Soviet extractive industries increased at the rate of 26 percent in the first half, and at the rate of 10 percent in the second half of the 1970s, but at the rate of only 5 percent in the first half of the 1980s; and the growth index for capital investment dropped from 44 percent in the first half, and 23 percent in the second half of the 1970s to 17 percent in the first half of the 1980s. Aganbegian has predicted a further deceleration in the expansion of these basic and crucial inputs.

Faced with these economic trends, Soviet leaders have for a good many years talked about the necessity of shifting the Soviet economy from extensive to intensive development. Thus far, however, this campaign has not succeeded. On the contrary, the contribution of intensification to Soviet economic growth, according to one Soviet study, has actually declined in recent years—from 40 percent in 1966-1970 to 25 percent in 1981-

1982.[19] The Soviet economy, it appears, is suffering from a basic inability to create and/or assimilate modern technology and to develop high labor productivity—essential prerequisites for intensive economic growth. Not only are there labor shortages in the Soviet Union, but labor productivity is extremely low (about 40 percent of the US level). In spite of the great emphasis given by the Soviet leadership to intensive development, increases in labor productivity have been very disappointing. From 1981-1982 to 1983-1984, for example, labor productivity grew by only 0.5 percent[20]—hardly a satisfactory result for the Soviet leadership, especially in view of its concerted efforts to "shift the economy to the rails of intensive development," as they like to put it.

The combination of falling growth rates and the resulting reduction in the availability of new capital; skyrocketing raw material costs; chronic bottlenecks even in priority sectors of the economy, such as steel, machine building, and transportation; the inefficiencies arising from an aging and in many cases obsolete machine plant, from a backward infrastructure in industry and especially in agriculture and construction, and from the rigid compartmentalization of the military from the civilian economy; and the inflexibility of the system of central and direct planning—in addition to large-scale waste, mismanagement and corruption—present the Soviet leadership with "titanic" tasks, as Gorbachev has acknowledged on numerous occasions.

It remains to be seen whether these problems can and will be solved by the Gorbachev administration. What is important for an understanding of Soviet foreign policy is the fact that the Soviet economy, as presently organized and managed, cannot provide the underpinnings for Soviet power in the long run. In other words, without a reversal of current economic trends in the Soviet Union, the performance of the Soviet economy is likely to become an increasingly limiting factor in the conduct of Soviet foreign policy, affecting not only the country's ability to maintain and expand its military power, but also its foreign assistance programs, its foreign trade posture, and its relationships with its allies in Eastern Europe. Continuing problems in agriculture may increase the Soviet Union's dependence on foreign sources of grain and other agricultural products. Technological underdevelopment and the imbalance in overall economic development may become increasingly serious obstacles to further economic growth. The long-term effects of these weaknesses in the Soviet economy, should they persist, will undermine the position of the Soviet Union in international affairs.

In assessing economic strength as a factor in Soviet foreign policy, however, we should not lose sight of the fact that, in spite of the present problems, the potential of the Soviet economy is enormous. Considered in absolute terms, economic progress under the Soviet regime has been considerable. Although the Soviet economy today is still substantially smaller than the American economy in terms of overall size, the disparity between the industrial sectors of the economies of the two superpowers is not nearly as great. As a matter of fact, in a number of areas of industry the Soviet Union leads the United States. Moreover, in most of the crucial defense-related scientific and industrial areas the Soviet Union is the equal of the United States. In terms of self-sufficiency with respect to essential raw materials and energy resources, the Soviet Union is clearly in a stronger position than the United States, which has to import many vital raw materials, including oil.

A good case can be made for the argument that during much of its history the Soviet Union has exerted a degree of influence in world affairs that has been disproportionate to the level of its socioeconomic development and economic power. Even today, it might be argued, the political influence of the Soviet Union is disproportionately great compared to its overall economic strength. In addition to being a reflection of the skill, persistence and resourcefulness of Soviet diplomacy, the most important reason for this must be sought in the high priority that the Soviet regime has accorded to the development, expansion, and maintenance of military power. The spectacular technological breakthrough of Sputnik in 1957 and more recent accomplishments in space notwithstanding, the Soviet Union has not compiled a strong record in scientific and technological innovation. Increasingly, therefore, its influence, power, and prestige in the world have become a function of its military power.

In the sphere of military power, the Soviet Union has indeed achieved enormous progress since 1918, when Lenin caustically described his country as "a military zero."[21] In spite of the great losses suffered in World War II, the USSR emerged as the strongest military power in Europe. Since 1945 the Soviet ground forces have been transformed into a modern army, well equipped with sophisticated weaponry and supported by thousands of tactical aircraft and a large assortment of nuclear missile units. Although Soviet leaders have on occasion complained about the lack of patriotism among the young, the Soviet Union, unlike the NATO countries, has not had to contend with large-scale demonstrations fueled by anti-militaristic sentiments and directed against military service and weapon deployments. On the contrary, in the USSR the military is a high-prestige profession.

In addition to its enormous strength in conventional forces, enhanced by its East European allies, the Soviet Union has also succeeded in achieving nuclear parity with the United States. The first nuclear weapons introduced by the Soviet Union in the early 1950s were short-range weapons intended to be used against targets in Europe and near the Soviet border. Throughout the 1950s and early 1960s, the USSR refrained from building strategic nuclear weapons and delivery systems—although it possessed the requisite technology. However, in the aftermath of the Cuban Missile Crisis, the decision was evidently taken by Soviet leaders to deploy intercontinental missiles. It was precisely the development of ICBMs which transformed the USSR from a regional or continental into a global military power.

Since the Soviet Union, under the leadership of Brezhnev, went "intercontinental" with its nuclear strike force, Soviet military power has been further enhanced by the buildup of a first-rate navy, a totally unprecedented development in Russian history, and the addition of extensive airlift capacities. As a consequence, the potential "reach" of Soviet conventional forces has been greatly extended and there has been a substantial increase in the flexibility and options available to the Soviet leadership in situations requiring the use of military power. In addition, the overall Soviet military posture has been strengthened by the buildup of a preponderance of conventional military power (in numerical terms) in Europe and the development of greater conventional and strategic power in the Far East, by the deployment of significant naval forces around the world, especially in the Mediterranean, and by its demonstrated capability and willingness to use surrogate forces on a large scale far from its own shores to fight proxy wars in the pursuit of its foreign policy objectives.

IDEOLOGY AND BELIEFS

Although a frequent subject of scholarly inquiry, discussion, and debate, the important question of the role of ideology in the formulation of Soviet foreign policy has never been resolved—and most likely never will be. One reason for this has to do with the lack of hard information and testable data. Another and more important reason is the inherent ambiguity of the role which ideology plays in human affairs, including the conduct of foreign policy. At the same time, in spite of the elusiveness of the subject matter, a number of observations can be made about Soviet ideology, that is, the officially approved political doctrine of the USSR, serving not only to guide Soviet leaders and other members of the political elite in their approach to politics and decision-making, but also to play an important role in the legitimization of the Soviet regime and in the mobilization of the population in support of that regime.

Unlike most other states, the USSR has an "official ideology," i.e., a political doctrine, called Marxism-Leninism, which is sanctioned, endorsed, and propagated (ad nauseam) by the CPSU and the communist-controlled mass organizations, and which is supported by the enormous resources of the Soviet state. Taken as a whole, this body of doctrine is much more coherent, systematic, developed, specific, logical, and internally consistent than the rather diffuse and ambiguous, frequently inconsistent, and often irrational set of beliefs that constitute the ideology of the individual, i.e., the "cognitive map" that in any political system helps shape the individual's relationship to political authority and the state. Our discussion of Soviet ideology will focus on the former, that is the political doctrine of the USSR, called Marxism-Leninism, which presumably affects how Soviet leaders and members of the political elite perceive and interpret the world around them, the behavior of nation states, the relations of the Soviet Union with other countries, and the relationship between domestic policy requirements and foreign policy objectives.

In considering the impact of ideology on Soviet foreign policy, it is important to recognize that Soviet leaders and decision makers are not only members of the CPSU or political elites at a given level, but also individuals. Their "cognitive map," therefore, includes not only ideas, values, and perspectives that have their source in Marxism-Leninism, but presumably also reflect orientations and points of reference acquired as the result of socialization, which may or may not be consistent with the precepts of the "official ideology." Thus, in a given case, the total "cognitive map" of a Soviet leader—e.g., the present USSR minister of foreign affairs, Eduard Shevardnadze, a Georgian—may be influenced and complicated by the fact that he is a member of a non-Russian nationality, that he grew up in the Caucasus rather than in one of the Baltic States or in Soviet Central Asia, and so forth.

To begin with, Soviet "official ideology" or doctrine is not unrelated to the Russian past. The cognitive map of Soviet leaders contains a good many components which have nothing to do with communism, but reflect thought patterns and perspectives that constitute important links with Russian history. The supposedly international character of the Russian Revolution of 1917 notwithstanding, Soviet leaders have frequently identified themselves with historic Russia or with the nineteenth-century Russian Empire. Thus, for example, in the already-cited speech to Soviet economic managers in 1931, Stalin drew instructive parallels between the backwardness of old Russia and the beatings it suffered at the hands of the Mongols, Turks, Swedes, Poles, Lithuanians, British, French, Germans, and Japanese. In his famous V-J Day speech, marking the end of World War II, he said that the victory over Japan had removed "the dark stain" of defeat suffered by prerevolutionary Russia in the Russo-Japanese War of 1904-1905. "For forty years have we, the men of the older generation, waited for this day."[22] Similarly, the advent of the modern ocean-going Soviet navy was linked with Peter the Great, who at one time apparently had designs on the Island of Madagascar off the East African coast and dreamed about the "penetration" of the Indian Ocean. In April 1970, when the Soviet Union celebrated the 100th anniversary of Lenin's birth and held the largest naval exercises in Soviet history (over 200 warships) to celebrate the occasion, *Krasnaia zvezda (Red Star)*, the press organ of the Soviet military, wrote: "The age-old dreams of our people have become a reality. The pennants of Soviet ships now flutter in the most remote corners of the seas and oceans."[23]

Some of the historical thought and behavior patterns of Tsarist Russia—its traditional xenophobia, its suspicion of and contempt for the outside world, its disdainful treatment of foreign diplomats, its fear of the potentially dangerous and subversive impact of foreign ideas, its avoidance of close contact with the West, its obsession with secretiveness and espionage, its self-image as the center of the universe and bearer of a historic mission—have parallels in Soviet ideology as it has evolved since 1917. Both Tsarist and Soviet Russia have been captive of a "siege mentality"—a powerful impetus for the establishment of a more or less omnipotent state and the concomitant subjugation of society and the individual. Both Tsarist and Soviet Russia have suffered from a legacy of backwardness and have had to cope with the challenge of a technologically superior West on their doorstep—a circumstance which has influenced the development of a highly ambiguous attitude toward the West. Finally, the long history of successive invasions, in the words of George F. Kennan, has produced a "traditional and instinctive Russian sense of insecurity," resulting in a "neurotic view of world affairs" and a world view in which "all foreigners are potential enemies."[24] For a number of decades now, the Soviet Union has not had to worry about the invasion of its territory and since the 1970s, it might be argued, it has enjoyed an unprecedented sense of security—thanks to its spectacular success in the buildup of its military power. However, as yet there is no evidence that its obsession with national security has diminished let alone disappeared.

Even if we had the ability to understand more fully the many and complex ways in which ideology influences human thought and behavior, in general, and the manner in which Marxism-Leninism affects the perception and judgment of Soviet decision makers in particular, ideology alone could not provide definitive answers to these questions. A knowledge of Marxism-Leninism, however, may give us some insight into the Soviet leadership's general frame of reference with respect to international affairs and into the basic beliefs and assumptions of Soviet decision makers as pertaining to their own role in international politics and that of their opponents. A knowledge of the "official ideology" of the Soviet Union and some of the traditional beliefs its people have inherited from the past may also contribute to our understanding of the hopes and fears of Soviet leaders and their predisposition to embark on a given course of action under certain circumstances. Therefore, in spite of the problems involved in any attempt to understand the impact of ideology on Soviet foreign policy, ideology is clearly an important and relevant factor to be considered.

Marxism-Leninism is an important factor in Soviet foreign policy, first of all, because it provides Soviet leaders with a systematic, if not always entirely consistent, conceptual framework for understanding international politics and the world outside the Soviet Union. Along with the concepts and categories drawn from Marxism-Leninism that are employed in the discussion of foreign policy issues come certain substantive ideas and a distinctive mode of thought and perspective. Thus for example, according to Marxism-Leninism, the Soviet Union is surrounded by hostile forces. Its relationship with the capitalist world is one of indefinite tension and conflict—albeit conflict in limited and controlled forms, and no genuine and lasting modus vivendi between the two hostile camps or systems, i.e., between the capitalist and the socialist worlds, is possible. In the words of Khrushchev: "No treaties or agreements between states can overcome the radical confrontation between the two social systems."[25] Consequently, while Soviet political doctrine proclaims its acceptance of "peaceful coexistence," the Marxist-Leninist understanding of this relationship calls for continued (and in the realm of ideology, intense) rivalry and conflict between capitalism and socialism.

Similarly, Marxism-Leninism teaches that Soviet foreign policy is superior to the foreign policy of any other state and always correct because of its scientific character and because of its being in tune with the "objective laws of history"; that the tide of history is with socialism and against capitalism; that the collapse of capitalism is inexorable (though no longer imminent) and the victory of socialism is foreordained and assured—although a long struggle lies ahead; that Soviet foreign policy, reflecting the absence of hostile social classes in Soviet society, is always peaceful and democratic, whereas the policy of capitalist countries, by definition, is aggressive, expansionist, and exploitative; that international conflict is natural and normal, given the existence of imperialism and the class nature of the non-communist countries; that all non-communist governments are illegitimate; that the United States, the citadel of world imperialism, in the words of Brezhnev, is a "rotten, degrading, decaying society,"[26] whose collapse, although no longer imminent, is inevitable, etc.

In assessing the impact of ideology on Soviet foreign policy, we can make a number of general observations: (1) The overall influence of the doctrine of Marxism-Leninism on Soviet foreign policy has declined with the passage of time. In response to changes in the international situation and in the definition of the Soviet national interest, major doctrinal principles have been abandoned. Soviet foreign policy, as it were, has become secularized, evolving into the policy of a state preoccupied with the pursuit of traditional foreign policy objectives: national security, power, and prestige. (2) The specific content and substance of Marxism-Leninism have changed over the years. In response to such important events as the development of nuclear weapons, important doctrinal modifications have been made. The *kto-kogo?* (literally: Who-whom? i.e., who will destroy whom?) of Lenin and Stalin has given way to Khrushchev's concept of "peaceful coexistence"—a concept also embraced by Khrushchev's successors. The Leninist concept of "temporary" coexistence has been amended to reflect the necessity of the prolonged "peaceful coexistence" of the two hostile social systems in the nuclear age. For the same reason, the Leninist doctrine of the inevitability of war between capitalism and socialism was abandoned by Khrushchev. (3) Soviet official ideology, which has always centered around the concept of internationalism and an international revolution, has increasingly been replaced by nationalism as the major bond within the Soviet elite and between the elite and the masses. As Seweryn Bialer has pointed out, this is a nationalism which reflects the historical experience of Russia and the Soviet Union, in particular the numerous invasions, and emphasizes the degree to which Russia is different, unique, and separate from the rest of the world, which is assumed to be at least potentially hostile. It is a nationalism which is imperial in nature and committed to the empire Stalin established in Eastern Europe. It is the nationalism of an ascendant great power with global interests and capabilities. It is, finally a nationalism that is wedded to the idea of a universal mission.[27] (4) Taken as a whole, the present-day official ideology of the Soviet Union, as modified by doctrinal changes and the impact of nationalism, advocates a world view which is inherently opposed to any long-term, let alone permanent, accommodation with the non-communist world and to any genuine modus vivendi with the United States.

The question of the influence of ideology on Soviet foreign policy is a relevant question to ask because (1) the Soviet Union, during most of its history, has been a state with a mission supposedly ordained and legitimized by history—viz., to transform the world and to further the interests of world communism, and (2) for the first time in its history, the Soviet Union has acquired the capabilities that are more nearly commensurate with that mission. The fact that the USSR has achieved nuclear parity with the United States and has become a global power makes the question of Soviet intentions and, therefore, the question of the influence of Soviet ideology more pertinent today than ever before.

As Zbigniew Brzezinski has noted, "power tempts—not only serves—policy."[28] The question uppermost in the minds of Western statesmen and policymakers today is: What will the Soviet Union do with its enormous military power that by now clearly exceeds any reasonable defensive needs? With the capabilities of the Soviet Union no longer in doubt, the key question concerns the motivations and intentions of the Soviet leadership in accumulating this vast military power. In part the urgency of this question stems from recent Soviet behavior in international politics. Soviet military intervention in Angola (through surrogate Cuban troops), Ethiopia, and Afghanistan, where the Soviet Union was involved longer than in World War II, gives rise to a series of questions. Will the unprecedented use of military power by the Soviet Union outside its own immediate security sphere—in the case of Angola and Ethiopia far away from its own shores—in the long run turn out to be a passing episode or is it the harbinger of a generally more assertive and aggressive stance on the part of the USSR? Will the Soviet Union, now that it has greatly expanded its capabilities, actively seek to translate its military power into political gains? Will the tension between the transformational (revolutionary) and the conventional (state) goals, which has historically characterized the foreign policy of the USSR, once again increase, now that the Soviet Union is clearly capable of exerting its influence on a global scale? Is Afghanistan a special case, where massive military intervention by the Soviet Union was prompted by legitimate security concerns, or is it a case of imperial expansion into yet another hapless borderland? Having objectively achieved an unprecedented degree of national security (to the extent to which there is security in the nuclear age), will the Soviet leadership subjectively respond to this circumstance and recognize the significance of its achievement by modifying its world view and overcoming its siege mentality? Having become a highly conservative power with respect to its domestic policies, will the Soviet Union come to perceive its interests to be best served by international stability and, in general, by the acceptance and preservation of the existing international order, or will it seek to maximize Soviet interests by pursuing a policy of destabilization, thus adding to the already considerable turmoil of international politics?

There is little doubt that the legitimacy of the Soviet regime in the eyes of its people is based on the successes of Soviet foreign policy, which are a source of pride for Soviet citizens. On the other hand, the history of Soviet foreign policy is not an unmitigated success story. It remains to be seen what ultimate impact the stalemate in Afghanistan will have on the Soviet military, the political leadership and elites, and the masses. Similarly, it remains to be seen to what extent the Soviet regime will be able to translate its awesome military power, acquired and maintained at great cost to its population, into demonstrable and lasting political advantage, both at home and abroad.

INSTITUTIONS AND PROCESS OF SOVIET FOREIGN POLICY

Like all other important political decisions in the Soviet Union, foreign policy decisions are made in the Politburo, the key decision-making organ of the CPSU and the Soviet state. During some periods of Soviet history, e.g., under Stalin, the decision-making process has been highly personal, involving little or no consultation with other members of the Soviet elite and entailing a minimum of input from the institutions formally charged with responsibilities in the sphere of foreign policy. Not surprisingly, during the long era of Stalin both institutions and subordinate members of the elite were overshadowed by the superhuman figure of Stalin, the Kremlin's sole real decision-maker.

During the post-Stalin period, according to the available evidence, the formulation of foreign policy has been the responsibility of the Politburo and a prerogative—at least most of the time—of the collective leadership that replaced the one-man rule of Stalin. The predominance of the Politburo in the determination of foreign policy was publicly acknowledged by no less a figure than Andrei Gromyko, the foreign minister of the USSR from 1957 to 1985, in his speech to the twenty-fourth CPSU Congress in 1971.[29] Gromyko's statement clearly suggests that the Politburo routinely considers and decides questions of foreign policy and that the role of other institutions involved in the foreign policy process—e.g., the USSR Supreme Soviet and the foreign affairs committees of its two houses, the CPSU Central Committee, and the Ministry of Foreign Affairs—at least as far as decision-making is concerned, is a minor one.

The available evidence suggests that the foreign policy machinery at the apex of the Soviet political system has undergone significant changes during the past few decades. (1) Foreign policy-making in the USSR, it appears, has become much more institutionalized and routinized than at any previous time in Soviet history. (2) There has been a significant expansion in the amount and quality of information that goes into the formulation of Soviet foreign policy. In addition to policy inputs from such traditional sources as its own Central Committee staff, the USSR Ministry of Foreign Affairs, the USSR Ministry of Defense, and the KGB, the Politburo today benefits from the assessments, proposals, and expert advice of highly trained specialists working in such institutions as the United States and Canada Institute and the World Economics and International Relations Institute. (3) There has been a decline in the compartmentalization of foreign and domestic policy issues, resulting in greater access to the decision-making process for a larger number of institutional groups and a concomitant decline in the influence of traditionally preponderant groups, such as the USSR Ministry of Defense. (4) There is considerable evidence that the top Soviet leadership does not always see eye to eye on matters of foreign policy. Disagreement over foreign policy apparently played a role in the dismissal of Molotov and Malenkov from the top Soviet leadership in 1955, Khrushchev in 1964, Shelest in 1972, and possibly Podgorny in 1977.[30] Evidence of differences in opinion on foreign policy matters can also be found in statements on foreign policy questions by Soviet leaders—e.g., at Party Congresses, anniversary speeches, and other public addresses.

If the formulation of foreign policy is the prerogative of the Politburo, the day-to-day administration and implementation is the responsibility of the USSR Ministry of Foreign Affairs, until 1985 the domain of Gromyko and now headed by Shevardnadze, who, like his predecessor, is a member of the Politburo.

Like the US Department of State, the USSR Ministry of Foreign Affairs is organized along both geographical and functional lines. Thus, for example, in 1982 it had three departments dealing with Africa, five departments dealing with Europe, two each dealing with Latin America and the Far East, a separate department concerned with the United States, and departments for the Middle East, the Near East, Scandinavia, South Asia, and Southeast Asia. In addition, it had two dozen functional departments concerned with consular affairs, currency and finance matters, treaties and legal questions, press relations, cultural relations with foreign countries, and the like.[31] Although the geographical and functional basis of organization has been preserved thus far, a major reorganization of the central apparatus of the ministry was undertaken by Gorbachev in 1986. Four new units have thus far been set up within the ministry to deal with arms control questions, humanitarian issues, information, and relations with the Pacific Island nations: (1) The Administration for Problems of Arms Reduction and Disarmament, (2) the Department for Humanitarian and Cultural Ties, (3) the Administration for Information, and (4) the Pacific Ocean Department. In addition, there has been a major personnel shake-up in the former fiefdom of Gromyko, who himself was dismissed from his post as foreign minister in 1985 and promoted to the largely ceremonial post of chairman of the USSR Supreme Soviet, i.e., to the presidency of the USSR. Soviet ambassadors in over forty countries have been replaced since Gorbachev became the new General Secretary of the CPSU, including those in such key countries as the United States, China, Japan, England, France, and West Germany.[32]

The Soviet Union's relations with other communist countries, which—according to the canons of Marxism-Leninism—are qualitatively different from relations with capitalist countries, are for the most part the responsibility of the Central Committee Department for Liaison with Communist and Workers' Parties of the Socialist Countries. Consequently, the USSR

Ministry of Foreign Affairs plays a more significant role in the Soviet Union's relations with non-communist countries.

Another important party organ involved in foreign policy is the International Department, now headed by Anatoly Dobrynin, the former USSR ambassador to the United States. The International Department is concerned with the relations between the CPSU and non-ruling communist and socialist parties in the capitalist countries and in the Third World, as well as with the Soviet Union's relations with national liberation movements, such as the Palestine Liberation Organization (PLO) and the ruling MPLA of Angola. Whereas the USSR Ministry of Foreign Affairs has been primarily concerned with the conduct of the conventional foreign policy of the Soviet Union, the International Department of the CPSU Central Committee, as the successor to the Comintern (Communist International) and the Cominform (Communist Information Bureau), has overseen the unconventional or revolutionary aspects and dimensions of Soviet foreign policy.[33]

During the long tenure of Gromyko as foreign minister, the USSR Ministry of Foreign Affairs acquired increasing autonomy. The replacement of Gromyko by Shevardnadze, who had virtually no foreign affairs experience prior to his appointment, would appear as an attempt by Gorbachev to reestablish central party control over the administration of foreign policy and over the diplomatic service, and at the same time to reduce the role of the Soviet foreign ministry in the formulation of foreign policy. There is little question that Gorbachev himself intends to play a very active role in foreign affairs—an astute move on his part, considering the enormous difficulties he faces in the domestic policy arena. If Gorbachev is going to be his own architect in developing the overall design of Soviet foreign policy, his right-hand man, at least for the time being, will be Dobrynin, the former Soviet ambassador to the United States, who—in a totally unprecedented move—was appointed secretary of the CPSU Central Committee and, as head of the reorganized International Department, was made responsible for foreign policy within the central party apparatus.

Taken together, the reorganization of the Soviet foreign ministry now underway and the far-reaching personnel changes in the Soviet diplomatic service and its nerve center in Moscow suggest that Gorbachev intends to be "a man on the move" in foreign policy as well. There is little question that as a result of the changes that have already taken place—in particular the removal of Gromyko and his replacement with a party official relatively inexperienced in foreign policy matters, as well as the appointment of the highly experienced Dobrynin as Central Committee secretary and head of the International Department—the status and role of the USSR Ministry of Foreign Affairs have been significantly reduced while the status and role of the International Department have been substantially increased. This interpretation is corroborated by the report that significant control over the *nomenklatura* of the foreign ministry has been transferred to the International Department under Dobrynin.[34] Under Gorbachev, it appears, foreign policy matters, including the composition of the Soviet diplomatic corps, will be under much closer party scrutiny and control than in the recent past.

It remains to be seen to what extent the changes in the personnel and organization of the Soviet foreign ministry are indicative of substantial changes in Soviet foreign policy. In this sphere, it would seem, the Gorbachev Administration is cross-pressured. The attainment of strategic parity with the United States and the greatly enhanced capability of the USSR to project its enormous conventional military power on a global scale, no doubt, create a powerful impetus toward the pursuit of a policy designed to translate these recognized capabilities into political gains, such as a substantial increase in the general influence of the USSR in world affairs. The domestic economic difficulties, on the other hand, would seem to dictate a conciliatory policy towards the outside world and especially toward the industrialized nations of the West and Japan—a policy designed to minimize the likelihood of an unrestricted arms race, to facilitate the development of cooperative economic relations and, above all, to create a political atmosphere in which the large-scale transfer of high technology becomes possible and likely.

Whatever the ultimate shape of Soviet foreign policy under Gorbachev, it will—to a very significant degree—reflect the interplay of various domestic factors. There is little question that the overall weight and significance of foreign policy has increased in the Soviet scheme of things. The interrelationship between key domestic political issues, such as the economy, and foreign policy is recognized in the Soviet Union, both at the level of the top Soviet leadership and at the level of ideology and scholarly discourse. The moves made by Gorbachev in the foreign policy sphere thus far suggest an awareness that the domestic political agenda cannot be tackled successfully without significant changes in the Soviet Union's relationship to the outside world.

NOTES

1. For a discussion of the nationality problem in Soviet foreign policy, see Jeremy Azrael, "The 'Nationality Problem' in the USSR: Domestic Pressures and Foreign Policy Constraints," in Seweryn Bialer, ed., *The Domestic Context of Soviet Foreign Policy* (Boulder, CO: Westview Press, 1981), pp. 139-153.

2. S.H. Steinberg, ed., *The Statesman's Yearbook* (New York: St. Martin's Press, 1968), p. 1527.

3. David J. M. Hooson, *A New Soviet Heartland?* (Princeton, NJ: D. Van Nostrand Company, 1964), p. 34.

4. Robert C. Kingsbury and Robert N. Taffee, *An Atlas of Soviet Affairs* (New York: Frederick A. Praeger, 1965), p. 58.

5. Robert C. Tucker, "Swollen State, Spent Society: Stalin's Legacy to Brezhnev," *Foreign Affairs*, Vol. 60, No. 2 (Winter 1981-1982), pp. 414-435.

6. Hooson, *A New Soviet Heartland?* p. 8.

7. This figure represents an estimate. The latest census figure (1979) is 262,436,200. See "Britannica World Data. Comparative National Statistics," in *1986 Britannica Book of the Year* (Chicago: Encyclopedia Britannica, 1986), p. 830.

8. Between 1970 and 1985, the Soviet population grew by 35.8 million, whereas the US population increased by 34.0 million. The annual growth rate for the Soviet population during 1980-1985 was 0.9 percent, for the United States, 1.0 percent. (Ibid.).

9. According to Harvard historian Richard Pipes, Russia lost 2 million people during World War I, 14 million during the Civil War and the famine, 10 million during the collectivization of agriculture, 10 million during the purges, and 20 million during World War II. See *The Limitation of Strategic Arms*. Hearings before the Subcommittee on

Strategic Arms Limitation Talks of the Committee on Armed Services, United States Senate, 91st Congress, 2nd Session, March 18, 1970, Pt. I (Washington, D.C.: Government Printing Office, 1970), p. 23. For the population growth estimates, see Murray Feshbach, "The Soviet Union: Population Trends and Dilemmas," *Population Bulletin*, Vol. 37, No. 3 (August 1982), p. 7.

10. Of the 20 million casualties suffered in World War II, 15 million are estimated to have been males.

11. Murray Feshbach, "The Soviet Union: Population Trends and Dilemmas," p. 26.

12. Ibid., p. 29

13. See N.V. Ogarkov, *All in Readiness for Defense of the Fatherland* (Moscow: Voenizdat, 1981), p. 61.

14. For a summary of these measures, see Cynthia Weber and Ann Goodman, "The Demographic Policy Debate in the USSR," *Population and Development Review*, Vol. 7, No. 2 (June 1981), pp. 279-295. For an excellent overview of the population problems of the USSR, see Feshbach, "The Soviet Union: Population Trends and Dilemmas."

15. I. Stalin, *Voprosy leninizma* (Moscow: Gosudarstvennoe izdatel'stvo politicheskoi literatury, 1953), 11th ed., p. 361. For an English translation, see Joseph Stalin, *Leninism* (Moscow: Co-operative Publishing Society of Foreign Workers in the USSR, 1933), Vol. II, p. 365.

16. Stalin, *Voprosy*, p. 362; English translation in Stalin, *Leninism*, p. 366.

17. See Roger A. Clarke and Dubravko J.I. Matko, *Soviet Economic Facts, 1917-1981* (London: The Macmillan Ltd. Press, 1983), p. 10. See also *Strana sovetov za 50 let. Sbornik statisticheskikh materialov* (Moscow: "Statistika," 1967), pp. 28ff.

18. See Harry Schwartz, *An Introduction to the Soviet Economy* (Columbus, O: Charles E. Merrill Publishing Company, 1968), p. 21.

19. See D. Chemikov, "Scientific-Technological Progress and Structural Shifts in Social Production," *Ekonomika i Matematicheskie Metody*, No. 4 (1984), p. 593, cited in Boris Rumer, "Realities of Gorbachev's Economic Program," *Problems of Communism*, Vol. 35, No. 3 (May-June 1986), p. 20.

20. Ibid.

21. See Louis Fisher, *Russia's Road from Peace to War. Soviet Foreign Relations, 1917-1941* (New York: Harper & Row, 1969), p. 4.

22. I.V. Stalin, *Sochineniia* (Stanford: The Hoover Institution on War, Revolution, and Peace, 1967), Vol. 2 [XV], p. 214.

23. Quoted in C.L. Sulzberger, "The Dream of Czar Peter," *The New York Times*, May 7, 1971.

24. George F. Kennan, *Memoirs, 1925-1950* (Boston: Little, Brown and Company, 1967), pp. 549, 560.

25. Quoted in *The Economist*, March 8, 1969, p. 16.

26. *Pravda*, July 4, 1968.

27. Seweryn Bialer, "Soviet Foreign Policy: Sources, Perceptions, Trends," in Bialer, ed., *The Domestic Context of Soviet Foreign Policy*, pp. 427-428.

28. Zbigniew Brzezinski, "Peace and Power," *Encounter*, Vol. XXXI, No. 5 (November 1968), p. 3.

29. *Pravda*, April 4, 1971.

30. Bialer, "Soviet Foreign Policy: Sources, Perceptions, Trends," p. 438, n.12.

31. Central Intelligence Agency, Directorate of Intelligence, *Directory of the USSR Ministry of Foreign Affairs* (Washington, D.C.: 1982).

32. See Central Intelligence Agency, Directorate of Intelligence, *Directory of Soviet Officials: National Organizations* (Washington, D.C.: 1986), pp. 69-79; Alexander Rahr, "Winds of Change Hit Foreign Ministry," *Radio Liberty Research Bulletin*, RL 274/86, July 16, 1986.

33. On the role of the International Department and the CPSU Central Committee in foreign policy, see Elizabeth Teague, "The Foreign Departments of the Central Committee of the CPSU," *Supplement to the Radio Liberty Research Bulletin*, October 27, 1980.
34. Alexander Rahr, "Winds of Change Hit Foreign Ministry," p. 4.

SUGGESTED READINGS

Aspaturian, Vernon V. *Process and Power in Soviet Foreign Policy* (Boston: Little, Brown and Company, 1971).

Bialer, Seweryn, ed., *The Domestic Context of Soviet Foreign Policy* (Boulder, Co: Westview Press, 1981).

Byrnes, Robert F., ed., *After Brezhnev: Sources of Soviet Conduct in the 1980s* (Bloomington: Indiana University Press, 1983).

Cohen, Saul B. *Geography and Politics in a World Divided* (New York: Random House, 1963).

Currie, Kenneth M. and Gregory Varhall, eds., *The Soviet Union: What Lies Ahead? Military-Political Affairs in the 1980s* (Studies in Communist Affairs, No. 6), Washington D.C., 1985.

Dallin, Alexander and Condoleezza Rice, eds., *The Gorbachev Era* (Stanford: The Portable Stanford, 1986).

Edmonds, Robin. *Soviet Foreign Policy: The Brezhnev Years* (Oxford: Oxford University Press, 1983).

Rubinstein, A.Z. *Soviet Foreign Policy Since World War II: Imperial and Global* (Boston: Little, Brown and Company, 1985), 2nd ed.

Schwartz, Morton. *The Foreign Policy of the USSR: Domestic Factors* (Encino, CA: Dickenson Publishing Company, 1975).

Staar, Richard F. *USSR Foreign Policies After Detente* (Stanford: Hoover Institution Press, 1985).

Triska, Jan F. and David D. Finley, *Soviet Foreign Policy* (London: Macmillan, 1968).

Veen, Hans-Joachim, ed. *Wohin entwickelt sich die Sowjetunion? Zur aussenpolitischen Relevanz innenpolitischer Entwicklungen* (Konrad-Adenauer Stiftung, Forschungsbericht 38) (Melle: Verlag Ernst Knoth, 1984).

THREE

TRIPLE DETENTE? THE STRATEGIC TRIANGLE IN THE LATE TWENTIETH CENTURY

Thomas W. Robinson

T he US-Soviet-Chinese strategic triangle entered a new phase in the mid-1980s, a consequence of changing conditions. Most importantly, in each of the three countries, the configuration of domestic forces changed both in direction and intensity, and caused all three states to seek a respite from mutual competition for power. Moreover, improvement was notable in bilateral relations along all three legs of the triangle, particularly the Sino-Soviet. Further, the several regional systems as well as the overall international system entered a new period of relative stability. The result of all three trends—at the domestic, foreign policy, and systemic levels—was a reshaping of the triangle into a rough equilateral form such that for the first time the prospect existed for mutually harmonious relations among the three. To be sure, that did not signal major withdrawal from the international arena by any of the three. On the contrary, foreign policy activism was the order of the day in Washington, Beijing, and Moscow. But theirs was the activism of positive involvement, wherein the gains of one triangular member were not always perceived to be at the expense of the others. Undercurrents still pulled in the opposite direction, especially concerning Soviet policy dualism. Nonetheless, the threat of direct military clashes receded, and competition was increasingly directed into the economic sphere. If the status quo would hold for a decade or so, conditions could change the primitive and dangerous nature of the triangle into a four- or even five-sided system. Japan and Western Europe stood the best chances of entering the scene as "nth" entities.

These are the themes of this chapter. Before setting them forth in detail, it is useful to recall briefly the history and operation of the strategic triangle. That exercise will demonstrate that the situation beginning around 1985 was both unique and promising, as well as illustrate how the dynamics of the system could bring about a new and perhaps felicitous equilibrium.

The triangle assumed three "forms" between its inception in the early 1950s and the 1980s. Each lasted roughly a decade. During the 1950s, it was obtuse in shape, as the Sino-Soviet alliance and the Cold War drew Moscow and Beijing together and as Washington assessed China and Russia as superior and subordinate enemies. That changed during the 1960s, thanks to the Sino-Soviet split. Since the political distance between Washington and Moscow did not vary greatly (the first arms control agreements and the Khrushchev visit were balanced by the Berlin, U-2, and Cuban missile crises), the triangle became more equilateral in form. It was, however, a system of all against all, accentuated by the Vietnam War and the Chinese Cultural Revolution. In the 1970s, two sets of shocks, inside and outside the triangle, precipitated a redistribution of power and policy within the system and throughout the globe. Inside the triangle, the Sino-Soviet military clashes in 1969, the subsequent Soviet military buildup in Asia against China, and the similar general buildup against the United States throughout the 1970s caused joint Sino-American reassessment of the situation and eventual rapprochement between Washington and Beijing. Outside the triangle, the international economic crisis stemming from the end of the Bretton Woods system and the two OPEC oil shocks weakened American domination of the global economy, while the resurgence of West Europe and Japan, together with the emergence of a series of middle powers across the Northern Hemisphere, shook the triangle. With the American decision to rearm after Afghanistan, the triangle took on a third, isosceles, shape, wherein China and the US lessened their political distance while each remained strongly opposed to Moscow. There things stood at the beginning of the 1980s.

What were the operational characteristics of the triangle during the three decades after 1950? First, the Soviet-American leg of the triangle was by far the most important but, because of its unchanging nature, provided the stabilizing base of the system. Second, the history of the triangle stemmed from variations— quite large, over thirty-plus years—in Chinese foreign policy, since Beijing's relative power was small compared with that of the United States and the Soviet Union. Third, the strategic triangle was a balance of power system, albeit primitive and vicious, and exhibited all the distinctive features of such a system. Thus, the lessons and known regularities of balance of power politics could be applied to relations among the three, as well as to their respective policies toward outside states and issues. Last, because of the enormous size of the three members of the triangle—each being in fact an internal empire—and the very great differences among them in terms of culture, history, geography, and level of modernization, the most important determinant of their respective foreign policies was the complex of domestic influences. International influences, while obviously important, were in fact disturbances to foreign policies made essentially in response to internal factors.

These four operational characteristics of the strategic triangle continued to operate in the 1980s and would undoubtedly persist in the period beyond. Already, however, forces welling up within the triangle were, by 1985, quite visible. Domestically, these included the Soviet tendency to pay more policy attention to solution of internal problems; Chinese focus on economic modernization as the cure for all its shortcomings; and American reordering of fiscal and economic priorities and defense against growing foreign competition. In foreign policy, the Soviet Union, despite its military preponderance, turned cautious during the late Brezhnev era and the Andropov and Chernenko years, as Moscow began to address domestic issues and as the Kremlin took note of the strident anti-Sovietism of the conservative Reagan administration. China opened itself to wholesale import of foreign technology and associated cultural influences, grew rapidly in power as a result, and consequently sought to free itself from the confines of too-close ties with the United States and restore balance in its relations with the Soviet Union. The United States undertook a strong rearmament program, began to refurbish its alliance systems, directly addressed such gnawing security issues as Nicaragua and Libya, and took the offensive in the international economic arena.

Outside the triangle, important changes were also occurring. While the international economic system continued in crisis, with low rates of growth, enormous Third World debt loads, and rising protectionism, changes for the better slowly emerged: oil prices plunged upon oversupply, inflationary pressures subsided, and interest rates dropped. Although America, the global economic leader, was most affected by these changes, China was hardly immune as it had chosen to bet its future on joining the market-oriented system: even the Soviet Union could not stand aloof, as it depended on oil sales for hard currency and had to prop up the economies of Eastern Europe, which in turn were quite dependent on international variations. As the globe proceeded along the path of further economic interdependence, the strategic triangle as a whole could only be affected the more. Added to this was a tendency for political and military developments outside the triangle to live a life of their own despite the best efforts of the three to modulate them or use them for their own purposes. Examples abound: the Iran-Iraq war, the North Korean military buildup and state terrorism, Ethiopian starvation of its own people, the terrorist activities of Libya, the Lebanese civil war and its Arab-Israeli implications, the activities of Solidarity in Poland, and the deepening black-white crisis in South Africa, to name a few. It was true that the politics of the strategic triangle were a vital element in keeping the peace (and hence indirectly fostering economic development) in several regions, especially those around the Chinese periphery. But more and more, global changes were beyond the means of the triangle to control.

When these changes, inside and outside the triangle, were summed, their net effect by the mid-1980s was to provide a kind of uneasy and perhaps temporary stability to relations among America, China, and Russia. A second effect, however, was to provide breathing space for decision-makers in the three capitals and an opportunity for both statesmen and analysts to plan and forecast the next stage of Sino-Soviet-American relations. Preliminary estimates arrived at three interesting conclusions. First, the need in all three capitals to pay attention to domestic problems and to try to stay out of harm's way abroad was so great that the time to deal with them, and hence the time of overall stability, could be lengthy indeed—as much as another ten to fifteen years. Second, the way was open to address many of the outstanding bilateral issues that had troubled all three legs of the triangle for many years. In the American-Soviet case, this meant renewed effort toward effective nuclear (and perhaps conventional) arms control. In Sino-Soviet relations, new policy departures sought to address the boundary question and the associated issue of Soviet and Chinese force dispositions in relevant areas; these led by 1985 to a general improvement in state-to-state ties. And in Sino-American developments, commercial and cultural ties of all kinds were strengthened considerably during the first half of the 1980s, while the all-important matter of Taiwan's future was kept off the top of the agenda. Third, extra-triangular forces more and more subtracted arenas and issues that previously had been hostage to the exigencies of relations among the three. Questions of international economics promised, for better or worse, to become the topic of supreme importance during the next decade or so. The two near-super-powers, Japan and Western Europe, together with an increasing number of middle powers, resisted the notion that their policies and futures would continue to be set in Washington, Moscow, and Beijing. And even in those nations of the Third World which could not play a major role in world affairs, the winds of modernization blew ever stronger. More and more they resisted, individually and collectively, the perceived domination of the strategic triangle, sought their own paths to development, refused to line up with one or the other against the third, marked out their own ideological paths, and took independent positions on key international issues. That they were only partly successful in the short run did not obscure the trend.

If in fact a major restructuring of the strategic triangle, and possibly even its transmutation into some other system, seems possible, it behooves us, in this preliminary inquiry, to cast a closer glance at these forces for change. First, let us look at the domestic situation as the most important factor in each of the three states, beginning with the United States.[1] Although there was plenty of room for argument, in the early 1980s America faced substantial socioeconomic problems which, if left to develop without redress, could have unwelcome political ramifications. Whatever the case, remedial measures would take at least a decade, during which Washington would, on balance, tend not to take startling initiatives abroad, induce conflict, intervene in existing disputes, or devote an increasing share of its policy and national attention or material wherewithal to the international sphere.

Continued economic problems were clearly the principal motivating force. Although inflation had been reduced during the early 1980s and interest rates had come down (although not rapidly and still not low enough to stimulate substantial growth), unemployment remained high, Federal budget deficits skyrocketed (and could not decline, thanks to the too low tax rates unwisely legislated by Reagan), deindustrialization accelerated, and the trade deficit mushroomed. There was no sign that these problems, all interrelated, would or could be healed satisfactorily in the foreseeable future. Only radical change would suffice, and that was not likely short of an acute economic crisis as a catalyst. Such a crisis could not be ruled out, since the normal economic cycle indicated that a recession could occur in the late 1980s. The system no longer possessed the cushion of a reasonably high rate of factory plant utilization, a monopoly or near-monopoly of high-technology industrial, farm, and service items for export, and a currency and a trading position that left little alternative for foreign customers. The recession, were it to come, would throw millions out of work rapidly, lead (at least before new economic solutions were found) to even higher budgetary debts, engender a stock market crash, induce high levels of protectionism and other beggar-thy-neighbor trade policies, and have a major impact on the international economic system. In an extreme case, only massive state intervention would be capable of turning around the situation, in effect reestablishing the World War II combination of planning, price controls, induced savings, and the like. Even wholesale restructuring—the only "solution" short of socialism yet known to the American economy—would take a good decade or perhaps more to set in place. During that period, it would be highly unlikely that the United States would want to involve itself unnecessarily in world affairs. Defense spending would be curtailed, foreign aid limited, international economic leadership in general foregone, Soviet military expansionism left unanswered, alliances left untended, and global leadership perhaps transferred elsewhere.

The coming economic crisis would probably be paralleled by social disjunctions of possibly equal severity. The root of the problem is social inequity born of the combination of human greed, changing economic conditions, and neglect (or refusal) by the political system to deal with the problem. Evidence of the situation was everywhere apparent by the mid-1980s: decline of the middle class, with attendant enlargement of the poorer levels of society and transfer of an increasing portion of wealth to the rich few; continued lack of solution to the problem of black integration into society (by the 1980s, the cultural separation of the two races had lessened only marginally); social disintegration and cultural decline of moral values; the massive drug problem, which appeared to be out of control, and the rise of crime directly attributed to its spread; the effects of long-term unemployment in certain sectors of industry and discrete regions; and the inability of the society to cope successfully with substantial illegal immigration across its southern borders, even after the new immigration law of 1987. Nothing less than direct assault against these growing problems would even begin to address their solution. But that would take not merely general recognition that the situation existed, but also admission that a concerted national effort over an extended period was imperative to set the problems straight. Since there was little indication that either condition was being met, the social crisis produced by these advancing conditions could soon emerge into full view and threaten the social fabric.

The question for the rest of the century for the United States was whether the polity could deal successfully with the combination of economic and social difficulties it faced or whether it too would be thrown into crisis. Some danger signs of the latter were already evident. An ideological bifurcation between extreme right and all other, more moderate, approaches had existed for more than a decade. Continued economic and social crises could well supply a massive dose of extreme leftist radicalism that established political institutions would find difficult to handle. Moreover, the political system was not producing a steady supply of seasoned and respected political leaders capable and willing to attack the issues. Many capable leaders preferred to avoid the political infighting and chose to remain in or return to the private sector. But the point is that it would take America time, probably as much time as it took to work itself out of the Great Depression, i.e., more than a decade, to emerge from the current economic and related social difficulties.

If the United States was thus entering a period of uncertainty which demanded greater attention to domestic problems, the Soviet Union was already proceeding along a similar path.[2] A large number of problems had been accumulating or had been left untended since the removal of Khrushchev in 1964 and particularly since the last years of Brezhnev in the early 1980s. The Andropov and Chernenko periods had proven too brief to address them adequately and the latter was not willing to do so. It seemed clear, on the other hand, that Gorbachev not only had a "mandate" (if limited) to confront problems and carry out reforms but also (given his comparative youth and his rapid control of the Party bureaucracy) would have the necessary time to get a reasonable start on their solution. The first order of business was to admit that the Kremlin could no longer avoid addressing the accumulated economic shortcomings and that wholesale changes were needed. In all probability, the Politburo possessed a good grasp of the magnitude and seriousness of the situation. But it continued to assume that solutions "within the system," i.e., top-down reforms, would suffice and that sufficient time was available to carry them out. Although the Russian people had always demonstrated an amazing tolerance for misrule and privation, and hence the Party leadership's presumption concerning time availability might prove correct, most observers agreed that wholesale changes of the system were required. The alternative was ultimate failure even of the reform effort and emergence of a revolutionary potential in the Soviet Union.

It was easy to perceive what the major problems were. Both agriculture and industry were performing poorly. In the countryside, productivity, while adequate in gross terms, was poor in per capita measures and in terms of quality and variety of output. The maladministration and inappropriate structure of the collective farm economy had long since become a familiar feature of the Soviet scene. It could probably continue that way indefinitely, since there was neither threat of malnutrition nor risk of running out of arable land, although the costs of irrigation and drainage were rising. But if Moscow wanted to make good on its promise of a better life under socialism, to say nothing of using food as an instrument of foreign policy or pointing to the successes, for propaganda purposes, of rural Russia under Party rule, it would have to make significant modifications in the system. There was time-urgency concerning rural demographics: most of the young people, especially men, fled to the cities, leaving the bulk of the work to be performed by a declining number of old women. Only a combination of much improved incentives and modern farming methods would alleviate the situation. This might mean replacing the collective farm with another system founded on individual incentive and the market price as the main mechanism for resource allocation. Major overhaul of the system was unlikely, and agriculture would probably remain a drag on Soviet economic and social life.

The problem was, if anything, worse in the non-agricultural sector. Low quality of output, technological content that slipped farther and farther behind world standards, prices of practically all commodities set by central planners instead of the market, over-centralization and vertical integration of industry, a basic mismatch between heavy and consumer sectors, too much emphasis on producer and military goods, universal shortages of essentials versus vast over-production of shoddy goods that could not be sold at any price, state ownership of all enterprises down to the smallest shops, shortage of standard services—the list was endless. As in agriculture, the problem was endemic and the result of the system of socialism, but not yet severe enough to induce revolutionary change from below. Soviet citizens in fact perceived their life getting better, if at a snail's pace. The problem was not so much domestic; the system could probably persevere indefinitely. Rather, international comparison and competition were what troubled the Gorbachev leadership. Most Soviet goods could not be sold abroad, the ruble was not convertible, the Soviet Union was not an important actor in the world trading system, and the Soviet system could not be touted as the best example of socialism and harbinger of communism. (Even developing countries like India looked down on the Russian example.) In short, Leninist-style socialism was in disrepute seven decades after the Bolshevik Revolution, and Soviet foreign policy was shorn of a vital instrument of policy influence and power projection.

Economic problems could probably be dealt with at leisure by the Politburo or even left to fester. The system would not be in danger internally for a few more decades. But ideology was another matter. Here it was quite clear that the younger generations had fallen away from the faith of their revolutionary-cum-wartime forebears. Moreover, the Party itself was generally regarded as an institution that sought to satisfy ambition and private gain of wealth and power but not an organization of the carriers of wisdom or the repository of enlightened, self-abnegating leadership. Few believed any longer in the innate verities of Marxism and certainly not in the current revised version purveyed by the Kremlin. Welfare socialism, yes; patriotism, certainly; but not continual sacrifice of present pleasures for the sake of the increasingly distant chimera of "full communism."

Thus the enormous alcohol problem within the Soviet population, the malingering at the workplace, the "I-don't-care" attitude
throughout the society, the escape into science fiction or wor-
ship of the past, and the continued rise of religious belief. As in
the economy, these matters could be dealt with for a while longer
either by ignoring them or through "administrative" methods
(the KGB, tighter controls over the individual's movements and
needs and, if necessary—but unlikely—outright use of force and
terror, i.e., a return to Stalinism). But in the end of ends, as the
Russians like to say, the system itself would risk toppling over.
It had occurred before in Hungary, Czechoslovakia, and Poland,
and could take place in Russia itself, if rising popular expectations were not attended to.

So the time to begin was right away, before a vicious circle set
in with the choice being repression or revolution. The trouble
was that the Gorbachev leadership seemed to have no effective
short run policy remedies other than more decrees, campaigns,
promises, declarations, and changes in material incentives. No
systemic changes appeared to be under serious consideration.
Words such as *perestroika* and *glasnost* would not suffice. And it
was also clear that the ideological blinders that had so troubled
previous rulers were still a deliberate feature of Gorbachev's own
headgear, despite his decision to surround himself with younger,
well-trained advisors and to travel around the country decrying
sloth and corruption. Leninist personalism was still in operation, shown by the tendency not merely to think but to argue
out loud to Western listeners in terms of crude, unsophisticated
Marxism.

The larger question was whether the Soviet Union was capable
of making itself into a modern society. The whole Russian political culture, which had not changed much in hundreds of years,
still stood in the way. To that was added the composition of the
USSR, a Union of Republics in which the latter had little
autonomy and in which all the constituent nationalities but one
(the Great Russians) were kept subordinate and subdued as

under the Stalinist formula. By the 1980s, the nationalities "problem" had still not been resolved; it was the direct product of the Leninist decision to provide cultural autonomy but forbid the large-scale movement of peoples (except by administrative decree, once again, as in World War II), locate industries largely in the RSFSR and not in Moslem Central Asia, and outlaw any kind of local political autonomy, much less a balanced federal system. Finally, was a society based on the idea that materialism was everything capable of becoming truly "modern?" What was one to think when basic indicators of modernization, such as infant mortality and longevity of life, had reversed and returned to premodern levels?

Once again, so long as Russia could get away with insulating itself from the outer world, it might not have mattered. But so long as the Kremlin stuck to its pretension that it was leading the world to a brighter future, the Soviet leadership had to care. It had to try to modernize (or remodernize) its people. The trouble was that it chose to do so through continuing the bankrupt combination of Marxist-Leninist ideological norms and material incentives. This in the face of a skeptical, generally demoralized populace. And it had to reform (dare one also say modernize?) itself, a much more difficult task, since the Party remained a political system whose main features were a contemporary version of medieval monarchism, Byzantine factionalism, and bureaucratic obfuscation. Although the future of Leninism itself was obviously not on the Party's agenda, at least publicly, any true attempt at systemic upgrading would sooner or later have to confront the basic cause of the comparative backwardness of Soviet society: the union of unreconstructed Marxism with primitive Leninism.

And so the Soviet Union had to be regarded as in serious trouble, which probably could not be resolved definitively for a decade or more. Hence the Kremlin's willingness to open the door to genuine compromises, however temporary, with the United States and to offer more lasting reconciliation with China.

As for Beijing, it had had its catharsis during the Cultural Revolution and Mao's last years. His successors had vowed never again to undergo such a purgatory and to move onto the track, once and for all, of thoroughgoing modernization of all spheres of life—led by the economic but not excluding the political. During the ten years following Mao's demise in 1976, the Deng Xiaoping leadership had carried out programmatic reforms in practically all areas.[3] The chronic agricultural problem was solved by abolishing the commune system, in effect returning the land to the tiller by making the state the long-term landlord, freeing the farmer to make most decisions concerning production and marketing; creating a revolution by allowing market prices, rather than state procurements, to rule; and privatizing much of local commerce and local light industry. A similar revolution was initiated in the urban areas and in management and ownership of heavy industry. Moreover, Deng swung open the door to high levels of trade and investment, deliberately allowing Western cultural currents to blow in at the same time. Thousands of students were sent abroad; they returned not only with technical skills but changed attitudes. The planning system continued to exist but shifted more and more to the incentive pattern. Wages were raised considerably and a startling variety of consumer goods were made available. People were encouraged to become consumers and make money. Cultural affairs were less closely supervised by the Party. The Army returned to the barracks. The Party was purged of many of its Cultural Revolution entrants, the old revolutionary generation retired, and education and skill level were made criteria for entrance and advancement.

The list could easily be extended. The point is that revolution from above had taken place in China, and one that met with widespread popular support. The question was not, therefore, what path Beijing should take or even how fast it should move. These issues had already been settled. Rather, the problem was: Could Deng's successors keep it up? Could they eschew the temptation to reimpose Leninist norms, shut off further reforms, and perhaps even jeopardize the modernization process as a whole? Would Deng's successors manage to stay together and not fall into factional infighting and outright conflict over differing ways to continue modernization? There was obviously no way to answer these questions until the post-Deng era had begun. Short of that, however, one could argue that it was in China's best interests to stick to the path so successfully laid out, i.e., that it was rational for China's new rulers to continue Deng's reforms and even to expand them. Indeed, it could be argued that they had no other choice, since to deviate would be to throw away China's best (and perhaps last) chance to modernize and to cast aside the high level of popular support so carefully repurchased after having skirted the edge of disaster during the two decades after 1957. As in the Soviet case, the Chinese Party could probably reimpose strict Leninist controls, stop modernization in its tracks, and demand absolute obedience of the populace. But the price would be much too high and the risk—eventual anti-Party popular revolution— much too great. If the post-Deng leadership were rational, therefore, the probability was reasonably high that China would more or less continue the policies set in place during this rule. It followed that Chinese foreign policy goals would also remain approximately what they had been since 1976: free trade, peace, and security.[4] And as a means to those ends, China would likely continue its modus vivendi with the United States and seek a significant rapprochement with the Soviet Union.

If these arguments had merit, then all three members of the strategic triangle had reason to smooth out their relations with each of the others, to maintain reasonably good ties, but certainly not to exacerbate matters deliberately by bringing to the fore unresolved issues. These kinds of ties are generally characteristic of the bilateral relations of states that have few or unimportant policy differences, no matter what, in general, the state of their respective internal orders is. But that had not been the case among America, China, and Russia since 1950. Relations between Washington and Moscow were usually poor throughout the period, the brief era of detente in the 1970s being the only exception. Relations between Beijing and Moscow were quite good during the early 1950s but deteriorated thereafter. American-Chinese attitudes and policies toward each other were uniformly negative until 1971, when they slowly and substantially improved to the mid-1980s. Nonetheless, the last years of the twentieth century could be different in that all three had pressing domestic reasons, as outlined above, to reshape the triangle into a roughly equilateral form characterized by all-around harmony. And when one inspected the catalogue of foreign policy issues along each leg of the triangle, it became clear that quite enough was on the platter. Indeed, it could be argued that national interests in each case mitigated in favor of settlement of a range of outstanding problems. The crucial change was that, for the first time, domestic conditions pointed to the same conclusion.

No miraculous nor permanent settlement of Soviet-American differences was to be expected, since the Washington-Moscow rivalry stemmed chiefly from the enormous and unique power of the two nations, the major incongruity between their modes of social organization, and their mutually exclusive ideologies.[5] But each desired a reduction of tensions with the other while it worked to resolve domestic problems. The list of possible areas of agreement was as long as that of zones of competition. Thus, the prolonged threat of mutual nuclear destruction gave rise to the need for new and meaningful strategic arms control agreements. The Soviet threat to West Europe could be dealt with by detailed force reductions along the Central Front, agreements not to deploy or to limit the numbers of new weaponry (especially mobile missiles and chemical-biological munitions), and more direct and immediate modes of communication in a crisis. Every region throughout the globe was witness to American-Soviet competition for influence, directly or in terms of third parties. Some locally initiated disputes could quickly involve the superpowers in direct conflict, as for instance Korea, the Middle East, Iran, and Pakistan. It would be relatively simple to defuse these time bombs by dealing directly with the regional parties and with each other's interests, strategies, and deployments in those places. The interesting and, to some extent, reciprocal, case of East Europe and Central America could also be addressed directly, if the White House and the Kremlin were willing to arrange mutual noninterference agreements. And domestic considerations would rekindle both parties' interest in trade. All these questions had been on the table of American-Soviet relations for many years. Each was capable of being worked on, set aside for the time being, or even definitively solved if the superpowers wished. Only motivation was lacking, something that could be supplied in the necessary amount by the changed domestic necessities in Washington and Moscow.[6]

A similar set of conclusions, albeit on a more limited scale, could be derived from the issues separating Moscow and Beijing. Both saw the gains that would flow from diminution of conflict. The Soviet Communist Party Politburo found it had two choices vis-a-vis China. Moscow could arm against a comparatively weak China, try to slow down its modernization drive, threaten it with punishment if it violated Soviet interests, withhold trade and investments, try to surround it with Soviet allies, or even move against it militarily. That was indeed the policy from 1969 to the mid-1980s. Or the Politburo could try to negotiate a settlement with China before the latter became too strong and thus either lost interest in compromise or drove a much harder bargain. The most important benefits of such an agreement would be, first, security from an otherwise growing Chinese military threat against difficult-to-defend areas of Siberia and the Soviet Far East, and second, freeing military resources for use elsewhere and shifting budgetary and material stocks into more productive civilian purposes. The cost would be decline in Soviet military influence (the only kind the Kremlin had in

Asia, as the Chinese price for a border agreement/arms control arrangement would be Soviet withdrawal from Southeast Asia). This latter Soviet policy came to the fore in 1986, signified by the Gorbachev Vladivostok speech, in August and its sequelae the next year, all of which stressed compromise of differences, optimism for the future, and willingness to seek solutions to various Asian problems. (It also signified the ascendancy of a group of Party "liberals" in the Soviet foreign policy establishment and their supporters in the relevant research institutes.)

Sino-Soviet relations had much potential for improvement, merely on the merits of the several issues separating the two communist-ruled giants. The border question by itself was not important and could be resolved overnight if the will and the preconditions were present. The Russians had long since supplied their share of both—and even went an extra distance by publicly giving way on the ownership of riverine islands in dispute and by announcing unilaterally a partial withdrawal of troops from Mongolia. The question was whether Beijing would seize the opportunity and compromise with Moscow on the so-called Three Obstacles (the border, Vietnam, and Afghanistan), and whether China should risk alienating its American support, which was predicated in part on the assumption of continued anti-Sovietism by Beijing. The Russian offer did make sense— it would cut costs, augment security, and lead to economic benefits for both sides—and would eliminate a major foreign policy obstacle to domestic house cleaning on the Soviet side and supply added impetus for modernization on the Chinese. The probability was thus high that a major improvement in Moscow-Beijing relations would soon occur. And if so, the second condition for establishment of an equilateral, nonthreatening triangle would have been set in place.

The last was already extant in the sense that American-Chinese relations had been good for over a decade and were constantly improving in both quality and quantity. The questions were, first, whether they would remain so during the period of Sino-

Soviet rapprochement, the post-Deng succession, and the Chinese drive for "independence" in foreign policy (e.g., movement away from Washington and toward the Third World); second, whether China would continue to refrain from calling a crisis over the Taiwan issue; and third, whether in the new era Beijing would maintain its policy of accepting economic interdependence and undertaking strategic guardianship, along with Washington, of South Korea, Thailand, and Pakistan. As to the first, rationality (that lovely word) would dictate maintenance of the status quo with Washington. China was receiving a large and increasing stream of benefits in all fields from that relationship; to throw it away would be to court disaster, at home and internationally. But the Party's Standing Committee had done just that several times before—under Mao, to be sure, who was thankfully gone—but there was no certainty that a significant policy swing would not take place again. For its part, Washington was willing to tolerate considerable separation of policy (there was no longer much talk about "parallel" tracks) and even a certain level of verbal abuse (lumping America with Russia as the two superpowers against whom the Third World should unite) in the United Nations and elsewhere. There were limits, however, as the White House and the Congress had already made clear. Only time would tell whether Beijing would understand its long-term interests clearly and not push itself too far away from Washington.

The most important issue was Taiwan. China had decided to put off resolution of the future of the island as early as the Shanghai Communique in 1972 and had continued that policy, despite its fervent desires, in the 1978 and 1982 declarations. In so doing, the Standing Committee took a calculated risk: that the material and strategic benefits that would flow from America would be great while, at the same time, neither would Taiwan move toward independence nor would Washington encourage Taipei along that path. Benefits did indeed come and the United States did discourage independence. But political trends on the island pointed sharply in the direction of a major opening of the political system eventuating in a multiparty arrangement, guaranteed political rights, direct election of top officials, and other signposts of democracy. With a population heavily weighted toward native Taiwanese who owed no loyalty to the Nationalist pretense of ruling all of China again someday, the door to independence was more than slightly ajar. A Taiwanese was even due to succeed Chiang Ching-kuo as head of the Kuomintang. A few overt steps in that direction might well cause Beijing to take fright and throw down the military gauntlet. That would, of course, destroy the American-Chinese relationship, since under the Taiwan Relations Act Washington remained the security guarantor of Taiwan.

Of equal importance, the United States was engaging in a sleight of hand over its commitments to the Mainland regarding Taiwan arms supply. In the 1982 Communique, Washington had pledged, among other things, to place a cap on the dollar amount of military sales to Taiwan, to decrease it on a regular annual basis, and eventually to phase it out entirely. But then the White House declared that the base amount for computational purposes would be the highest amount possible, about $860 million per annum, further stated that there would be an inflation differential (so that in some years the amount of sales might actually rise), later established a very low gradient, some $20 million per year, such that the total time involved could be as much as 35 years, and still later let it be known that American companies on a private basis could sell military technology to Taiwan entirely outside the 1982 agreement. Beijing forwarded protests on each occasion but did not take counteraction, despite the appearance that at least the last-named American action did contravene the letter, as well as the intent, of the agreement. It was not clear how much longer China would put up with such unilateral changes; the only reason it had allowed them in the first place was the establishment on a firm base of more important (at least in the short term) economic matters, technology transfer, and trade with America. At some point, Chinese patience was likely to wear out and the Standing Committee would bring the matter back onto the front burner, probably during the early post-Deng era and no later than the post-Reagan period in the United States. The resulting crisis could severely jeopardize American-Chinese harmony and both states would have to decide how much Taiwan was worth.

The third question involved the intersection of international economics and balance of power politics in American and Chinese foreign policies. For the sake of economic modernization, China had gone a long way toward integrating itself into the American-led system of economic interdependence. The benefits were manifold in terms of the contribution of foreign technology, training, capital, and trade to China's astonishing economic growth during the decade after Mao. The costs—cultural baggage inseparable from economic-technological goodies, requirements and standards set by foreign institutions, partial integration of Chinese industry with those in states at vast distances from Chinese shores, and meshing of Chinese fiscal and monetary policies with those set by central bankers obeying the dictates of foreign capitalist interests, to name a few—could prove high to a leadership that claimed to be Marxist in outlook and that prided itself on its autarky and extreme nationalism. It was not clear that the hybrid mix of Chinese-style socialism, selective Western imported technologies and managerial styles, and the imperatives of a systems-dominated international economy would survive in the long run. For America, the question was whether the benefits in Chinese eyes would outweigh the costs. The task for businessmen, scholars, and diplomats alike was to point to the concrete gains already in hand and promise much more to come in hopes that, when the post-Deng evaluation came, the essence of the economic relationship would have survived. Convincing Beijing of the merits of interdependence would always be an uphill struggle.

A strong degree of Sino-American strategic interdependence

had also appeared. Its foundation was both countries' need to maintain stability in Asia, the consequent necessity to deter Soviet aggression and expansion of influence around the Chinese periphery, and the shortfall in resources each possessed individually to carry out those tasks. The linkage with China's economic drive was clear: modernization, trade, and technology transfer, all necessitated peace and stability, both globally and in Asia. That meant that Beijing as well as Washington would cooperate not merely concerning deterrents of Soviet military aggression but, equally importantly, regarding maintenance of a balance of power in each of Asia's sub-regions. It was relatively easy to deter the Russians directly: the combination of American rearmament and Chinese military modernization, essentially separate tasks, would see to that. Nonetheless, the strategic bond was cemented by a limited agreement to transfer certain kinds of American military technology, training, and techniques to China, so long as no large dollar amounts were involved and no undue Chinese dependence resulted.

Perhaps of greater importance, although not often noted or even acknowledged, was regional cooperation in Northeast, Southeast, and South Asia in support of the status quo. The putative enemy in Northeast Asia was North Korea, for only Pyongyang could drag China into conflict by invading the South. Beijing therefore not only severely limited its willingness to assist the North (in the unlikely event of an American-South Korean invasion) but also withheld military assistance to the North and even threatened to take (unspecified) direct action if Pyongyang moved south. Thereby China in fact became a security guarantor of Seoul, along with Washington. That shift, occupying the late 1970s and early 1980s, caused Kim Il-sung to lean progressively toward Moscow, thereby exacerbating further Chinese-North Korean difficulties. In Southeast Asia, the same structural framework was present, with a similar outcome. There it was Vietnamese expansionism that had to be countered and the means thereto was to support the "frontline" state in

Hanoi's path, Thailand. Since Washington was already Bangkok's security guarantor of long standing, but since the United States after the end of the Vietnamese War was severely constrained in carrying out its commitment, it fell to China to supply much of the content to the threat of retribution were Hanoi to try to conquer Thailand. Thus, more than tacit security cooperation took place between America and China: Beijing as well as Washington stood behind Bangkok, both materially buttressed the anti-Pnom Penh guerrilla opposition in Cambodia. Also both punished Hanoi for its transgressions, China through direct military action whenever called for and America through refusing to recognize Hanoi as well as denying economic assistance. That drove Hanoi more completely into Moscow's hands, with the upshot that the Soviet Navy installed itself in Camn Ranh Bay and Da Nang and the Kremlin fastened a hammerhold on the Vietnamese economy. Nonetheless, war between Vietnam and the ASEAN states was prevented and a reasonably stable balance of power established. In South Asia, there was a slight variation to the pattern. The local contest was between India and Pakistan, with New Delhi aligned with Moscow and Islamabad oriented to Washington. But since India was by far the larger power, had become China's enemy after 1959, and was especially threatening to Pakistan after establishing a firm Russian connection in 1965, China had no choice but to prop up Pakistan. This it did in fact from 1960, but particularly after the Soviet invasion of Afghanistan in 1979. The difference stemmed from India's hugeness and the direct nature of Soviet aggression, both of which prompted Beijing to try to make peace with New Delhi by offering to compromise on the Sino-Indian border controversy, as well as use Pakistan as a base area to support the anti-Soviet Afghan resistance. The United States also sent assistance to the Afghans through Pakistan but, unlike China, refused to guarantee Pakistan against India, trusting instead to Indian good will and benign intentions. A contradiction thus existed in American and Chinese support of Pakistan. But as in the other two areas, the consequence was a reasonably stable balance internationally. It could be upset more by internal Pakistani weakness than by Soviet-supported aggression, which was also the case in Thailand and South Korea.

From the above analysis, it seemed reasonable to conclude that the strategic triangle, for both domestic and bilateral reasons, appeared on the verge of reasonable stability. Perhaps, by 1986, that had already taken place. Three considerations, two internal to the triangle and one external, remained to be addressed. The first internal issue was whether or not America, China, and Russia, despite their respective needs for international quiescence as a condition for solution to internal difficulties, might find the relative absence of threat within the triangle an invitation to play more active roles in pursuit of their various interests in other areas. Would not that greater opportunity for involvement heighten the prospects for clashes of interest as, say, the Soviets attempted to move further into Asia, China expanded its reach into the Middle East, and America decided it could wait no longer for events to move in its favor in Central America? Signs already existed that that was already occurring in the Soviet Union under Gorbachev, as supposedly "new" and more outgoing, positivistic orientation was replacing the negative and stodgy image produced by Gromyko, Brezhnev, and the like. And as the United States attempted to deal with its defense, trade, and fiscal problems, it had become much more active in negotiations with, and putting pressure on, its allies and trading partners. Finally, China was already experiencing a new freedom within the triangle derived from having moved a good way toward "relative equidistance" between Washington and Moscow, and would surely become even more active as its national power grew and its range of interests expanded. Such a propensity, on the part of all three members of the triangle, would undoubtedly continue. But two factors would serve to ameliorate those drives. On the one hand, if the situation worsened in the United States and the Soviet Union, and if China thrashed about during the post-Deng period trying to decide whether or not to remain faithful to the Dengist outline, which was possible, all three nations would tend to impart more caution into their international activities. On the other hand, the nature of their involvement would tend to be nonthreatening, both to each other and to outside entities. The idea of an equilateral, harmonious triangle was that its tension quotient would decline considerably. Thus, it would not matter so much to Washington if Moscow became a factor of consequence, say, in the South Pacific economy; Moscow would worry less if Beijing were to improve its relations with Hanoi or New Delhi; and Beijing would not be overly concerned were Washington and Moscow to sign arms control agreements concerning conventional force dispositions and nuclear weapons systems in Europe.

The second internal issue concerned the "lessons of history" of American, Chinese, and Soviet foreign policies. In each case, disconcerting regularities presented themselves. In the American instance, the certitude of foreign policy direction was often unclear to outsiders, first because of the four-year cycle of the presidency, and second because of the popular tendency to turn diametrically at times and adopt quite different foreign policy stances. Usually, a sudden, serious, and specific provocation needed to be present, as for instance Pearl Harbor or Korea. Although for the most part those departures brought foreign policy back into line with national interest, when they occurred, the international system received a shock. Even in an era of a harmonious, equilateral triangle, plenty of issues held such potential. To that was added the latter-day tendency for American policy to be made, independently, in many centers of the national government. Foreign powers often experienced considerable difficulty in determining what American policy was, therefore, or who was making it.

In the Soviet instance, the problem was equally severe. The Kremlin quite often chose to make a *volte face*, thinking nothing of the ensuing criticism or consequences to others, and acting as if nothing in particular was wrong. Indeed, Moscow always worked two policy lines, major and minor, public and secret, frequently opposed to each other. Soviet foreign policy from its inception has reflected such policy dualism. Thus, even though the Kremlin might negotiate in seeming good faith on arms control, it would at the same time arm itself as quickly as possible; it would officially support a government in power but simultaneously undermine it through propaganda, munitions, and training delivered to its domestic communist opponents; the KGB, so important an element in Soviet attitudes and policies, would take policy actions quite at variance to those adopted by the Foreign Ministry. Periodically, the contradiction between the two lines would be exposed, and the Kremlin would have to decide which to abandon. But whatever the outcome, the propensity to policy dualism caused others rightfully to be suspicious of stated Soviet policy and for Moscow to be capable at any time of moving in quite a different direction.

As for China, the problem was the regularity of the unpredictability of its domestic politics. Mao brought a sea change to Chinese domestic life four times after 1949, each of which came without much warning. Mao's successors threw out all his programs and proceeded in a totally different direction as quickly as they could. Who was to say that economic modernization *über alles* would outlast Deng? As noted above, rationality pointed toward continuity. But history indicated the contrary. And a China that could throw itself into turmoil could also quickly upset the nicely balanced nature of an equilateral triangle.

The best that could be said concerning the net effect of these two phenomena internal to the triangle is that they introduced notes of uncertainty and complexity into the analysis. While an equilateral, harmonious triangle based on domestic primacy and the need to settle outstanding bilateral differences ought to result in a decade or more of peace and development, it might not turn out that way. Too many unknowns still lurked in the equation.

On the other hand, the third and last consideration, this one external to the triangle, clearly supported the principal conclusion. External forces on the triangle, and others independent of it, would more and more constrain the three members to change the rules of the game they played among themselves and their respective approaches to the outside. Three features characterized that trend. First, as the volume of international transactions, principally economic rose in intensity and scale, the degree of interdependence would grow correspondingly. All nations, including America, China, and Russia, increasingly felt the pressures of interdependence.[7] It was perhaps not too much to say that the late twentieth century would be described principally by this development and that economic concerns would replace military threats as the center of international attention. If so, the "strategic" triangle would become somewhat less strategic in two senses: it would no longer be so central to world affairs, and its *raison d'etre* would decline in comparative importance. If security was the "name of the game" in the third of a century after 1950, development would be "where it was at" in the two or three decades thereafter.

The second feature was the rise of Japan, and possibly of West Europe, to near-superpower status. The former lacked the necessary military requisites and perhaps the vast expanse of territory to qualify in every sense, but it did hold the potential to augment its military power quickly. And it could well do so if trends already established within Japan and in American-Japanese relations persisted. As for Western Europe, only the will was yet lacking to act as a unit on the international scene, and that appeared to be in process of supply. An international system in which these two players rose to prominence in many (if not all) ways equal to that of the three members of the strategic triangle would transform the system; for the strategic triangle would no longer exist as such, having been replaced by a four- or five-sided strategic system, one that—merely because of the much larger number of internal arrangements (alliances, alignments, neutralities, and the like)—could prove to be inherently safer and more stable than the triangle.

The final feature was the rise of new middle powers, some of whom might seek a role in a transformed strategic system and others of whom might try to avoid that arrangement altogether. India and Brazil already had such pretensions, and certainly the potential, for the former. Other, essentially regional, powers sought to dominate their respective areas or to play a role on the world scene out of proportion to their objective capability. North and South Korea, Vietnam, possibly Indonesia, Iran, Israel, Egypt, Canada, Mexico, and Argentina were states that fell into that category. Others, such as Libya, Syria, and Cuba, exercised temporary influence out of proportion to their size for special reasons, as did some oil-exporting states. Even such non-state entities as multinational corporations and terrorist organizations ought to be registered as contributors to this feature. The point was that an increasing percentage of global transactions and the attention of policy-makers everywhere were being drawn out of the strategic triangle's arena and capability for influence and onto a broader stage.

In the end, these three external forces could spell the demise of the strategic triangle as it was known into the early 1980s. And given the opportunity provided by the more benign nature of the triangle internally, perhaps that was a legitimate policy goal for the United States, if not (yet) China or the Soviet Union. The dozen years left in the twentieth century could therefore prove to be the century's most significant.

NOTES

1. See *Statistical Abstract of the United States, 1986* (Washington: Superintendent of Documents, 1986); and Andrew Hacker, ed., *A Statistical Portrait of the American People* (New York: Viking, 1983).

2. See Robert F. Byrnes, ed., *After Brezhnev: Sources of Soviet Conduct in the 1980s* (Bloomington: Indiana University Press, 1983); and Seweryn Bialer, *The Soviet Paradox* (New York: Knopf, 1986).

3. See A. Doak Barnett and Ralph M. Clough, eds., *Modernizing China: Post-Mao Form and Development* (Boulder: Westview, 1986); and 99th US Congress, Joint Economic Committee, *China's Economy Looks Toward the Year 2000* (Washington: GPO, 1986).

4. On Chinese foreign policy generally, see Harry Harding Jr., ed., *China's Foreign Relations in the 1980s* (New Haven: Yale, 1984); and Lillian C. Harris and Robert L. Worden, eds., *China and the Third World* (Dover, Mass.: Arden House, 1986).

5. See Adam Ulam, *Dangerous Relations: The Soviet Union and World Politics, 1970-1982* (New York: Oxford, 1983); and Joseph Whelan and Michael Dixon, *The Soviet Union in the Third World: Threat to World Peace?* (New York: Pergamon-Brassey's, 1986).

6. On US-Soviet relations, see Raymond L. Garthoff, *Detente and Confrontation: American-Soviet Relations from Nixon to Reagan* (Washington: Brookings, 1985). On US foreign policy generally, see Thomas Thornton, *A Challenge to US Policy in the Third World* (Boulder: Westview, 1986).

7. See Robert Keohane and Joseph S. Nye, *Power and Interdependence: World Politics in Transition* (Boston: Little Brown, 1977).

SUGGESTED READINGS

Barnett, A. Doak and Ralph M. Clough, eds. *Modernizing China: Post-Mao Forms and Development* (Boulder: Westview, 1986).

Garthoff, Raymond L. *Detente and Confrontation: American-Soviet Relations from Nixon to Reagan* (Washington: Brookings, 1985).

Hacker, Andrew, ed. *A Statistical Portait of the American People* (New York: Viking, 1983).

Harding, Harry, Jr., ed. *China's Foreign Relations in the 1980s* (New Haven: Yale, 1984).

Keohane, Robert and Joseph S. Nye. *Power and Interdependence: World Politics in Transition* (Boston: Little Brown, 1977).

99th US Congress. Joint Economic Committee. *China's Economy Looks Toward the Year 2000* (Washington: GPO, 1986).

Thornton, Thomas. *A Challenge to US Policy in the Third World* (Boulder: Westview, 1986).

Thurow, Lester. *The Zero Sum Society: Distribution and the Possibilities of Economic Change* (New York: Basic Books, 1980).

Ulam, Adam. *Dangerous Relations: The Soviet Union and World Politics, 1970-1982* (New York: Oxford, 1983).

Whelan, Joseph and Michael Dixon. *The Soviet Union in the Third World: Threat to World Peace?* (New York: Pergamon-Brassey's, 1986).

FOUR

SOVIET POLICY TOWARD WESTERN EUROPE

Trond Gilberg

An examination of Soviet policy towards any region of the world must take into account the various roles that the Kremlin plays globally and regionally. First of all, the Soviet Union is a global power, at least in military terms. This fact has a direct impact upon Moscow's policies towards a region or a particular state, because such policies must be subordinated to the broader needs of Soviet global interests. Furthermore, the leaders in the Kremlin must reckon with the fact that its policies anywhere will be watched closely by the other global power, the United States, and Washington's actual or potential countermoves are factors to be considered as policy is debated, formulated, and implemented.

Second, the Soviet Union is also a regional power. In fact, its location on the Eurasian land mass makes it a regional power in Northern and Western Europe, Southeast Europe and the Mid-

Middle East, Southeast Asia, and the Far East. Thus, Moscow plays this part in more areas of the world than any other state.

Third, Moscow, as a European power, maintains relations with all of the other European states, East or West. Its policy towards any one of these states will be fashioned in part by such bilateral considerations.

So far the focus has been on the Soviet Union when it acts as a state in the interstate system. We also know that the leaders in the Kremlin traditionally have considered themselves leaders of an international movement known variously as "the international working class movement," or "world communism." This focus was in fact the dominant one in the Kremlin for a few years after the Russian Revolution, but it soon became secondary to the needs and interests of the new Soviet state. Despite such a secondary position, the Kremlin maintains that it represents the interests of the communist movement, and a leadership role is also claimed in that movement, despite the controversies caused by such a stance.[1]

Soviet policy towards any region, including Western Europe, is fashioned in part by this self-proclaimed role as leader of the world communist movement. In order to further these interests, the Soviets attempt to maintain strong and multifaceted ties with the local communist parties.

Finally, Soviet leaders claim that they represent "progressive forces" throughout the world, and they maintain ties with organizations that fall into this category. For example, socialists and social democrats occasionally are classified as "progressive," and the Soviets play on the old notion in the European working class that there are ties that bind among left-of-center groups and individuals, despite a number of policy differences and a host of controversies over the years. At times, this notion is expressed as "no enemies on the left," and it has a certain nostalgic value for some non-communist leftists in Europe and elsewhere. By the same token, the Soviets have assiduously supported peace movements of various kinds, and they have tried to capitalize on residual anti-Americanism throughout the world, including Europe.[2]

Soviet policy towards the region of Western Europe will be fashioned by the interplay of the various roles outlined above. Finally, factions and personalities in the Soviet political system itself will have an effect upon the creation and execution of specific policies. In addition, historical antecedents can be expected to play a part in the complex process which one can call "the formulation and execution of Soviet policy towards Western Europe." Indeed, many of the policies pursued by the Soviet Union in Western Europe are a continuation of traditional approaches, which we will now examine.

HISTORICAL ANTECEDENTS

The revolutionaries who captured power in Petrograd and elsewhere in November 1917 were mostly Europeans, both in ethnic terms and by educational background. They had been educated in Western Europe, or had spent time there, either voluntarily or in exile. Their intellectual inspiration stemmed from traditions originating in Western Europe, such as the Renaissance, the Enlightenment, and the French Revolution. Their ideological mentors, Karl Marx and Friedrich Engels, were quintessential Europeans who had little understanding or sympathy for the East, for Asia, or for the "great unwashed" Russian Empire. As Westernizers, the Bolsheviks admired the urban proletariat, itself a product of Western-style industrialization, but looked down upon the vast peasant masses which constituted the heart and soul of Russia. Both as revolutionaries and as leaders of the Soviet state, these individuals focused upon the West in general and Western Europe in particular. It was here that they expected the revolution to occur, and it was in this heartland that actual or potential enemies lurked.[3]

Western Europe had traditionally dominated Russian foreign policy thoughts and actions, a legacy the Bolsheviks inherited. The main policies emanating from the Kremlin, now adorned with a red star, in the decades up to World War II, had the following characteristics:

WESTERN EUROPE AS THE NEXT BATTLEGROUND OF WORLD REVOLUTION

Early in the rule of the Bolsheviks, Western Europe was seen as an area in which the revolutionary struggle must be successful, or the entire revolutionary movement, including that which had captured power in Russia, would be lost. By 1922-1923, it was clear that the revolutionary potential in Western Europe had abated if not disappeared. The revolutionary phase of Soviet foreign policy was very nearly over; expansion of "Marxism-Leninism" would have to come as the result of expansion in the Kremlin's power as a state.[4]

WESTERN EUROPE AS A HOSTILE AREA: THE NOTION OF "AREA DENIAL"

Having determined that Western Europe could not be won by revolutionary means, the Kremlin set about ensuring that the area would not be used as a springboard for hostile actions against the fledgling state. This could be accomplished in a number of ways. Specifically, the Soviets sought to establish friendly relations (or at least workable diplomatic relations) with individual West European states, while encouraging the development of political parties and groups that could undermine the strength of the existing systems of the area, thus reducing the potential for anti-Soviet actions. The goals remained constant: the states of Western Europe must be prevented from forming a coalition that could successfully smash the Soviet Union politically, economically, or militarily. The area must be denied to the "class enemies" of Soviet socialism.[5]

THE CAPITALIST CAMP DIVIDED

While the Kremlin was concerned about reducing or eliminating threats from Western Europe as a whole, it also realized the opportunities that existed through bilateral relations. A differentiated policy towards the various states of the region produced the opportunity to split the capitalist camp, to enhance economic relations with selected countries, and to gain political advantage, possibly up to the point where a revolution might in fact take place.

During the period of 1923 (when state relations assumed predominance over the pursuit of world revolution in Soviet foreign policy) to 1939 (the advent of World War II), the Kremlin paid particular attention to Germany. In fact, the preoccupation with Germany continued after the war and became a capstone of the Kremlin's approach to Western Europe even in the contemporary era.[6]

Other West European states also played an important part in the foreign policies emanating from Moscow. While Germany was of central concern, France and Great Britain were seen as important, both in terms of preventing their participation in hostile alliances, and of establishing good bilateral relations, both politically and economically. Thus, the Soviet leadership assiduously cultivated the British in order to obtain diplomatic recognition from London. Once this had been arranged, most other West European states followed suit. France was also a major element in the Soviet quest for legitimacy in the concert of nations. After the rise to power of the Nazis in January 1933, Soviet policy towards France aimed at the establishment of alliances and the securing of "collective security" in the League of Nations as the Nazi menace cast an increasingly deep shadow over the European continent.[7]

THE SOVIET UNION AS REVOLUTIONARY LEADER

While Stalin (and his predecessors) conducted Realpolitik at the state level, they also sought to fulfill their self-appointed roles as leaders of the revolutionary movement of the international working class. This policy went through a number of changes between 1917 and 1939, ranging from revolutionary optimism and the promotion of upheavals (1919-1921) through the tactical device of the united front (1921/22-1927/28), the struggle with the "social fascists" (1928-1933), and the "popular front" (1933-1939).[8]

SOVIET FOREIGN POLICY 1945-1980: THE EMERGING BIPOLAR SYSTEM

World War II changed the political map of Europe and fundamentally transformed the nature of international relations. Part of the European continent was now controlled by local communist parties under the protection of the Soviet Union and the occupying forces of the Red Army. The notion of "Western Europe" took on a different meaning; it now basically included all those states which had not fallen under communist control. Geographically, this included the territories west of the Elbe River, while politically it also contained states such as Finland and Austria, technically neutral but clearly in the Western "camp" in terms of the traditions, political culture, and political process.

In addition to the massive political changes in Eastern Europe there now emerged another extra-European power which exerted profound impact on European politics, namely the United States. The emergence of the United States as a global power and the leader of the Western alliance, which was clearly directed against Soviet expansionism (as seen in Washington), altered the balance of power on the European continent, and forced a change in basic aspects of Soviet foreign policy towards that region.

A new element in the Kremlin's policy was the focus on the United States as the main enemy and chief contender. The Kremlin increasingly found itself in competition with the most powerful capitalist state. This competition occurred first in Europe, but as Soviet foreign policy interests began to extend into the Third World, Stalin's successors also found the political, economic, and sometimes military presence of the United

States very much a factor there. In Western Europe, the Marshall Plan, the establishment of NATO, and the reemergence of West Germany as a major military power in close alliance with the United States represented serious obstacles to Soviet interests in the region. Soviet policy towards Europe in the three decades from 1945-1975 was in large measure preoccupied with these matters.[9]

During this period, there were a number of issues that could be utilized by the Kremlin for the purpose of reducing American influence in Europe. A concerted campaign was launched to prevent the formation of NATO. Later, West German membership in that organization was protested through a number of front organizations and other vehicles. During the 1960s and early 1970s, the war in Vietnam provided a useful tool as Moscow tried to capitalize on the outrage felt in many sectors of European society over the war, which was perceived as a manifestation of US imperialism against genuine national liberation forces. The Soviets also actively opposed the formation of the Common Market and its subsequent expansion. And, throughout the entire period, there was an ongoing campaign to reduce or eliminate American economic influence and US military presence in the region as a whole or in individual countries.[10]

The Kremlin's bilateral relations with West European countries were determined, in large measure, by the overriding needs of US-Soviet competition. Thus, the goal of bilateral relations was to reduce US influence in a particular country and, if possible, to wean that state away from the NATO alliance. To this end, the Soviets utilized a mixture of threats and blandishments. The threats referred to the vulnerabilities of the country in question in military terms or, conversely, Moscow emphasized the dangers of local cultures and economic systems succumbing to American imperialism. In each case, Soviet leaders exhibited greater sophistication and a deeper knowledge of local conditions than had previously been the case, and policies were frequently tailor-made to an extent previously unknown in the Kremlin's foreign policy. At times, Moscow overplayed its hand, as evident in its efforts to influence some West German elections. But on the whole, the Soviet Union gradually emerged as a more formidable opponent for the United States than had previously been the case.[11]

The 1970s saw increased Soviet efforts to capitalize on the remnants of working class solidarity—a notion which had once been so powerful within the European working class. There was a renewed effort to expand relations with the socialists and social democrats of Western Europe and to work with this united front against aspects of US foreign policy. The issues identified were first the Vietnam war and later US policy in Central America. Here there emerged a common ground which the Kremlin sought to utilize to its advantage. Its success was limited, however, because the social democrats retained considerable skepticism about close relations with a regime that had been largely responsible for the destruction of working class unity in the interwar period and then again after World War II. Improved ties were nevertheless established—a far cry from the animosity that had characterized relations among elements of the left during the Stalin era.[12]

Throughout the entire period, West Germany remained the primary focus of Soviet policies towards Western Europe. Great Britain and France were close behind in importance, but local political developments in those two countries produced disappointments in Moscow. In Great Britain a strong conservative trend propelled to power the "Iron Lady," Margaret Thatcher, well known for her anti-Soviet attitudes. In France, the election of Francois Mitterrand to the Presidency did not represent an advantage for Moscow, because Mitterrand was a socialist of the old school whose foreign policy was marked by strong anti-Sovietism and an emphasis on France's place in the Western alliance. Elsewhere, the Soviets attempted to capitalize on Scandinavian attitudes emphasizing the need for bridge-building between East and West, thus limiting the influence of the United

States in that important strategic region. Once again, Soviet policies were marked by a mixture of threats and positive incentives, as exemplified by relations with Norway, strategically located on the northern flank of the USSR. The Soviets tried to prevent prepositioning of NATO military materiel in Norway, but were unsuccessful, in part due to their heavy-handed approach. The leaders in the Kremlin nevertheless gained some satisfaction from the fact that the stockpiles were located in the middle of Norway and not in the north, where they would have more utility in case of conflict. Other issues in Soviet-Norwegian relations included territorial boundaries in the Barents Sea (of considerable importance because of oil drilling), and economic activities on Spitsbergen.[13]

Throughout the rest of Europe, too, Soviet policies pursued the dual track of limiting US influence while expanding the role of the Kremlin. The Mediterranean, particularly Italy and Greece, represented an area of opportunity. In Italy, the communists came close to acquiring power in the 1976 national elections. In Greece, a left socialist, Andreas Papandreou, produced an anti-American platform in some of his election campaigns and, after he came to power, a number of these campaign promises were actually translated into policy. These opportunities came at a time when the perennial controversy between Greece and Turkey had seriously weakened NATO's southern flank. The prospects for the 1980s were thus fairly good for the Soviets as they surveyed policy opportunities in Western Europe.[14]

WESTERN EUROPE IN THE 1980S: OPPORTUNITIES AND OBSTACLES

As the decade of the 1980s dawned, the leaders in the Kremlin could assess the political situation in Western Europe with equanimity, but also with doubts concerning further expansion of their influence in that part of the continent. On the plus side, the strategic military balance, which had been based on American superiority in nuclear arms, offsetting the Warsaw Pact advantage in conventional forces, had been altered. The Soviet Union had achieved rough parity with the United States in strategic nuclear arms while maintaining its conventional superiority. Despite Soviet disclaimers, this reality was clear to most political leaders in Western Europe, and it confronted them with a painful dilemma: to rally around the United States in greater measure than before, or to try to live with the altered balance, possibly through some limited form of accommodation to Soviet wishes. This provided the Kremlin with an overall advantage that had not been present earlier.[15]

Even a neutralization of the Soviet advantage presented the leaders in Moscow with certain opportunities. Specifically, West European leaders and US statesmen alike envisioned the placement of American missiles in NATO countries to offset both Soviet conventional superiority and intermediate range missiles targeted at Western Europe. Furthermore, Washington continued to pressure its European allies to make more substantial commitments to conventional arms. Each of these policies created controversies among some of the political elites of the region. But the greatest opportunity presented itself among the masses of Western Europe, where substantial numbers fervently opposed US missiles and increased conventional armaments. Even if the Kremlin could not control the various segments that composed the European peace movement (which it did not), the movement itself presented the Americans with considerable problems, thus indirectly serving Soviet purposes.

Domestic developments in the United States as well as some aspects of US foreign policy further enhanced European doubts and fears about the "American colossus," thus potentially increasing the opportunities for Soviet maneuvers. President Ronald Reagan was perceived as the "grade-B actor" and the "cowboy" who would impulsively use the power of the American giant to create confrontations with the other global power, with dire repercussions for Western Europe. Intellectually and ideologically, many West Europeans also disagreed with Reagan's "new revolution" approach to welfare state programs, and they looked askance at the White House's infatuation with supply side economics and "rugged individualism." Furthermore, increased US assertiveness around the globe, and particularly in Central America, met with skepticism and at times outright opposition in some Western European elites. These fears and concerns were further magnified among certain political strata and within the public in general.[16]

Political trends in Western Europe in the second half of the 1970s and early 1980s also created an unusual and clearly inadvertent "alliance" between Soviet interests and the needs of some political forces in the area. The conservative trend which had swept much of Western Europe during the second half of the 1970s had brought down a number of social democratic governments and pushed these parties into opposition. In almost all cases, this trend produced a great deal of soul searching among the social democratic leaders. Had they lost because they had moved too far to the political center? Was it time to move back to the traditional leftism that had characterized them earlier? In any case it was necessary to establish a clear profile against the ruling conservatives, and this could be done with considerable fanfare in foreign policy, by questioning the "Americanism" of the rulers and emphasizing "Europeanism" and nationalism. Insofar as this meant reduced US influence among such parties (which might well capture power in a future election), the Kremlin could be pleased.[17]

Additionally, US policies in Central America, which were one specific example of a generally more assertive stance by Washington everywhere, created considerable controversy in Western Europe and provided a rallying point for many political forces of the moderate left. Once again, there was a commonality of interests among these elements, despite the fact that they had little else in common. The leaders in the Kremlin were quick to capitalize on these aspects of West European political reality.

Finally, the Reagan administration's emphasis on the Strategic Defense Initiative ("Star Wars") sparked considerable controversy in Western Europe, where public opinion as well as many political elites questioned the policy and perceived it as a potential hindrance to substantive arms negotiations. This doubt about a major aspect of US defense policy produced yet another area of opportunity for the Soviet leadership. And, as we shall see below, the Kremlin made this issue one of its focal points in determining policies towards Western Europe in the 1980s.[18]

While conditions in Western Europe and the United States produced numerous opportunities for the enhancement of Soviet interests, Moscow also faced a number of problems which made policy implementation difficult. At home, the early 1980s produced the inevitable results of rule by gerontocracy. The death of Leonid Brezhnev in late 1982 set in motion a political succession which brought to the top first Yuri Andropov and then Konstantin Chernenko before a more youthful leader finally emerged, in Mikhail Gorbachev. This rapid turnover at the top inevitably reduced the vigor and initiative with which Moscow could pursue its policy aims in Western Europe and elsewhere, limiting the likelihood that the Soviets could fully utilize the opportunities that presented themselves. But the advent to power of the younger, more vigorous Gorbachev ushered in a period in which the Soviet Union far more actively pursued its goals and objectives everywhere, including Western Europe. This revitalized leadership currently fashions policies towards Bonn and London, Paris and Rome. And, as we shall see, these policies represent a major challenge to the United States.

Leadership turnover was one of the liabilities facing Moscow in the early 1980s. Among other problems that still persist are the chronic inefficiency of the economy and the bloated size of the bureaucracy. These are systemic problems that cannot be solved by mere rejuvenation of the top political leadership. Indeed, it will require a massive investment of political power to get rid of the old and inefficient Party and state bureaucrats at all levels of authority. The current campaign of *glasnost*, sponsored by Gorbachev, has already run into considerable opposition and appears to require much of the General Secretary's time. Preoccupation with domestic matters inevitably reduces the vigor with which foreign policies can be pursued.[19]

Occasionally, accidents take place that reduce the efficacy of any policy. Such an accident, for example, was the nuclear disaster at Chernobyl, which had major policy ramifications in Western Europe. Soviet reticence about the accident and the cavalier attitude displayed by the Kremlin towards the leaders and people of Western (and Eastern) Europe after nuclear fallout occurred cost the Kremlin dearly. This was particularly true among those political leaders and mass publics who appeared favorably disposed towards the Soviets or at least questioned many aspects of US foreign policy. Subsequent Soviet openness in discussions about the accident alleviated some of these negative aspects. Still, Moscow will suffer from its own "political fallout" in the region for a considerable period as a result of Chernobyl.[20]

A number of other problems as well demanded Gorbachev's attention. The war in Afghanistan, for example, remained a liability of major proportions, both in terms of actual losses sustained and a tarnished Soviet reputation among many leftists everywhere, including Western Europe. The socioeconomic problems of Eastern Europe, particularly in Poland, further reduced the maneuverability of the Kremlin and drained precious economic resources that were needed at home. Relations with China, although somewhat improved, demanded continued Soviet concern and expenditures. Finally, the Kremlin got entangled in the Middle East morass, not unlike the other major powers. The volatility of that region has demanded a presence but makes real control or influence impossible. Once again, policies towards Western Europe occasionally were given a back seat vis-a-vis the many other areas of Soviet involvement and concern.[21]

Given the opportunities and liabilities discussed above, Soviet policy towards Western Europe has undergone a revitalization within the past several years. The region has again become a major target for Soviet approaches of various kinds. These approaches show a greater sophistication in Moscow's understanding of the political and socioeconomic realities of the region as a whole and also of conditions in individual countries. Taken together, these factors have produced policies that must be reckoned with both in Washington and in the West European capitals.

During the last few years, the Soviet Union has continued its dual track approach to Western Europe by acting both as a state in the interstate system and as the self-proclaimed leader of the international communist movement. The former role is clearly much more important. In that role, the Soviets distinguish between relations with the political elites of West European states, on the one hand, and relations with the public and various unofficial political structures on the other.

In relations with the political elites of Western Europe, Gorbachev pursues a number of policies that are common to the entire region. Other policies are aimed at groups of states which in some way are different from the others. Finally, certain policies are aimed exclusively at individual states. The most general policies of the Kremlin toward Western Europe include continued emphasis on the need to reduce US influence in the region as a whole.

This goal has been one of the mainstays of Soviet policy in Western Europe since World War II, and the Gorbachev regime has pursued it with increased vigor. The Soviets attempt to reduce US influence through a variety of mechanisms that are important individually but even more crucial if taken together as an integrated package. First of all, the Kremlin has cultivated an image of modernity in its relations with the West Europeans. Thus, Mikhail Gorbachev and his wife Raisa presented themselves as worldly and sophisticated individuals in their visits to

Great Britain and Iceland. The campaign to make Soviet leaders look more sophisticated is designed to eliminate the old impression of them as wooden, dull, dogmatic, and untrustworthy. Foreign Minister Shevardnadze has also done much to promote the idea that the current Soviet leaders are modern, well educated and, above all, "businesslike" and reasonable. This campaign testifies to greater Soviet awareness of the role of public impressions and public opinion in democratic societies.[22]

Second, Kremlin leaders have tried to portray themselves as sensible and peace-loving. The Soviets, in their campaign to limit the emplacement of US missiles on European soil, emphasized this message with great consistency. Similarly, Moscow has portrayed the Strategic Defense Initiative ("Star Wars") as yet another example of American warmongering that must be denounced by all reasonable men and women. Various Soviet proposals have sought to eliminate SDI from the American arsenal while offering a variety of concessions designed to establish the image that Moscow is reasonable, but the "cowboy in the White House" is not. This message was last sent forth after the Reykjavik Summit, with mixed results (see below).[23]

Third, Gorbachev has worked hard to promote the notion that all Europeans must act together for the purpose of promoting solutions to problems that face all of Europe. The US, which is manifestly not a European power, cannot possibly offer meaningful solutions to the problems facing Europeans; the Soviet Union, as a European state, can. The "Europeanness" of the Soviet Union has become a major aspect of Moscow's general approach to the region of Western Europe.[24]

Fourth, Gorbachev and Shevardnadze have tried to capitalize on some of the policies conducted by the United States in various parts of the world. Thus, Washington is depicted as a reactionary government dedicated to maintaining authoritarian systems everywhere, particularly in Latin and Central America. Continued US support for the contras in Nicaragua is unpopular with many political elites in Western Europe and the Soviets have consistently called upon "progressive leaders" to castigate Washington for its misguided policies. The US raid on Libya in the spring of 1986 was also criticized as an example of the trigger-happy nature of US foreign policy, thereby establishing a commonality between Soviet views and those expressed by some West European political leaders. This is clearly a continuation of policies established in the 1970s.[25]

These themes are the mainstay of Soviet policies towards the political elites of the region as a whole. They also constitute the backbone of the Kremlin's policies towards the West European public at large as well as selected public organizations.

While the Soviets are concerned about "denying" the area of Western Europe to the United States, they also have other designs on this important region. Western Europe is the third largest area of technological achievement in the world (after the US and Japan), and Moscow desperately needs technology transfer from this area to sustain its flagging economy. Furthermore, trade with Western Europe is important since the area provides opportunities for Soviet exports of raw materials and fuels in return for finished industrial goods. The larger the trade turnover, the better, for increased economic interaction may have political repercussions. For example, economic interests that have become heavily involved in trade with the Soviet Union and Comecon may serve as political interest groups demanding of their governments better relations with Moscow and the capitals of Eastern Europe. Any development in this direction potentially benefits the overall goals of Soviet policy in Western Europe.[26]

The combined effects of the altered strategic balance in Europe, European skepticism about aspects of US domestic developments and foreign policy, and increased economic interaction between the states of Western Europe and the Soviet Union and its allies may produce a greater willingness to seek accommodation with the Kremlin. This is a process, often called "Finlandization" (a term hated by the Finns), in which the states of Western Europe would retain their basic socioeconomic and political characteristics, but evidence greater willingness to accept major Soviet foreign policy demands. Such a development would substantiallly benefit the Soviet Union. Specifically, the economies of Western Europe would retain their productivity and could be used to bolster the troubled Soviet and Eastern European systems. The maintenance of political pluralism would eliminate costly control mechanisms, while "accommodationist" tendencies towards the Kremlin would produce desired results anyway. And, finally, such a Finlandized Western Europe would be much less likely to accept US influence.

There can be little doubt that Mikhail Gorbachev is pursuing Finlandization with increased vigor. This is done at the elite and mass levels, and there is some indication that it has policy makers in Washington and in the West European capitals worried.[27]

Moscow has continued its activity as self-proclaimed leader of the international communist movement during the decade of the 1980s. The policies pursued by the Kremlin were clearly coordinated with, and subordinated to, the needs of the Soviet Union as a global and regional power, but there were also other elements of importance. The threat of "Eurocommunism" has subsided. The Spanish Communist Party, once the spearhead of "Eurocommunism," split over the party's interpretation of concepts such as "dictatorship of the proletariat" and "the road to power," and no longer represented a meaningful challenge to Moscow's authority. The French party, which had flirted with "Eurocommunism" in the 1970s, moved back into the ranks of loyalists. Assorted other communist parties gradually reduced their challenge to Moscow. Among the major parties of Western Europe, only the Italians maintained their stance as the quintessential Eurocommunist party, and continued controversies with the Soviets on a large number of issues. This clearly represented a nuisance but, on the whole, the Gorbachev leadership can look with a certain amount of satisfaction on developments in this area.[28]

As interparty relations among communist parties improved during the 1980s, the leaders in the Kremlin attempted to expand their contacts with the socialists and social democrats of Western Europe. This was a natural tendency, insofar as these parties increasingly found themselves in opposition in a number of countries (as mentioned earlier), but the messages emanating from Moscow stressed the need for solidarity among progressive forces, thus reverting to a time when working class unity had been one of the main themes of Soviet policy toward Western Europe. These elements of Soviet policy clearly supported the needs and wishes of the Soviet Union as a global and regional power that made the ringing slogans somewhat hollow in the ears of many a European leftist. In the end, it was clear that the Kremlin pursued "working class solidarity" in a strictly utilitarian manner, as an auxiliary to its great power interests.[29]

Mikhail Gorbachev has continued a well-established Soviet policy of differentiated relations with the states of Western Europe. These policies are clearly subordinated to the overall goals of Moscow in the region, but within these limits are many opportunities for policy differentiation based on local conditions.

As Moscow surveys the map of Europe, a number of subgroups emerge, requiring policy differentiation. First of all, there is a group of key states, constituting the main Western European powers; in this category fall West Germany, France, and Great Britain. Italy is important, but appears relegated to a secondary position. Second, there are smaller states whose significance is determined by location and strategic value. In this category fall the Nordic countries (Finland, Sweden, Norway, Denmark), Portugal, and Spain. Third, some countries represent particular opportunities due to local political conditions (Greece, Iceland). Finally, some countries provide opportunities on specific issues, but are too small or dependent upon larger neighbors to warrant major attention (Benelux). Country-specific policies emanating from Moscow seem to follow this classification.

SOVIET POLICY TOWARD THE MAJOR EUROPEAN POWERS

During the past few years, the Kremlin's preoccupation with the "big three" (West Germany, France, and Great Britain) in Western Europe has continued, and relations have in fact expanded. This is consistent with the overall goals and objectives of Soviet policy and represents a relatively sophisticated reading of political conditions within the three major powers. During the last few years, these conditions have in fact provided the Kremlin with opportunities that were not present in the same measure earlier. In West Germany, for example, the debate over deployment of US missiles was particularly heated, and the peace movement mobilized large numbers against such activity. Part of that coalition is still intact and is being revived to protest US policies in disarmament talks, particularly pertaining to SDI. This debate has become a major focus for the leading political parties as well, as they established positions prior to the January 1987 national elections. The definite leftward trend of the SPD in West Germany has been followed with deep interest in Moscow, and Soviet commentary on this phenomenon has been quite favorable. All in all, recent developments in the Federal Republic have, from the Soviet viewpoint, tended to go in the desired direction.

West Germany is also important for the Soviet Union as an economic partner. The relationship has been maintained for a long period of time, independent of political vicissitudes, and Moscow is anxious to continue it, indeed to expand it. The Federal Republic represents the chief conduit for high technology to the Soviet Union, either directly or through the German Democratic Republic. West German industry and banking are also very interested in the relationship. This correlation of economic interests can also have political benefits for the Kremlin insofar as German ties with the East occasionally create controversies with the United States (e.g., the pipeline technology and West German imports of substantial amounts of Soviet natural gas).

Under these conditions, the Federal Republic will continue to be the key country for Soviet policies towards Western Europe. Moscow was clearly interested in a Social Democratic victory in the last election, because it might have meant a change in German policies on NATO, with less emphasis on solidarity with the US.

Furthermore, the SPD represents a form of German nationalism that tends to focus on specific German needs and the position of the Federal Republic as a Central European power. This, in turn, might lead to a reduction in Bonn's attachment to the Atlantic powers, particularly the United States. All of these tendencies are viewed positively in Moscow, because they could reduce US influence in a key country of the Western alliance.[30]

The Kremlin also watches Great Britain with a great deal of interest. Gorbachev's visit fascinated the British public and helped establish the image of a new Soviet leader—sophisticated, erudite, "Western." This is an important development in overall Soviet policy towards Western Europe, but has particular validity in Great Britain, where political conditions at this time look favorable from Moscow's vantage point. Continued political and economic problems have pushed Thatcher onto the defensive, while the Labour Party, under the leadership of Neil Kinnock, appears rejuvenated and strengthened after a decade of internal polarization, factionalism, and strife. Kinnock has publicly stated that Britain under his leadership would reevaluate the country's nuclear policy and work for changes in NATO's military posture. Such a policy stance is clearly favorable from Moscow's point of view, because it would reduce Britain's military value and would disrupt the strong ties on military policy that now exist between Washington and London. A Labour victory could also result in greater sympathy for overall Soviet goals and objectives. While not Finlandization, it is certainly much better than the staunchly pro-US and anti-Soviet policies pursued by Margaret Thatcher. And, finally, it may mean greater economic cooperation than is now the case. Thus, a Labour victory in Britain would be preferable to a Tory one for the achievement of all three overall goals set by the Soviets for the region as a whole. But it should be pointed out that Labourites have a tendency to disappoint Soviet expectations, as exemplified by Clement Attlee and Ernest Bevin after World War II. This indeed remains one of the unknowns in Moscow's calculation about Great Britain.[31]

France, by contrast, offers fewer political opportunities. Francois Mitterrand has conducted a consistently anti-Soviet foreign policy on many issues. Recent political developments have propelled conservatives back into power in crucial positions, and experiments with "socialization" of the economy have fizzled. The Soviets still need France as an economic partner, but economic relations must be conducted with a regime from which few political concessions can be expected. The only consolation for Moscow is the fact that French policy is often at loggerheads with US interests as well. In comparison to the Federal Republic and Great Britain, this is small comfort indeed.[32]

Italy is accorded less consideration in Soviet foreign policy plans than the three "majors." A decade ago, the expanded role of the Italian communists in internal politics provided the Kremlin with a certain amount of optimism, mixed with apprehension about the Eurocommunist stance of CP leader Enrico Berlinguer and his colleagues. Since then, the communist tide has crested in Italy. From Moscow's point of view, Italy's primary value is as an economic partner. The prospects of Finlandization are small, and the Italian commitment to NATO appears to have sufficient appeal across political lines so that US influence will remain a factor of importance.[33]

The Kremlin's policies in Northern Europe are geared towards the maintenance of Finnish and Swedish neutrality and further reduction of Danish and Norwegian commitments to NATO and the United States. Northern Europe is strategically crucial to the Soviet Union. Soviet access to the open sea is funneled through the straits of Oresund at the mouth of the Baltic Sea; a second access point is the Barents Sea bordering on the Kola Peninsula. Both of these access points could be controlled by the Danes, Swedes, and Norwegians in case of a military conflict. Furthermore, Norwegian airfields are within easy striking distance of the Soviet naval base at Murmansk, site of the Northern Fleet (and the single greatest concentration of naval power in the world). Therefore, Soviet strategic calculations must inevitably include the Nordic countries. Expanded influence there would be highly beneficial to the Soviets; expanded US influence in the region might be fatal for them. Thus, the Kremlin is looking for ways to expand the Finlandization of Finland westward and southward in this area.

In pursuit of these goals, the Kremlin can utilize a number of factors present in the local political environments of Northern Europe. Finland is neutral already, and its foreign policy stance is regulated by a number of political agreements with Moscow. Furthermore, economic relations with the giant neighbor have become important for Finnish industry. Relatively close relations with Moscow remain the guarantor for the continuation of Finnish independence and political pluralism. Basic changes in this relationship are not likely in the foreseeable future.[34]

Sweden is also neutral, but with much less dependence upon the Kremlin. In fact, Swedish neutrality is clearly westward leaning in most of its manifestations. Nevertheless, there are elements of anti-Americanism in some segments of Swedish society, and even the ruling Social Democrats and other parties of the moderate left have been critical of certain aspects of US foreign policy during the 1970s and 1980s. At the same time, most political leaders in Sweden consider neutrality as also implying bridge-building efforts between East and West. Such a mindset presupposes a willingness to examine Soviet arguments carefully and to take issue with those who reject them as mere posturing for maximum policy benefit. From the Soviet point of view, the continuation of Swedish neutrality and bridge-building efforts provide a more favorable political climate for "influence-mongering" than many other places do. It may also be that Moscow associates such efforts with weakness. For example, Soviet submarines have violated Swedish waters with relative impunity in the 1980s, and there is no indication that these incursions have been halted because of Swedish insistence. Soviet inquisitiveness about certain Swedish defense installations may have been caused by persistent rumors about operational nuclear weapons in the arsenal of this neutral state. In any case, spectacular revelations about these Soviet incursions have strained relations between Stockholm and Moscow, possibly reducing the expectations of the Soviet leaders about the results that may be achieved in Sweden. For now, Soviet goals are probably limited to the maintenance of Swedish neutrality and continued willingness among decision-makers and other members of the political elite in Stockholm to act as bridge-builders.[35]

Soviet policies towards Norway and Denmark focus on the membership of these two countries in NATO. The Kremlin is vitally interested in removing these two strategically located countries from the Western defense organization or, if this proves impossible, to reduce their contributions. The two countries currently forbid stationing of foreign troops on their territory in peace time and have rejected the positioning of tactical nuclear weapons in their countries. During recent discussions among NATO defense ministers, both the Danes and the Norwegians had a number of reservations about SDI. All of this indicates to the Soviets that, at the least, these two strategically important countries may be persuaded to keep their NATO contributions at present levels, or perhaps even to reduce them. Persistent pacifist sentiment in some strata of the population, particularly in the labor movement, further enhances Soviet hopes. But there is also solid support for NATO in other population segments, particularly in Norway, so the prospects for success in this Soviet quest are limited. Again, the Kremlin must be content with maintaining the status quo for the time being.[36]

Portugal and Spain are of obvious strategic importance, given their location at the entrance to the Mediterranean. The political history of both countries is also such that the Kremlin watches them with particular interest. This is especially the case in Portugal, where the communists, together with other leftist elements, almost succeeded in coming to power after the end of the Salazar dictatorship. Such opportunities are now largely gone, and both countries have established stable democratic systems. Still, elements in each country question aspects of US foreign policy as well as the commitment of their respective political leaders to the West in military and economic terms. Insofar as this attitude exists, there are possibilities for influence to be exerted.[37]

Domestic political conditions in two West European countries create a favorable atmosphere for Soviet approaches, be they political or economic. In Greece, the election of Andreas Papandreou ushered in a leadership that has taken a marked anti-American stance on a number of important issues, particularly strategic defense, US policy in the Middle East, and American support for the contras in Nicaragua. In Iceland, the strength of the communists in the domestic political spectrum is enhanced by the fact that substantial portions of the Icelandic public exhibit some anti-Americanism, largely because of the sizable US presence at Keflavik airport. Furthermore, most of Iceland's energy needs are met by Soviet exports. Thus, there is an economic factor of considerable proportion in this relationship as well.

Soviet approaches to these two countries at the opposite ends of Europe emphasize a number of common points. Most importantly, the Kremlin appeals to Greek and Icelandic nationalism. In both countries, nationalism is a pervasive political element whose intensity is fueled in part by domestic conditions, and partly by the fact that there is strong outside influence in the economic, political, and military spheres of national life. Together, these elements have helped leftist groups and parties in both countries. The exposed strategic location of Greece and the crucial part that would be played by Iceland in any maritime war in the Atlantic make these two countries a primary target for great power attention. This fact, in turn, intensifies feelings of inferiority and dependence, with an attendant rise in nationalist attitudes. In both countries, local communists have become the most vociferous spokesmen for national interests, emphasizing the need for neutrality and friendly relations with all major powers.

Soviet policies toward both countries stress these themes in an effort to capitalize on existing political conditions. A particularly important theme has been the Kremlin's desire to protect the social and economic spheres of both countries from succumbing to US imperialism. Furthermore, the Soviets paint the picture of small power involvement in big power schemes in dark hues for Greece and Iceland. It is indeed possible, Moscow warns, that these small and peace-loving countries may become pawns in the schemes of Washington imperialists.

The results of these approaches are mixed in both countries. The Greek government may have made loud noises about its disapproval of US actions in various areas, but practical policies have been much more moderate. Similarly, loud protestations of national feelings in Iceland have not resulted in official moves to withdraw from the NATO alliance. Again, the primary Soviet goal is to reduce the contributions of these two countries to the alliance; their withdrawal is probably beyond likelihood for the immediate future.[38]

The Benelux countries lack the characteristics of other states already considered. Their location is not particularly important in strategic terms, and their economies lack the size and complexity of the larger powers. Still, some political issues are particularly volatile in these countries, especially in Belgium and the Netherlands, and the Soviet Union has tried to capitalize on them. The most important was the question of placing US missiles on their territory. After considerable and heated debate, which produced major political crises in both countries, their respective parliaments finally ratified the government's decision to allow missiles on their territories. During the debate, the antimissile coalition was courted by the Kremlin in a variety of ways, but after the final decision, Soviet overtures towards the Benelux countries subsided. The current debate over SDI may renew Soviet interests.[39]

CONCLUSION

The 1980s have seen a rejuvenation of Soviet policy towards Western Europe. After the succession crises of the early years, the emergence of Mikhail Gorbachev as the leader in the Kremlin has led to a more forceful and sophisticated conduct of policy towards the region as a whole and also towards particular countries or groups of states. The specific goals and objectives of the Soviet Union in Western Europe have not changed in any major way since the Brezhnev era, but the style and vigor of the approach are clearly superior to the conduct of policies during the last decade. Gorbachev's approach reveals greater understanding of European political realities and capabilities for utilizing existing conditions and opportunities to maximum advantage, as discussed above. What have been the major successes and failures of this revitalized Soviet foreign policy?

An assessment of Soviet policy reveals a mixture of modest successes and some failures. No member of NATO has left the organization, while Spain has joined. In no country have Soviet efforts resulted in major gains for the local communists or the pro-Soviet elements of the left. There has been no serious defection from the ranks in Western Europe on major issues of strategic importance in the military field or in foreign policy orientation. Finlandization has not made much headway in state policy, and neutralism has been maintained at tolerable levels.

Washington is also pleased with the containment of these trends. Furthermore, Soviet attempts to use vehicles such as antiwar sentiment, protest against missile emplacement, and rejection of SDI for enhanced influence in Western Europe have met with scant success. Even the stalemate at Reykjavik, which was originally blamed on the US by many in Western Europe, has failed to produce real political gains for the Kremlin; US counter-moves and a concerted effort to communicate the real story of the Summit to the West European leaders have offset the early Soviet propaganda advantage. In fact, there may be a backlash in Western Europe against the possible effects of nuclear disarmament as proposed at the Summit meeting. Finally, West European concerns over US policies in Central America have not resulted in a major crisis in the alliance, despite Soviet efforts.

The limited successes of Soviet policy are partly the result of US decisions which in some cases have alienated elements of the West European public or parts of the policy-making elites. But the origin of these successes is not particularly relevant, as long as the outcome of policies is favorable for Moscow. For example, the Western European peace movement does provide a number of problems for US policy makers and local elites alike. The sense of increased Soviet vitality, coupled with the more sophisticated style of the Kremlin leadership, does have a psychological effect on those who must do business with Moscow. Mikhail Gorbachev's assertiveness in portraying the global reach of Soviet military powers as well as his determination to deal with the US from a position of strength, do instill a certain amount of fear in Western Europe. This psychological balance between the carrot and the stick helps set the environment in which negotiations are conducted and specific policies are formulated and executed. The Gorbachev regime is still young, and policy formulation is a time-consuming process, so positive results are not likely to be achieved quickly.

In some cases, Soviet policy may have been counterproductive. The increased activity of the Soviet secret services in Western Europe has resulted in spectacular spy cases and expulsions.

Many leaders of peace movements in the region resent Soviet attempts to attach them to the bandwagon of the Kremlin's foreign policy goals and objectives. Genuine neutralists resent Soviet policy as much as they reject US approaches to Europe. Assertive statements and thrusts issued in Moscow occasionally produce countermoves in the West. All in all, then, the negative results of the new Soviet style should not be overlooked.

Seen from Washington, the Soviet Union under Gorbachev represents a challenge in Western Europe. The challenge is not critical at the moment, because the self-interests of the peoples and leaders of the region dictate the maintenance of the Western alliance. Furthermore, there is a political and cultural affinity between the US and Europe that cannot easily be breached. The nature of the Soviet challenge is illustrated by the fact that Western Europe is once again high on the agenda of the revitalized Kremlin leadership. This means that the political, ideological, and propaganda struggle will be intensified in divided Europe. Given the style and sophistication of the Kremlin in the second half of the 1980s, this may become a formidable challenge indeed.

NOTES

1. One of the best discussions of Soviet roles in international affairs is still Vernon V. Aspaturian, *Process and Power in Soviet Foreign Policy*, (Boston: Little, Brown and Company, 1971), esp. "Introduction."
2. I have discussed some aspects of this in "The Soviets and the Noncommunist Left," Herbert J. Ellison ed. *Soviet Policy Toward Western Europe*, (Seattle: University of Washington Press, 1983), Ch. 5.
3. I have summarized a great deal of material here. See, for example, Franz Borkenau, *European Communism*, (London: Faber and Faber, 1953), and William E. Griffith, *Communism in Europe*, (2 vols.), (Cambridge: MIT Press, 1964).
4. There exists a great deal of documentary evidence on this topic; see, for example, Bela Kun, *Kommunisticheskii Internatsional v Dokumentakh* (Moscow: Partiinoe Izdatel'stvo, 1933).
5. Adam Ulam, *Expansion and Coexistence*, (2nd ed.), (New York: Praeger Publishers, 1974), esp. Chs. III, IV, and V.
6. George F. Kennan, *Russia and the West Under Lenin and Stalin*, (New York: Mentor Books, 1961), esp. Ch. 11.
7. This summary is based on many sources. For a concise overview of Soviet policy towards selected countries of Western Europe, see William E. Griffith, "The Soviets and Western Europe: An Overview," in Ellison, *Soviet Policy*, Ch. 1, esp. pp. 7-11.
8. Much has been written on this topic. My own book, *The Soviet Communist Party and Scandinavian Communism*, (Oslo: University of Oslo Press, 1973), discusses this in considerable detail. For a brief overview, see my conclusion, pp. 204-212.
9. Ulam, *Expansion and Coexistence*, esp. Ch. VIII-XIII.
10. One of the best discussions of this Soviet policy is still

Zbigniew K. Brzezinski, *The Soviet Bloc*, (Cambridge: Harvard University Press, 1969), esp. Ch. 6.

11. One of the recent syntheses of Soviet foreign policy is Adam B. Ulam, *Dangerous Relations: The Soviet Union in World Politics 1970-1982*, (New York: Oxford University Press, 1983).

12. Heinz Timmermann, "Moskau und die Linke in Westeuropa: Aspekte und Perspektiven des Verhaltnisses zu den Eurokommunisten und zu den Demokratischen Sozialisten," *Osteuropa*, May 1980, pp. 389-400.

13. See, for example, *Arbeiderbladet*, (Oslo), Dec. 10, 1979, on the subject of Soviet-Norwegian relations.

14. For a thorough discussion of the Greek communists, see Dimitri Kitsikis, "Greece: Communism in a Non-Western Setting," in David E. Albright, ed. *Communism and Political Systems in Western Europe*, (Boulder: Westview Press, 1979), Ch. 5. On Italy, see Giacomo Sani, "Italy: The Changing Role of the PCI," in Ibid., Ch. 1.

15. An excellent discussion of recent Soviet force posture under new conditions is William E. Odom, "Soviet Force Posture: Dilemmas and Directions," *Problems of Communism*, July-August 1985, pp. 1-15.

16. Alexander Bovin discussed the Soviet "European line" in a remarkably candid article in *Izvestia*, July 20, 1986.

17. Mikhail Gorbachev clearly made a pitch to leftist elements (and other "peace-loving elements") in an interview with a Czech correspondent, published in *Pravda*, September 9, 1986.

18. Ibid.

19. For an excellent analysis of the Gorbachev program and its liabilities, see Thane Gustafson and Dawn Mann, "Gorbachev's First Year: Building Power and Authority," *Problems of Communism*, May-June 1986, pp. 1-20.

20. The Soviets eventually became candid about the problems of Chernobyl and nuclear power; see, for example, inter-

view with A.M. Petrosyants, Chairman of the USSR State Committee on the Use of Atomic Energy in *Pravda*, July 31, 1986.

21. But by the summer of 1986 Europe came back to the forefront; see A. Bovin in *Izvestia*, July 20, 1986.

22. See ibid.; see also Soviet statements on the visit of West German Foreign Minister Genscher, (*Pravda*, July 22, 1986); French President Mitterrand, (ibid., July 8, 1986); and British MPs, (ibid., May 27, 1986).

23. Commentary by T. Kolesnichenko (ibid., March 27, 1986), on US policy generally. On Reykjavik, see Gorbachev's press conference in ibid., October 14, 1986, and editorial in ibid., October 16, 1986.

24. A message frequently sent to Europeans; see statements made to British, French, and West German dignitaries in Moscow, in ibid., May 27, July 8, and July 22, 1986.

25. Commentary by T. Kolesnichenko, ibid., March 27, 1986.

26. For a good overview, see John P. Hardt and Kate L. Tomlinson, "Soviet Economic Policies in Western Europe," in Ellison, ed. *Soviet Policy*, Ch. 6.

27. The theme is, naturally enough, not used by A. Bovin in his article on the turn to Europe, but the message is clear if implicit; see *Izvestia*, July 20, 1986.

28. The Italian Communist Party leader, A. Natta, visited Moscow in January 1986. The two party leaders agreed to disagree. For a detailed report, see *Pravda*, January 29, 1986. For a discussion of developments in the Spanish party, see Eusebio Mujal-Leon, "Decline and Fall of Spanish Communism," *Problems of Communism*, March-April 1986, pp. 1-28.

29. See Gorbachev's comments to Felipe Gonzalez, Premier of Spain (and a socialist) when the Spanish leader visited the USSR, in *Pravda*, May 20, 1986.

30. Much material has been summarized here; see, for ex-

ample, Elizabeth Pond, "Andropov, Kohl, and East-West Issues," *Problems of Communism*, July-August 1983, pp. 38-46; Fred Oldenbourg, "Sowjetische Deutschland–Politik–von Breshnev zu Gorbatchow," *Osteuropa*, May 1985, pp. 303-320; Boris Meissner, "Die Deutsch–Sowjetischen Beziehungen seit dem zweiten Weltkrieg," ibid., September 1985, pp. 631-653.

31. Soviet commentary on Britain can be found in the piece by A. Bovin, *Izvestia* (July 20, 1986), and in statements made to British MPs in *Pravda*, May 27, 1986.

32. The meager results in France did not come about because Gorbachev did not try; he visited France in October 1985 (see *Pravda* and *Izvestia*, October 2, 3, 1985), and French President Francois Mitterrand was in the Soviet capital in July 1986 (*Pravda*, July 8, 1986).

33. The Italian Premier, Benedetto Craxi, visited Moscow in May 1985, and the talks were "constructive." See ibid, May 30, 1985.

34. The Finns are acutely aware of the need for good relations with the Soviet Union. See, for example, statements by Kalevi Sorsa after he became Prime Minister (*Frankfurter Allgemeine*, March 7-8, 1982).

35. Despite problems of various kinds, the Soviets have made recent overtures to the Swedes; see, for example, statements made during the visit to Moscow of Ingmar Carlsson, the new Prime Minister, (reported in *Pravda*, April 16, 1986).

36. Such reservations are not new. The Danish position on a number of crucial defense issues was discussed in Hans-Henrik Holm and Nikolaj Pedersen, "Dansk INF-Politik," ("Danish INF Policy") in their book *Slaget om Missilerne: Dobbeltbeslutningen Og Sikkerheden i Europe* (*The Battle of the Missiles: The Double-Track Decision and European Security*), (Arhus: Forlaget Politika, 1983), esp. pp. 211-248. The Norwegian defense debate has been dis-

cussed by Trond Gilberg, et. al. in "The Soviet Union and Northern Europe," *Problems of Communism*, March-April 1981, pp. 1-25.

37. For recent Soviet approaches, see statements made to Felipe Gonzalez during his visit to Moscow, in *Pravda*, May 20, 1986.

38. The Greeks were wooed during the visit of Andreas Papandreou; see ibid., February 15, 1985. The Gorbachevs did their best to charm the Icelanders during the Reykjavik Summit. For Soviet reports on that Summit, see ibid, October 14, 15, and 16, 1986.

39. The Soviets put great hopes in the peace movements of the Benelux countries and elsewhere in Western Europe. For an analysis of the early stages of this, see J.A. Emerson Vermaat, "Moscow Fronts and the European Peace Movement," *Problems of Communism*, November-December 1982, pp. 43-57.

SUGGESTED READINGS

Ellison, Herbert J. (ed.), *Soviet Policy Toward Western Europe* (Seattle: University of Washington Press, 1983).

Griffith, William E. *The Superpowers and Regional Tensions: The USSR, the United States, and Europe* (Lexington: Lexington Books, 1981).

Hoeber, Amoretta and Joseph Douglass. *Conventional War and Escalation: The Soviet View* (New York: Crane, Russak, 1981).

Kanet, Roger (ed.), *Soviet Foreign Policy in the 1980s* (New York: Praeger, 1982).

THE FOLLOWING ARTICLES IN *PROBLEMS OF COMMUNISM*

Aspaturian, Vernon V. "Soviet Global Power and the Correlation of Forces," May-June 1980.

Gilberg, Trond et. al. "USSR and Northern Europe," March-April 1981.

Hassner, Pierre. "Moscow and the Western Alliance," May-June 1981.

Odom, William E. "Soviet Force Posture," July-August 1985.

Pond, Elizabeth. "Moscow and Bonn," July-August 1983.

Sodaro, Michael J. "Moscow and Mitterrand," July-August 1982.

Vermaat, J.A. Emerson. "Moscow and Europe's Peace Movements," November-December 1982.

FIVE

SOVIET CONTROLS OVER EASTERN EUROPE
ASSESSING THE GORBACHEV ERA

Ivan Volgyes

In June 1986, Mikhail Gorbachev, General Secretary of the Communist Party of the Soviet Union, stepped out of his gleaming Aeroflot plane to visit Hungary.[1] With deliberate strides, he walked down the ceremonial steps to be greeted by Comrade Janos Kadar and his wife, assembled dignitaries, assorted ambassadors and sundry KGB agents. Gorbachev, like his predecessors ever since the mid-1960s, had come to give his blessings to the course charted by Kadar. During the next two days of whirlwind visits and plenty of photo opportunities, lengthy discussions with senior officials within the party and government elite, as well as with a few factory managers, Gorbachev appeared pleased and conciliatory; after Chernobyl, it was as if he knew that no one would give him a hard time. In retrospect, he was right. As the official adoration continued, Gorbachev—already known in Hungary as Tsar Isotop I— received the assembled heads of the Warsaw Pact member states to ceremoniously pick up the mantle of Supreme Leader of the Communist Empire in Eastern Europe.[2]

As he sat with the leaders of the East European communist parties Gorbachev could survey the shape of his empire with satisfaction. There were no open or outward rifts evident; no Soviet tanks had been ordered in recently to quell unseemly riots, revolts or revolutions. There were no open challenges to Soviet rule, as there had been in 1948, 1956, 1968; even Romania appeared conciliatory. Outwardly, Soviet-East European relations seemed to be as "normal" as they have been for many a year.

The health of the Soviet empire appeared in relatively good order. The various nations of the alliance system appeared pliant and subdued, and there were few, if any, open challenges to contend with. The Poles had been "normalized" after the crushing of "Solidarity." The Czechoslovaks—even if economically and politically stagnant—showed a stodgy stability that kept the population sullen, dispirited, but unthreatening as far as the political order was concerned. The East Germans basked in a sunshine of economic prosperity, confident that when push came to shove, on the one hand, the West Germans would bail them out economically, while on the other, noted that the Soviet Union's overwhelming military presence within the country was to remain a fact of life. The Bulgarians were clearly "in control"; there were cautious calls for some "reformist innovations," but there was no perceived threat to the political order. The Hungarians were facing economic difficulties, although their relative prosperity was evident to the visiting Gorbachev and his delegation; compared to life in the USSR, Hungary seemed to be closer to the West than to the socialist camp. And while the Soviet leader noted the disgrace caused by Romanian mismanagement and totalitarianism, still there appeared to be no recognizable threat to the communist regime that maintained firm control.

Gorbachev and the Soviet leadership had reason to be content. Since 1945-1948 when the communists, under Soviet auspices, seized political power in the region, there had indeed been continuous challenges to Soviet leadership. As Stalinism grew harsher and harsher in the region, resistance also increased. The workers' riots in East Germany in 1953, in Czechoslovakia in 1954, the Polish events of October and the Hungarian revolution in October-November 1956, challenged both the Soviet/Stalinist style of rule, and Soviet control of the region. When de-Stalinization began to loosen the Soviet empire's hold over its own people and those in Eastern Europe, the Polish and Hungarian events of 1956 sent shockwaves to those who were afraid of losing both the empire and communist party rule. When, in 1968, the reformist policies of the Prague Spring appeared to threaten the stodgy party elite and create what Czech intellectuals called "socialism with a human face," the Soviet Union responded by sending in overwhelming forces to crush the Czechoslovak quest. And when, in 1980-1982 the Polish workers threatened the Soviet system by demanding independent trade unions and greater workers' power against an ailing and corrupt communist party, once again force—the power of the Polish military/security apparatus under Soviet tutelage—had to be used to crush their aspirations. But in 1986 the region remained calm, fraught with problems, but stable as far as Soviet control was concerned.

Much of this calm, of course, could be attributed to the fact that the USSR maintained relatively tight direct and indirect control over the region. Its direct control included the use of military, secret police, and political instruments, while its indirect means included the use of political and economic linkages. By keeping control of the Warsaw Pact, the military arm of its alliance structure, the USSR effectively kept peace in the region. With large masses of troops based in East Germany,

Czechoslovakia, and Hungary; with its logistical divisions deployed in Poland, no one in these states could realistically consider either making a separate deal with the West against the USSR, or of pulling out of the Warsaw Pact. With the local political and secret police organizations heavily dominated by the ever present KGB advisers and liaison officers, the population of these states could hardly breathe without Soviet knowledge of that act. And, with the political elites tied rigidly at the top by the political interrelationship among the communist leaders under Soviet "advice," leaders openly and avowedly hostile to the USSR were unlikely to emerge.

Indirect controls were also evident and well used by the Soviet leaders. In the political arena, the indirect controls included the frequent "consultations" by the East Europeans with the Soviet "older brother" that took place at all levels and in nearly all states. They included the fraternal visits, the Soviet infiltration of all types of cadres, the joint training and sharing of information, and even the formulation of policies at various levels within each system. Economically, it included the uses of the COMECON, the Council of Mutual Economic Assistance, an umbrella trade and economic development organization that was charged with facilitating Soviet economic control in the region. The East European states were not happy about the USSR's continuing exploitation through such techniques as charging higher than world prices for oil, or continuous Soviet demands that East Europeans help pay the costs for developing Soviet resources. However, because of trade with the USSR and because of reliance on Soviet raw materials, they were in no position to challenge the USSR. Altogether, the Soviets had reason to be satisfied with their continued control of the region.

Eastern Europe is, in reality, a collection of highly differentiated states. It includes Stalinist states, such as Romania that has been less supportive of Soviet foreign policy goals than the most liberal state in the region, Hungary. Poland, with its unsolved economic and social problems, with its social liberalism and semi-militarized rule, is vastly different from East Germany where the economy seems to work like clockwork but where there is hardly any room for independent ideas or experimentation. Bulgaria and Czechoslovakia maintain vastly different attitudes toward the USSR by their general populations, in spite of the striking similarities toward the USSR evident at the top party levels. For the Soviet leaders, however, the region is not merely a collection of different states; as far as they are concerned they treat Eastern Europe both officially and unofficially as the bloc, the "socialist commonwealth of nations." And in the view of the Soviet leaders, it is their region.

It is, of course, a natural human folly often occasioned by mental laziness that causes people to view human events in traditional methods of rendering facts. A mosaic fits trends and events into familiar places; the shapes and colors match deeply rooted patterns of cognition and recognition, and the human mind settles back with a sigh of relief. Only rarely do we try to look at events or ideas in a nonconventional manner, hoping to glimpse something new and different from hitherto familiar patterns.

As we examine the history of Soviet-East European relations, we often look at familiar patterns of recognition as well.[3] Litanies have been written about the Soviets' interests, pressure tactics, geopolitical considerations, fear of encirclement and the like, leaving the reader sunk in a mire of familiar terms to which he/she has long been conditioned. In the verbiage, no new patterns are introduced—only ideas that follow long-accepted patterns.

This essay seeks to challenge some of the conventionalities regarding Soviet-East European relations. It will (1) discuss, by way of background, some of the accepted pattern-relationships between the USSR and Eastern Europe; (2) analyze the issues that unite and divide the alliance system; and (3) project the likely policy changes that may be adopted during the Gorbachev era.

THE "RELATIONSHIP"

Conventional wisdom has always identified Soviet-East European relationships in precisely this context: Soviet-East European relations. The emphasis has been placed on Soviet desiderata, Soviet interests, and Soviet needs. Viewed from this perspective, it was clearly possible to establish the characteristics of such relations, their limits, and their mutualities. Although a large number of studies have dealt with Eastern Europe as a "liability" or the "costs" of Eastern Europe to the Soviet Union, those who examined Soviet-East European relations took it for granted that they must proceed from the perspective of the dominant power in the region.[4]

Is such a unilateral approach warranted today? I believe not, for today's Eastern Europe has far more divergent agendas toward the USSR than the USSR has toward Eastern Europe. While there are a few commonalities in such relations, there are also far more differences that should be briefly noted.[5] Among the commonalities, one can list: ideological conformity, mutual concern for the maintenance of communist party power, the painful advance into the post-industrial era, the inability to achieve relative satisfaction of consumer demands, the desire to control dissident activities, and the goal of maintaining domestic stability. These commonalities tie the alliance together, the implementation of which do not cause stress within the alliance system in Soviet-East European relations. Although there are substantial differences in the methods of implementation of these goals—notably regarding the payment of the costs involved—the real stresses appear when we look at the demands of the alliance from the perspective of East European-Soviet relations.

STRESSES IN THE ALLIANCE

The examination of stress in East European-Soviet relationships must begin with an understanding that it is normal in any alliance system to have a certain tension, especially if a hegemone dominates that system. The stresses in the communist alliance system are caused primarily by diverse perspectives regarding the goals of that alliance; Eastern European decision makers tend to emphasize issues that are divisive, while Soviet decision makers, not unnaturally, stress the issues that unite the alliance system. The divergent perspectives produce a certain dynamism that, in and of itself, establishes mutualities, misperceptions, and complexities both for the alliance system as a whole and the individual state-actors within the alliance.

If we examine the issues that are important from the Eastern European perspective, the reason they are largely divisive becomes relatively clear: the Eastern European state interests are clearly different from those of the USSR. For most Eastern Europeans, the most important and divisive problems, *inter alia*, include energy policies, external trade, external relations, and military integration. Viewed from the USSR, however, the most serious problems of the alliance system are slightly different: combating ideological divergence, establishing means for handling potential sociopolitical instability, and a prevention of the loosening of the alliance system's bonds.

In regard to energy policies, the heavy dependence of the Eastern European states on energy resources imported from the USSR has often been noted both in the West and in the East. During the past ten to fifteen years, the USSR guaranteed the delivery of oil in "adequate" quantities to Eastern Europe; the cost of the energy carriers—just as those of other COMECON products—was pegged to the five-year average price on a sliding scale. This worked relatively well during the period when price fluctuations in the West varied substantially and tended generally upward. East Europeans received these products at about 20 percent below the actual world market price, and were able to pay for them in soft currencies or through barter deals. But toward the beginning of the 1980s, two changes could be noted: on the one hand, the Soviet Union began to be strapped for oil and gas exports at previous levels, and it became less willing to sell to the East Europeans at prices below world market—and largely for soft currencies—products that could be sold to the West for hard dollars. The consequent decline in deliveries has caused a great deal of hardship for the East Europeans, especially during the severe winter of 1984-1985, when whole cities were without electricity, factories stood idle, and people were freezing. On the other hand, when world oil prices began to decline precipitously in 1985-1986, the East Europeans started to complain that the COMECON pricing system was unfair to them. While they admitted that they paid for some of the oil in soft currencies, and often in not the best quality goods, they still pointed to the enormous differences between the world price of oil—down to $8-10 a barrel on the world market in mid-1986—and the price charged by the USSR—still around $24 a barrel. The result of these developments, of course, has been such dislocations as, for instance, the necessity of the Hungarian government in 1985 to send 4,000 buses to the USSR instead of 800 in 1980 in payment for the same amount of oil, while on the world market they would have needed to sell only 1,500 of the same buses to get the same quality and amount.[6] We should, however, note that no one in the world market would have bought those same 1,500 or 4,000 buses even at the price the USSR was willing to pay for them.

But the Eastern Europeans' complaints did not stop there: the uniform dissatisfaction with their demanded contribution to the building of new pipelines, refineries, and drilling fields in the Soviet Far East had come to the fore by early 1984. They pointed out—rightfully—that in the COMECON discussions regarding these developments, never had they been given a firm and clear explanation of what their contributions actually would be, what they would pay for, or what part of the total costs they would bear in exchange for natural resources or semi-finished goods from the USSR. Moreover, economic experts within the policymaking apparatus in Eastern Europe also rejected *en masse* the Soviet demands that the Eastern Europeans contribute to

the infrastructural development of Siberia, for example, in helping to build Soviet cities and towns, such as Yamburg, in areas
where the new oil or gas fields, were to be developed. By and
large, however, with the probable exception of Hungary, the
Soviets expected these contributions as the only possible exchange for much needed energy and other natural resources
imported from the USSR.[7]

External trade is a divisive issue that does not seem to go away.
The USSR remains the largest trading partner of the region, the
supplier of many of the raw materials and a large percentage of
the semi-finished goods. Unlike the price of oil, other raw
material prices remain generally stable in the world market, and
the COMECON pricing system moderates price volatility. The
East European economic elites, however, are quick to claim that
while the goods shipped by the USSR to Eastern Europe reflect
the relatively unchanging price structure of the Soviet economy,
the goods that are shipped to the USSR at preestablished prices
could be sold on the world market for higher prices. Consequently, they hold that the COMECON price structure, even in
this respect, discriminates against them, for deliveries to the
USSR even at lower prices simply must be met. Thus, using the
example of Hungary, the whole heavy-industrial sector has had
to be maintained with a 60 percent plus price-support level, sole-
ly for the purpose of shipping industrial goods to the USSR at
prices for which such goods could never be produced in a market-
socialist economy where wages and costs have spiraled upward.[8]

Parenthetically, we must note that Soviet leaders seem genuinely baffled by these charges. They point out that the East
Europeans were not complaining when the oil products were
sold to them at lower than world prices through the COM-
ECON sliding scale. They also point out that the East Europeans
always received "adequate" energy supplies, and that—in order
to ship more oil and gas to Eastern Europe—the Soviets have
had to build new pipelines, discover and excavate new fields, invest in new factories. In short, for the benefit of the "little

brothers," the Soviets have had to invest heavily—something that they alone should not be required to do. Moreover, the Soviets, for their part, complain about the low quality of goods shipped to them from Eastern Europe; shoes that fall apart in the first rain, telephones without membranes, and other shoddy products are brought up as Soviet counterclaims, exacerbating still more the divisiveness of these issues.

As far as external relations are concerned, the Eastern Europeans are also eager to become Europeans living in the East, once again, rather than simply being "East Europeans." The rediscovery of the German past of East Germany, the efforts of Hungarians to become "bridgebuilders," the circuitous attachment of Romanians and Poles to policies that are altogether more European– than Soviet-oriented, are a few examples of these processes. The flap—or fiasco as some would say—over the visit of East German CP leader Honecker to West Germany, the resulting June 21, 1985 vituperative *Pravda* article attacking the "presumably" separate state interests, the August apologies in the CPSU journal, *Kommunist*, the subsequent and successful 1987-1988 Honecker visits to Bonn and Paris—are demonstrative of the desire of the East Europeans to follow external policies at variance with the views of some Soviet decision makers. And the cautious, ever so slightly more than subterranean, early support by some East European leaders for the "zero-option" in the elimination of nuclear intermediate range missiles—long before the conclusion of the 1987 INF agreement—is another indication of the deep divisions over external policies.[9]

Finally, the issue of defense expenditures also needs to be addressed, although divisiveness here may be less real than potential. This issue originated with the Warsaw Pact decision of November 22, 1978, and raised military expenditures three percent to meet NATO's Long Term Modernization Program. Although there were strong objections openly expressed by Romania, and obvious but muted objections indicated by others—by and large, the stated goals have been met. But at what price? Especially in Czechoslovakia, Hungary, Poland, and Romania, the growth in defense expenditures occurred simultaneously with substantial limitations in the civilian sectors, resulting in severe shortages, a decrease in health and social expenditures, and major societal dislocations. The demand by the Soviet elite for greater defense expenditures at a time when these economies have experienced major slowdowns ran counter to the national interests of the East European states.

As noted above, from the perspective of the Soviet hegemone, relationships with Eastern Europe depend upon those issues that enhance the unity rather than the diversity of the alliance system. The current leadership in Moscow is not about to discard the Marxist ideological bonds at home, and it should not be surprising that they are wary of major ideological divergence from Soviet desiderata. Gorbachev's first visit with Prime Minister Planinc of Yugoslavia, widely reported and discussed openly even on Austrian television, is a small illustration of the demands for ideological conformity. While it is clear that the Soviets do not plan to stop the existing divergences in the practical application of communist rule that are already in place—e.g., in Romania or Hungary—they are going to combat any ideological divergence expressed openly as a direct challenge to the Soviet system. The emphasis will be on unity-cum-conformity, even if toleration of practical differences are likely to be allowed.[10]

A second major issue of contention from the Soviet perspective is the problem of socioeconomic instability. In the Soviet view the avoidance of such instability lies in the maintenance of the "leading role of the party." While the Soviets approve of increasing productivity, stressing labor discipline, or even providing greater incentives, they do not wish—nor are likely to allow— the adoption and open propagation of measures potentially damaging to the party's elite position.[11] Reforms, maybe, but only if the party initiates, directs, and controls them. Thus, the success of future reform in Eastern Europe can be guaranteed only if accompanied by the strengthening of the party's domestic position—or, at least, if it appears dressed in such garb. One can call for multicandidate elections within the party as a measure of increasing "democratization," but one must never call for the establishment of a multiparty system. Instability must be avoided, perhaps even at a great cost, but especially so if that instability were to result in the diminution of the party's leading role.

The final aspect of concern to Soviet leaders lies in the future unification of the alliance structure, in its military, economic, and political manifestations. By unification—or integration—they refer to the closer collaboration (read subordination), both institutionally and individually, among the component parts of the alliance. It should be noted that since the establishment of the Gorbachev leadership, once again, increasing emphasis seems to be placed on the central function of the USSR, its "Third Rome" role, and the "fraternal duty" of the socialist states to assist the Soviet Union as it grapples with the economic and military threats it perceives from the West. The "besieged fortress" mentality, once more, is evident, and the stress on "unity" is noted nearly continuously.

As suggested above, East European-Soviet and Soviet-East European relations are the obverse sides of the same coin: relations among a hegemone and smaller powers within the alliance system. Precisely because they are the obverse sides of the common coin, both sides must be considered in order to get a composite picture. Students of international politics are aware that in relations between smaller powers and a superpower, the smaller powers seek to carve out greater room for maneuver through focusing on divisive issues, while the superpowers try to stress issues that "bind" the alliance together. The Soviet power sphere is no different in this respect, and the dynamism of this conflict will still define and determine Soviet-East European relations for the next few years.

EASTERN EUROPE AND THE USSR
DURING THE GORBACHEV ERA

The relationship between Eastern Europe and the USSR during the mid-1980s, so far at least, has not been characterized by the special mark of Mikhail Sergeievich Gorbachev. Contrary to many in the West, Eastern European leaders do not necessarily view the struggle for supremacy within the Kremlin as having irrevocably been won by Gorbachev at this point. Their caution is, perhaps, a sign of maturity from observing previous power struggles in the East. In their attitudes toward Gorbachev, however, there is much more than just caution; there is also weariness.

Eastern Europe's leaders look at Gorbachev through weary eyes for two reasons; the first has to do with their preoccupation with the man, his personality, and policies; the second with his age.[12] They view Gorbachev as a strong leader, the creator of the party apparatus, and a man who has been closely tied to Andropov and thus to the KGB, and to the centralizing forces within the USSR. They do not see in Gorbachev the deliberate and successful reformer, although they cautiously add that "perhaps with time..." while not at all certain what will happen with time. Their view, generally, is that Gorbachev is more of a centralizer than a reformist liberalizer, more of a strong leader who will try to get his way through the instruments of force, than through private incentives and true decentralization of the planned economy. While Gorbachev appears to be more liberal than the recently replaced Gustav Husak or the stridently adamant Erich Honecker, he does not seem to be the reformer who will loosen the reins of communism. Moreover, both reformist and Stalinist leaders in the region complain that the manner in which Gorbachev has dealt with them so far has been more curt and formal than friendly and supportive—lacking warmth and compassion.

The second reason is, perhaps, more personal with the East

European leaders than should be expected; they see Gorbachev as a young upstart—emphasizing young. At 56, Gorbachev is twenty years younger than they; taking guidance from one's senior is one thing; accepting orders from a young and brash individual—however much he represents the hegemone, is tough to take. When Gorbachev lectures them, as at the Budapest Summit or at the Polish Party Congress, in spite of the tough hide these veterans of communist politics possess, they simply cringe and inwardly grumble. In the dynamism of state-to-state relations, perhaps, this should not matter. But it does.

Curiously, this relationship may also explain, at least partially, the current lack of clear direction from Moscow toward Eastern Europe. To be sure, the lack of direction is also due to the fact that three years after his accession to the helm, there still is a domestic consolidation of power taking place within the USSR, that the Gorbachev leadership is far more interested in putting its domestic house in order than in conducting foreign policy, or to the fact that there are really no major crises in Eastern Europe. But the awkwardness of the personal relationship, the way these leaders view Gorbachev, and the way Gorbachev sees them, surely must be taken into consideration.

As a result of these circumstances, Eastern Europeans today seem to have unprecedented room to maneuver. After the most recent CPSU Congress (February-March 1986), they realize that they can expand some ties with the West but they are weary of Gorbachev's limits; stability-cum-ideological conformity, as Professor Charles Gati once observed, must be maintained through the traditional means currently available to them. But they want more from the Soviets than the Soviets in their economic malaise can provide, and the Soviets feel the same way toward the Eastern Europeans; each is looking toward the other for help out of their economic and social straits.

Perhaps it would be a godsend for all if they could return to the golden age of detente, when the Soviets could pump large amounts of money into military expenditures with the US content to cut back; when they could copy, take, or steal technology at will from the West, while proclaiming peaceful intentions. Eastern Europeans, to be sure, feel that they would benefit greatly from such a state of affairs; in an atmosphere free of tension between the USSR and the West, their room to maneuver, some think, would be much greater than it appears today. To proclaim then as some do that "changes in Eastern Europe are most likely to occur in an atmosphere of detente" is at least ahistorical and, I respectfully submit, incorrect.[13] It is worth noting that the events of 1956 occurred in the Cold War atmosphere after the Spirit of Geneva failed, the Prague Spring took place at the height of Vietnam, and the rise of Solidarity after the invasion of Afghanistan.

Lasting and positive changes in the loosening of the Soviet empire in Eastern Europe can take place by attempting to reach closer ties with the West and the integration of the Eastern European economies with the West to a greater extent than is now taking place. But that can only happen if these economies begin to produce things that can be sold profitably in the West, which in turn would involve a great deal of technology transfer from the West, with a simultaneous welcoming of Western processes and techniques into the economies of Eastern Europe. Could the East European elite take advantage of the Soviet interests in the "reformism" Gorbachev tries to push at home? Or could the Eastern European leaders take advantage of the hiatus in Soviet leadership in regard to Eastern Europe? I believe they could, slowly, cautiously, without bravado or grand pronouncement, always aware of the danger of tweaking the nose of the bear. The Hungarian "mechanism" could be expanded in Hungary and emulated elsewhere, provided that no one attaches a special name, a special challenge to it, one that would sound alarm bells in the Kremlin. No "Spring of Freedom," no "Socialism with a Human Face," no "Polish Renewal," but just slow, cautious steps of real reform: the incorporation of market mechanisms, modern technology and decentralization, and a significant growth in contact and trade with the West. By taking advantage of the continued differentiation in building relationships with the Eastern European states on the part of the US, and by recognizing the relative freedom of action offered to them by Gorbachev and the new Soviet leadership, the East European leaders might be able to inculcate more "European" attitudes in the citizenry. And then they could indeed make a greater commitment to the values that have given the West a system that is emulable and looked upon with envy by the regimes and people of the region. By undertaking these tasks, perhaps one day the East European leaders could save their own skins, their rule, and be regarded as legitimate defenders of the national interests of the states in this diverse region.

NOTES

1. This study is partially based on an earlier article, "Troubled Friendship or Mutual Dependence? Eastern Europe and the USSR in the Gorbachev Era," *Orbis*, Vol. 30, No. 2 (Summer 1986).

2. As elsewhere, the term "Eastern Europe" refers to the communist states of Europe with the exception of the USSR, Yugoslavia, and Albania.

3. For a partially successful attempt to break out of the mold by offering a new approach see Jiri Valenta, "Revolutionary Change, Soviet Intervention and 'Normalization' in East Central Europe," *Comparative Politics*, v. 16, No. 2 (January 1984), pp. 127-151.

4. Vernon V. Aspaturian, "Has Eastern Europe Become a Liability to the Soviet Union?" in Charles Gati (ed.), *The International Politics of Eastern Europe* (New York: Praeger, 1975), pp. 17-36.

5. For a broader treatment see Vernon V. Aspaturian, "Soviet Aims in East Europe," in *Current History* (October 1970), pp. 206-211, 244-246; Keith Crane, *The Soviet Economic Dilemma of Eastern Europe* (Santa Monica: Rand Corporation R-3368-AF, 1986).

6. For a detailed study see the three volume Joint Economic Committee studies, *East European Economies: Slow Growth in the 1980s* (Washington, D.C.: Government Printing Office, 1984-86).

7. It has been suspected, but never actually proven, that a certain portion of energy carriers imported by Eastern Europe from the USSR winds up being resold in the West for hard currency. Payment made for such energy carriers to the USSR—in convertible rubles, soft local currencies, and goods,—was still below the price that could be had for the re-exported oil products. When costs of infrastructural subsidies to the USSR are added on,

175

however, such products, especially with falling oil prices, are financially less attractive from the East Europeans' perspective.

8. For an excellent economic analysis see Paul Marer, "East European Economies: Achievements, Problems, Prospects," in Teresa Rakowska-Harmstone (ed.), *Communism in Eastern Europe* (Bloomington, IN: Indiana University Press, 1984), pp. 283-328.

9. For an interesting analysis of the impact of East European policies on the USSR see A. Ross Johnson, *The Impact of Eastern Europe on Soviet Policy toward Western Europe* (Santa Monica: Rand R-3332-AF, 1986).

10. An East European informant, a member of the top elite in Hungary, characterized this relationship simply by saying "As long as we do not try to shove a new policy under their noses and insist that it is a divergent model that works better, as long as we proceed without fanfare and insistence on policies as ideologically different from the Soviet model, they seem to leave us alone." June 1986 interview in Budapest.

11. Whether the Soviets realize that in Hungary and Poland especially the local organs of the party have become irrelevant, is an oft-debated question among the top elites in the East European parties. Cf. Ivan Volgyes, "Hungary: Before the Storm Breaks," *Current History* (November 1987), pp. 373-37; and Ivan Volgyes, "Gorbachev and Eastern Europe," *International Review*, (November 1987), pp. 6-9.

12. The question of Eastern European elites' perception of Gorbachev is problematic for analysts; lacking direct interviews with such elites, we can only make surmises from indirect evidence available to researchers. During the summer of 1986, several American scholars visited the region and brought back a great deal of information from these states—mostly from Poland, Hungary, Czechoslovakia

and East Germany, but also from Bulgaria—regarding the elites' perception of Gorbachev. On the more broadly based, popular levels, similar evidence can be obtained through the public opinion research projects of Radio Free Europe. While one cannot maintain that public and elite opinions are congruent in regard to Gorbachev, the fact that the same weariness appears consistently tends to back our elite interviews on the subject.

13. F. Stephen Larrabee, "For Eastern Europe, Soviet Ties Must Be Rethought," *International Herald Tribune*, March 12, 1986.

SUGGESTED READINGS

Drachkovitch, Milorad M., ed. *East Central Europe: Yesterday, Today, and Tomorrow*. Stanford, CA: Hoover Institute Press, 1982.

Fischer-Galati, Stephen, ed. *The Communist Parties of Eastern Europe*. New York: Columbia University Press, 1979.

Herspring, Dale R., and Ivan Volgyes. *Civil-Military Relations in Communist States*. Boulder, CO: Westview, 1979.

Johnson, A. Ross, R.W. Dean, and Alex Alexiev. *East European Military Establishments: The Warsaw Pact Northern Tier*. Santa Monica, CA: Rand Corporation, 1980.

Kuhlman, James A. *The Foreign Policy of Eastern Europe*. Leyden, Neth.: Sijthoff, 1978.

Linden, Ronald H. *Bear and Foxes: The International Relations of East European States*. New York: Columbia University Press, 1979.

Marer, Paul, and John Michael Montias. *East European Integration and East-West Trade*. Bloomington, IN: Indiana University Press, 1980.

Nelson, Daniel N. *Soviet Allies*. Boulder, CO: Westview, 1984.

Rakowska-Harmstone, Teresa, and Andrew Gyorgy, eds. *Communism in East Europe*. Bloomington, IN: Indiana University Press, 1984.

Schopflin, George. *Eastern European Handbook*. London: St. Martin's Press, 1982.

Starr, Richard F., ed. *Communist Regimes in Eastern Europe*. 4th ed. Stanford, CA: Hoover, 1982.

Tokes, Rudolf L., ed. *Opposition in Eastern Europe*. Baltimore, MD: Johns Hopkins University Press, 1979.

Volgyes, Ivan. *The Reliability of the East European Armies: The Southern Tier*. Chapel Hill, NC: Duke University Press, 1983.

Volgyes, Ivan. *Politics in Eastern Europe*. Chicago: Dorsey, 1986.

White, Stephen, John Gardner, and George Schopflin. *Communist Political Systems: An Introduction*. London: Macmillan, 1982.

SIX

SOVIET POLICY IN SUB-SAHARAN AFRICA

PROSPECTS AND PROBLEMS FOR MODEL AND ALLY STRATEGIES

Daniel R. Kempton and Roger E. Kanet

By the end of the 1970s it appeared to many observers that the Soviet Union had made unparalleled advances into sub-Saharan Africa during the prior decade, thereby marking the beginning of a qualitatively new Soviet role on the continent. A review of the events of the 1970s provided ample evidence to support this conclusion. In December 1969 the new leaders of the Congo (Brazzaville) forcefully reaffirmed their country's commitment to Marxism-Leninism and renamed their country the People's Republic of Congo.[1] In 1974 Benin's leaders also declared their adherence to Marxism-Leninism, and in 1977 Siad Barre, a long-time Soviet ally, formally declared Somalia a Marxist-Leninist state. But the events that most dramatically opened the way for Soviet involvement in Africa were the Ethiopian revolution and the collapse of the Portuguese colonial empire, which led to the creation of self-proclaimed Marxist-Leninist regimes in Angola, Guinea-Bissau, Sao Tome and Principe, and Mozambique. These events also prompted the two most extensive cases of Soviet military involvement in sub-Saharan Africa.

The Soviets spent more than $800 million to install the MPLA (Popular Movement for the Liberation of Angola) in power in Angola. Not only did they provide significant financial and material assistance, but it was Soviet willingness to equip and transport more than 12,000 well-trained Cuban troops that swung the conflict in the MPLA's favor by early 1976. Never before had the Soviet Union and its allies successfully determined the outcome of an African conflict in such dramatic fashion. Just two years later, the Soviet-Cuban connection provided an encore performance. In 1978 Soviet advisors, with Cuban troops, led Ethiopia to victory over Somalia in the Ogaden War. Once again, without Cuban troops and Soviet military support, the results could have been quite different.[2] By the end of the 1970s, Soviet influence seemed to be growing even among non-Marxist-Leninist regimes such as those of Tanzania, Seychelles, and Zambia.

The 1980s have witnessed an equally important, though admittedly less dramatic, decline in Soviet fortunes in Sub-Saharan Africa, although the Soviet Union has made limited gains such as the growth of diplomatic ties with Botswana, Zambia, and Zimbabwe. More importantly, the Soviets have experienced declining relations with a number of African states, including some of their closest Marxist-Leninist allies such as Angola and Mozambique.

SOVIET OBJECTIVES AND STRATEGY IN THE THIRD WORLD

Before discussing in detail Soviet fortunes in Africa during the 1980s, it is important to examine the place of the Third World, particularly of Africa, in the overall foreign policy of the Soviet Union. Soviet policy in the Third World in the years since World War II can be divided into at least three periods.[3] During the first of these periods, the last eight years of Stalin's rule, the Soviets were preoccupied with the reconstruction of their war-ravaged economy and the consolidation of their control over areas that had come under the domination of the Red Army in 1945. With few exceptions, little attention was given to the colonial areas of the world. Stalin's death in 1953 and the coming to power of Nikita Khrushchev ushered in a period in Soviet policy toward the Third World characterized by growing awareness of the importance of the developing world and an almost frantic effort to break out of the political isolation in which the USSR still found itself. In an attempt to benefit from the growing conflicts between the West and national liberation movements or recently-independent states in the Third World, the Soviets offered economic and political assistance and attempted to establish a wide range of political ties with Third World leaders. During this period, which extended through the 1960s, the major Soviet weakness in relations with developing countries stemmed from their inability to project military power beyond the confines of the territory that they dominated. In addition, however, the limited economic base from which the Soviets competed with the United States represented another long-term weakness.

A third period in Soviet relations with the Third World began about 1970, at the time when the Soviets had approached relative strategic nuclear parity with the United States and had created the military infrastructure that would permit it to use military power effectively in the attempt to determine the outcome of events outside Soviet-dominated territory. Throughout the 1970s military power became the single most important element in the Soviet drive to expand its role throughout the Third World. The introduction of Soviet (and Cuban) military support into local conflicts in Angola and Ethiopia were decisive to their initial outcomes. Soviet arms transfers to countries such as Syria and Libya were also essential to the efforts of the leaders of those countries to accomplish their international objectives.

During the three periods, the USSR has grown from a predominantly regional power with regional interests and limited capabilities into a global superpower. Among the first changes introduced after 1953 by the post-Stalin leadership was the fact that it no longer viewed countries such as India and Egypt as mere appendages of Western imperialism, but rather as independent states whose interests overlapped in many areas those of the Soviet Union and the other members of the redefined "Socialist Community."[4]

In the mid-1950s, Khrushchev initiated an attempt to expand the Soviet role in international affairs. In the Middle East, for example, the beginnings of Soviet military and economic support in Afghanistan, Egypt, and later in other Arab states, effectively challenged Western dominance and reduced Soviet isolation in that region of strategic significance for Soviet security. The wave of decolonization that swept over Africa after Ghanaian independence in 1957 found the Soviets willing to provide assistance to a variety of new African states. The attempted deployment of missiles in Cuba in the fall of 1962 was probably the high point of Khrushchev's efforts to challenge the United States' dominance in world affairs; however, it also indicated most clearly the continuing inferiority of the Soviet Union's position.

In the early 1960s, the Soviet Union still lacked the economic, military, and political capabilities necessary to compete effectively in most regions of the world. The United States commanded substantial strategic superiority which forced the Soviets to move cautiously. Moreover, the absence of an effective Soviet capability to project conventional military power outside its own area of control meant that Soviet leaders had great difficulty in supporting clients or allies in areas outside the core region of Soviet power. In 1956, for example, it was primarily US opposition to the joint British-French-Israeli attack on Egypt—not Soviet threats to intervene—that brought the Suez War to a conclusion. In 1960, during the Congolese Civil War, the closing of the airport in Leopoldville by UN officials effectively cut off Soviet support for the forces of Patrice Lumumba. In the mid-to late 1960s Soviet-oriented political leaders in several African countries were overthrown with virtual impunity (Ben Bella in Algeria, Nkrumah in Ghana, and Keita in Mali). In sum, during this period the Soviet Union was unable to provide effective support to stabilize the Third World regimes which it viewed as friendly and supportive of Soviet interests.

The Khrushchev era in Soviet politics witnessed a major break from the past in the expansion of Soviet interests and the attempt of the USSR to play a greater role in the international system. However, the results of this change in orientation were mixed. Even though the Soviet Union had begun to close the military gap between itself and the United States and had established the foundations for the development of relations with a number of Third World countries—and was, therefore, no longer isolated—these relations remained fragile and provided the Soviets with few concrete returns on their investment of support.

In late 1964, when Brezhnev came to power in the Soviet Union, the position of the USSR in the noncommunist international system was stronger than it had been a decade earlier. Still, the USSR remained primarily a regional power. Its interests and, in some cases, its commitments had expanded beyond the confines of Stalin's empire, but inadequate capabilities severely limited its ability to affect significantly events in other areas of the world.

Even prior to Khrushchev's overthrow, several developments had occurred that would have a major impact on the growth of the role of the Soviet Union in the international system, and in particular in the Third World, in the 1970s. The first of these was the collapse of the European colonial empires and the "radicalization" of many of the newly independent states. Conflicts of interest between the industrial West and the less developed countries provided the Soviet leadership with possibilities to expand their involvement in countries or regions that earlier were closed to them. Related to this was the reduction of Western power—and involvement—in much of the Third World, as evidenced by the British withdrawal by 1970 from the regions "east of Suez."

Just as important was the initiation by the early 1960s—reinforced by the debacle of the Cuban Missile Crisis—of a program of military buildup in both the nuclear and conventional arenas and the Soviet military expansion into areas that until that time were outside the range of Soviet military capabilities. By the end of the decade the Soviets had approximated strategic parity with the United States.[5] Since the beginning of the 1970s, therefore, the strategic nuclear power of the United States has been largely neutralized by countervailing Soviet strategic capabilities. This "balance of terror" provided the Soviets with an international strategic environment in which they were able to employ their expanded conventional military—as well as political and economic—capabilities in ways conducive to the protection and expansion of their own state interests. Far from making conventional military capabilities obsolete, the nuclear stalemate between the superpowers in fact reestablished an environment in which conventional weapons could be employed—at least in certain circumstances.

Besides the expansion of Soviet strategic power begun in the Khrushchev era and continued until the present, the Soviets also built up their conventional military capabilities—both in Europe and throughout Asia and Africa and even Latin America—to the point where by the 1970s they were capable of projecting power throughout a substantial portion of the world. Among the most important aspects of this development was the construction of both an ocean-going navy and a worldwide merchant fleet that also engaged in military-related reconnaissance. Although the expansion of the Soviet fleet became most visible only after Khrushchev's fall from power, the decision to develop a surface fleet was made prior to the Cuban missile crisis.[6] By the 1970s the Soviets had created a navy that permitted them to play an important military role in various international crisis situations, such as the 1971 Indo-Pakistani War, the Middle East War of 1973, and other conflicts.[7]

Moreover, they had also created a network of agreements with a number of developing countries that gave them access to the naval facilities necessary for the maintenance of this new ocean-going fleet. The production of long-range transport aircraft and the signing of agreements for overflight rights and the use of landing facilities provided an important complement to the expanded naval power, as evident during the Soviet military interventions in Angola and Ethiopia.[8]

In many respects Soviet objectives benefited from events in the Third World during the 1970s over which the Soviets themselves exercised only minimal influence. First of all, the continuing drive toward independence in the developing world and the inability of moderate governments in many developing countries to deal effectively with the problems of economic backwardness and political instability combined to bring to power throughout portions of Asia, Africa, and the Western Hemisphere a group of governments more strongly anti-Western than their predecessors. This provided the Soviets and their Cuban and East European allies with opportunities to gain access to—if not always influence over—leaders in a substantial number of developing states. At the same time the position of the United States and its Western allies deteriorated throughout the Third World.

Associated with the relative change of position of the Soviet Union and the West in developing countries during the 1970s was the unwillingness or inability of the West, including the United States, to pursue a coherent course of action in its policies. The US debacle in Vietnam, the Watergate scandal, and the exposure of various CIA operations in the mid-1970s made it virtually impossible for the US government to initiate an effective response to Soviet activities in the Third World. Moreover, given the political environment of detente and the apparent conviction of some US leaders that the period of US-Soviet conflict characteristic of the Cold War had come to an end, the political atmosphere in the United States was not conducive to checking Soviet expansion of their international role by taking advantage of conflict situations throughout the Third World. Both in Angola in 1975-1976 and in Ethiopia two years later the Soviets assumed correctly that they would be able to intervene without the danger of effective American counteraction, since the United States did not have the will to challenge the expansion of Soviet involvement in regions then considered far from the centers of primary US interest.

In the Third World itself the Soviets indicated during the 1970s that the political and military foundations that they had laid during the prior decade—and into the 1970s as well—provided them with the ability to support outcomes that they deemed favorable to their own interests. In Angola, Ethiopia, and Southeast Asia, for example, Soviet (and Cuban) support was essential in either bringing to power or consolidating regimes friendly toward and dependent on the USSR. By the middle of the 1970s, the Soviet Union had become a state with both global interests and global capabilities. In Angola and again in Ethiopia it provided allies with significant military assistance which was adequate to change the local balance of power in favor of the recipients of Soviet support. In return, the Soviets have been provided with access to naval and air facilities that are useful in potential future conflicts with the West.[9]

Since the early 1970s the Soviets have continued to support political movements or countries of potential importance to their strategic and global interests, despite what seems to be a preference for supporting "progressive" regimes and movements. Although an upsurge of Soviet involvement in Sub-Saharan Africa occurred in the mid-1970s, Soviet interest is still concentrated heavily in the band of countries that border the southern flank of the USSR. Here the Soviet goal has remained the reduction of Western influence and military capabilities and the concomitant expansion of the military and political capabilities of the Soviet state. This has meant that the Soviets have continued to provide military and political support to such countries as Afghanistan, Iraq, Libya, Syria, and South Yemen. In several cases they have signed treaties of friendship and cooperation with important South Asian, Middle Eastern, and African countries, for example, Iraq and India. In fact, during the 1970s they also increased their efforts to improve relations with countries formally allied with the West, such as Turkey and Iran (prior to the overthrow of the Shah) by offering economic assistance and even military sales as a means of reducing these countries' dependence on their Western allies—in particular the United States. Another important element in Soviet policy has been the search for access to both naval and airport facilities that would enable them to expand the reach of their military capabilities.

From the initial establishment of contacts with Third World states more than thirty years ago the Soviets have relied heavily on the provision of economic and military assistance as means of developing and consolidating relations.[10] In general the terms of Soviet assistance are favorable when compared with commercial loans available to emerging nations on the international market, though the Soviets offer virtually no nonrepayable grants and virtually all aid is provided in the form of credits for the purchase of Soviet goods and equipment. Soviet trade with Asia and Africa has grown rapidly as well, though an important aspect of this trade has been its relationship to the provision of economic assistance. With relatively few exceptions (e.g., the purchase of rubber from Malaysia and grain from Argentina), trade has resulted from agreements between the Soviet leaders and their Afro-Asian counterparts which include the commitment of Soviet economic and technical assistance. Examples of this type of agreement have been those with Egypt and India which called for the Soviet Union to provide capital equipment on the basis of long-term credits. These loans were to be repaid with the products of the recipient country over a period of twelve years at an interest rate of 2.0-2.5 percent. Such agreements have been especially attractive to those countries which have had problems obtaining the convertible currency necessary to purchase on the world market machinery and equipment needed for economic projects.

By the end of the 1970s, then, the relative position of the two major power blocs in the Third World had changed markedly. The collapse of the Western colonial empires and the ensuing rise of numerous anti-Western political regimes in the developing world, unilateral Western military retrenchment, and various other developments resulted in the contraction of the Western military presence and of Western political influence throughout most of Asia and Africa. At the same time, the Soviets were able to establish a network of economic, political, and military relationships that permitted them for the first time in their history to play the role of a global power with worldwide interests and the capabilities to pursue many of those interests effectively. The change in the relative position of the Soviet Union in the international political system stems in part from the continued buildup of Soviet military power and the willingness and ability of the Soviet leadership to take advantage of the conflicts between the less developed states and the major Western powers.[11] Already in the 1970s the Soviets were able to employ their newly developed military power—including an ocean-going fleet and long-range transport aircraft—in conjunction with access to port and air facilities in order to support distant and dispersed political and strategic goals. Examples include the use of the Soviet fleet in the Bay of Bengal to demonstrate support for India in the 1971 war with Pakistan, the transport of large numbers of Cuban troops into Angola four years later to support the MPLA, a virtual repeat of this operation in Ethiopia in 1978, and the provision of substantial military supplies to revolutionary groups in Central America in the 1980s.

By 1980 the Soviet Union had become a true superpower with the ability to influence developments in areas far from Soviet territory. Although the primary means available to the Soviets in their attempts to accomplish their short- and long-term objectives throughout the Third World has been the provision of various forms of military support, that support has been accompanied by a wide range of other Soviet activities: relations with revolutionary movements and political parties, modest amounts of economic assistance, political support in various international forums, and a vast assortment of propaganda activities.

SOVIET STRATEGY IN AFRICA

When we turn to the question of Soviet involvement in Africa we find that they have been especially concerned with accomplishing a number of foreign policy objectives:[12]

- To reduce both Western and Chinese influence in Africa;
- To increase the Soviet presence (and influence) in African domestic and international affairs and to increase Soviet international prestige;
- To gain African support on international issues;
- To obtain access to air bases, naval facilities, military storage facilities, and to obtain overflight and transit agreements;
- To obtain needed commodities and profits from arms sales;

- To support the spread of Marxism-Leninism.

Although there is consensus among Western political analysts concerning Soviet motivations and objectives, these are not logically derived from a coherent theory of Soviet behavior, nor have propositions concerning Soviet behavior been rigorously tested. One recent study has attempted to resolve this problem by using Soviet arms transfers policy as one indicator of Soviet motives. What the author found was that of the five sub-Saharan African states which received the largest increases in Soviet arms over the last decade, three (Angola, Ethiopia, and Mozambique) were self-declared Marxist-Leninist states. However, these three also happened to be relatively larger and more strategically located states and had major port facilities to offer. The other two states, Tanzania and Zambia, both have had politically influential leaders.[13] In short, the study seems to demonstrate what long-time observers of Soviet policy have contended; Soviet policy toward sub-Saharan Africa appears to be guided by a multiplicity of goals that are inconsistently discernible in Soviet behavior.

The question of Soviet strategy toward sub-Saharan Africa is easier to answer. Although equally controversial, Soviet strategy is more directly visible in Soviet activities than are their objectives. Over time the Soviet Union has pursued two basic strategies to achieve its objectives in the developing world—a model and an ally strategy. The evolution of Soviet strategy can be seen as the fluctuation between, and various attempts to combine, these two strategies.[14] The key difference between the two strategies is that with a model strategy the Soviet Union seeks to promote the creation of regimes modeled closely after the Soviet political system in the belief that they will prove to be more stable and durable allies and provide more opportunities for influence, while with an ally strategy the Soviet Union ignores the domestic characteristics of regimes and seeks to build its relationships to developing countries on the basis of shared international positions. In reality this dichotomy is shared by the United States and other past great powers. Historically, the United States has vacillated considerably in the emphasis it places on either promoting its model of democracy or finding reliable allies in its competition with the Soviet Union, regardless of their domestic characteristics. The choice between model and ally must be made by all great powers.

Finally, before discussing the strategies themselves it should be firmly stated that, while arguing that Soviet policy towards sub-Saharan Africa has been guided by two discernible strategies, the authors do not intend to imply that Soviet behavior is not opportunistic or does not take African realities into account. Quite the contrary. Soviet strategy toward sub-Saharan Africa has undergone numerous changes based on new Soviet understandings of the African terrain. Not only is Soviet strategy founded on the Soviet assessment of African conditions, but it also applied flexibly to individual cases. In this sense strategy is simply a general pattern for Soviet policy that is designed to achieve a preconceived set of goals.

With a model strategy the Soviet Union supports the creation of regimes modeled on itself. There are two major variants of the model strategy. The first, more common, variant occurs when the Soviet Union supports the revolutionary struggle of communist parties or Marxist-Leninist movements roughly modeled on the Communist Party of the Soviet Union (CPSU). Soviet support for the MPLA may be placed in this category. The second variant is a nonrevolutionary strategy in which established Soviet allies are pushed to adopt elements of the Soviet model. This second, nonrevolutionary variant was used to a limited extent by both Khrushchev and Brezhnev. For example, after the overthrow of a number of pro-Soviet governments in Africa in the mid-1960s, the Soviet Union actively encouraged Sekou Toure to turn the PDC of Guinea into a vanguard party, or at least to create a vanguard within the party. A similar effort was made in Egypt in the late 1960s.

The apparent logic of a model strategy is that Soviet leaders believe that regimes modeled on the CPSU will make better allies.[15] First, if these regimes establish a Soviet-style vanguard party, they are likely to be more stable than other regimes in the developing world. This is particularly important for Soviet leaders because many of their previous relationships with developing states, particularly in Africa, collapsed when leaders allied with the Soviet Union were overthrown or died in office. During the 1960s, the Soviet Union developed close ties to numerous radical African leaders, including Ahmed Ben Bella of Algeria, Kwame Nkrumah of Ghana, Modibo Keita of Mali, and Gamal Abdul Nasser of Egypt. In each of these cases, except that of Algeria, the removal of the individual leader crippled Soviet ties to the state in question. In contrast, a centralized vanguard party could more effectively institutionalize the revolutionary process and thus prevent coups and better guarantee continuity when a leader died in office.

A second advantage of a model strategy is that it provides extensive opportunities for the Soviet Union to maximize its influence over clients. This is particularly true for the more common, revolutionary variant. During the often long and bitter revolutionary struggle, national liberation movements (NLMs) require significant amounts of foreign economic and military assistance. In most cases the Soviet Union has been the most willing and capable supplier of this assistance. This close supplier-recipient relationship offers a great deal of leverage to both parties involved. Particularly important for the Soviet Union is the fact that in its advising and training capacities it can develop close ties to the leading cadres of these NLMs. Not only does Soviet ideological training typically accompany Soviet military training, but many of the leading political cadres of these NLMs are sent to the Soviet Union itself for political training. Although close personal contact certainly does not guarantee enduring ties, it does provide opportunities to establish working relationships with individuals below the NLM's current leaders who represent potential successors.[16] From the Soviet perspective this increases the possibility its ties to a given developing state will survive the tenure of any particular leader. Furthermore, the second generation of leaders typically does not have the same revolutionary legitimacy as the first generation, and thus is more likely to rely on the party organization and external assistance to maintain itself in power.

A third advantage is that, by promoting itself as a model for developing states, the Soviet Union also promotes its own worldview. In short, the Soviet worldview is based on the premise that the central conflict of the contemporary world is between the progressive forces, led by the Soviet Union, and the capitalist forces, led by the United States. Presumably, as the members of an NLM undergo military and political training with Soviet bloc advisors, they will absorb aspects of the Soviet worldview. Reinforcing explicit ideological training is the natural process of radicalization which typically occurs during a revolutionary struggle.[17] As a revolutionary struggle progresses without significant concessions on the part of the colonial power or ruling regime, moderate leaders and their tactics are frequently forsaken for more radical leaders and tactics. In most cases of revolutionary struggle in the developing world, as policies become more radical, they also become more anti-Western, since the colonial powers or ruling regimes are typically more closely associated with the West.

A final factor to consider is that many revolutionary movements and states in the developing world may adopt a socialist orientation initially for self-defense.[18] Kenneth Jowitt argues that, by adopting a Marxist-Leninist doctrine, a revolutionary movement or government makes itself politically visible and intelligible to potential socialist allies, most importantly the Soviet Union. But whether or not a Marxist-Leninist ideology is adopted because of the conviction of a local leader, or more to win external assistance as Jowitt contends, its international effect is roughly the same. The acceptance of a Marxist-Leninist doctrine frequently brings Soviet-bloc support and more consistently leads to the permanent antagonism of the United States.

Over time this reinforces and strengthens a government's or revolutionary movement's ties to the Soviet Union and adds credibility to Soviet claims of the West's inherent antagonism toward the needs of the developing world.

Writing separately, two Western analysts, Jerry Hough and Peter Zwick, have aptly noted the central problem with the Soviet Union's model strategy,[19] the fact that many of the states modeled on the Soviet Union are no longer Soviet allies. Zwick suggests that the Soviet Union really does not need any more Albanias, Chinas, or Romanias. In retrospect, " ...the risks involved in promoting communist revolution may outweigh the benefits."[20] Both Zwick and Hough conclude that the Soviet Union may be willing to abandon the model strategy (i.e., communist revolution). However, the point of a model strategy is not so much that it guarantees that states will never break away from the Soviet Union, but rather that it provides the Soviet Union greater opportunity to prevent this from occurring and generally makes such a total break less probable. What Zwick and Hough fail to consider are the numerous problems the Soviet Union has experienced with non-model strategies in the developing world. In this light, a model strategy may appear to the Soviets as the best of rather mediocre options.

In the case of an ally strategy, the Soviet Union principally supports established governments in the developing world largely on the basis of international alignments. Any government that is pro-Soviet or even clearly anti-American is seen as a potential Soviet ally, regardless of its domestic orientation. The logic of an ally strategy is quite different from that of a model strategy. First, it recognizes that in most developing countries true communist parties modeled on the CPSU are unlikely to gain power. They lack the domestic support required to assume and hold power. Also, despite more alarmist Western predictions, there are relatively few cases where the prospects are favorable for Marxist-Leninist movements to gain power. When the Portuguese colonial empire collapsed in 1975, all the major colonial empires are now gone. Colonial territories have historically provided some of the most fruitful opportunities for NLMs. A second criticism of a model strategy, especially its revolutionary variant, is that it is more likely to have a negative impact on Soviet relations with the West. For example, the Soviet use of a model strategy, particularly in Angola and Afghanistan, was a contributing factor in the collapse of detente.[21]

There are also important problems with the nonrevolutionary variant of the model strategy. Most importantly, allies who are pushed to adopt elements of the Soviet model are likely to resent this pressure and view it as meddling in their internal affairs. For example, over the last decade the Soviet Union has pressured Ethiopia's ruling council, the Dergue, to create a formal party organization. Some of the members of the Dergue, which is made up primarily of younger military officers, view this policy as an attempt to subvert their authority. Particularly worrisome to the Dergue has been the fact that the Soviet Union has apparently attempted to establish contacts directly to the emerging party organization, staffed primarily by radical civilians, rather than conduct its relations through the Dergue.[22] Despite Soviet pressure, the Dergue has moved extremely slowly. In 1977 the Union of Marxist-Leninist Organizations was formed, only to be disbanded in 1980. Next, the Dergue established the COPWE (Commission for Organizing the Party of Workers of Ethiopia). Although this commission is clearly only a preparatory organ, the Soviet Union warmly welcomed it as a "vanguard party."[23] In 1984 a vanguard Marxist-Leninist party was finally created in Ethiopia and now seems to be progressing according to the Soviet model. Although Soviet pressure for the creation of a vanguard party has not seriously jeopardized the Soviet-Ethiopian relationship (in large part because of Ethiopia's continuing dependence on the USSR for security support), it has been a source of considerable tension.

The basic tenet of an ally strategy is to build the political relationships of alliances with developing states on the basis of existing mutual interests. During the Khrushchev years Soviet strategy toward the developing world was primarily an ally strategy. Although many of these governments were to some degree socialist, others were not. In all cases, however, they had adopted anti-American or anti-Western policies for either domestic or regional reasons. For Ghana and Guinea, vehement opposition to colonialism made close ties to the West embarrassing and, in some contexts, impossible. For Egypt and Iraq it was American support for Israel which eventually made an alliance with the West anathema; for them the Soviet bloc was the only reliable source of military assistance. Relatively close United States-Pakistani relations have also put India in opposition to the United States. In Africa the Soviet Union actively courted the radical leaders of the governments of Algeria, the Congo (now Zaire), Ghana, Guinea, and Mali. Although many of these governments were clearly socialist, others were not. In all of these cases, however, the respective leaders had, for various reasons, adopted anti-Western stances. Thus, the relationship was built on a shared antagonism toward the West, rather than on the basis of shared domestic traits. In concluding this discussion of ally and model strategies, it should be reiterated that these two types of strategies are essentially ideal types. Soviet strategy toward a particular country at any given time may be decidedly closer to one or the other strategy. But frequently elements of both strategies occur simultaneously in Soviet behavior.

Although Soviet strategy toward the developing world underwent numerous vacillations prior to Khrushchev's assent to power, these changes had little bearing on sub-Saharan Africa since the Soviet Union only became actively involved there in the 1950s. During the Khrushchev years a dramatic increase in the level of Soviet involvement in Africa occurred, based largely on an ally strategy. Instead of supporting revolutionary communist parties dedicated to the duplication of the Soviet political and economic model, Khrushchev actively courted individual African leaders. But by the late 1960s, as noted earlier, all of these leaders, with the exception of Sekou Toure, had been removed from office, resulting in a significant decline in the Soviet presence. In the case of Sekou Toure a number of Soviet advisors stationed in Guinea were accused of involvement in a planned coup d'etat; whereupon Toure, an ordinarily suspicious individual, also dramatically reduced the Soviet presence in Guinea. From this experience the Soviet leaders learned the precariousness of basing international relationships on the shoulders of individual African leaders. The African political context was volatile. Furthermore, it became increasingly clear by the mid-1960s that Khrushchev's allies in Africa were nationalists first and socialists second.[24]

By the early 1970s the Soviet Union had considerably diversified its policy toward sub-Saharan Africa to the point where there existed two separate, clearly discernible strategies. First, the Soviets actively sought to develop their diplomatic ties to all African regimes—particularly those which were relatively more powerful, influential or strategically located—irrespective of the nature of their domestic regimes. In 1969 during the Nigerian Civil War, for example, the Soviet Union broke with past precedents and provided military assistance to the unequivocally pro-Western Nigerian government. Although Nigeria maintained its close relations with the West after the war, Soviet relations with Nigeria progressed throughout most of the 1970s. Soviet involvement in defending a moderate African government also helped open the way for an increase in Soviet ties to moderate regimes throughout Africa.

During the 1970s the Soviet Union also developed a strategy of support for national liberation movements, particularly but not exclusively those which advocated some form of Marxism-Leninism. Recipients of Soviet support included the African National Congress in South Africa, Frelimo in Mozambique, the MPLA in Angola, the PAIGC in Guinea-Bissau, SWAPO in Namibia, and ZAPU in Rhodesia. During the revolutionary struggle the Soviet Union developed close ties to these movements by providing them with political, economic, and military support, with a considerable emphasis on the last. Throughout this period the Soviets have undeniably been the most willing and capable supplier of military assistance to national liberation movements. When Soviet strategy succeeds, a given national liberation movement achieves power at the end of a long, Soviet-assisted military struggle. During the struggle the Soviet Union will develop close and friendly ties not only to the leader of the national liberation movement, but also to the cadres at various levels of the organization who receive political or military training from Soviet bloc advisors. In this way over time the relationship is institutionalized at a party to party level, rather than merely remaining dependent on the good will of an individual friendly leader. This increases the possibility of Soviet ties surviving an individual African leader. Furthermore, if a vanguard party is formed during the revolutionary struggle—a process strongly encouraged by the Soviet Union—it will likely result in a more firmly entrenched post-independence role for the Soviet Union. As Mark Katz argues, while Marxist-Leninists have broken with the Soviet Union in the past, the presence of a large number of Soviet advisors and Soviet assistance in the day-to-day administration of government make such a break considerably more difficult.[25]

At least three of the Soviet Union's most dramatic gains in sub-Saharan Africa—Angola, Guinea-Bissau, and Mozambique —came as a direct result of the national liberation process described above. However, events in Ethiopia, probably the Soviet Union's most valued ally, proceeded somewhat differently. In Ethiopia, the revolution of 1974 developed so suddenly that there were no contacts between the Soviet Union and the Dergue, or military council, which led the revolution. The initial Soviet response to the revolution was cautious and, in fact, at the time of the revolution the Dergue's domestic program and international alignment were very much in doubt. Despite subsequent Ethiopian requests for military assistance it was not until 1975 that an arms agreement with the Soviet Union was signed. One of the major reasons for Soviet hesitation was fear of antagonizing neighboring Somalia, a self-declared Marxist-Leninist state and Ethiopia's historical enemy. Initial Soviet fears were confirmed when in November of 1977 the Somali government unilaterally repudiated its treaty of friendship with the Soviet Union. In many ways the 1977-1978 Ogaden War between Somalia and Ethiopia helped to solidify Soviet ties to the Dergue in the same manner as Soviet ties to the national liberation movements in southern Africa were solidified by their respective wars of national liberation. During the war Ethiopia depended heavily on Soviet-bloc advisors and Cuban troops for success in their war effort and to a more limited extent for assistance in day-to-day governmental administration. As was true of Soviet assistance to the government of Nigeria in 1969, the decisive Soviet and Cuban assistance to the governments of Angola and Ethiopia during the late 1970s was well-received throughout most of sub-Saharan Africa. Thus, the Soviet interventions in sub-Saharan Africa were, at least initially, beneficial rather than harmful in the Soviet Union's effort to develop diplomatic ties to non-Marxist-Leninist regimes. First of all, the interventions demonstrated that the Soviet Union could be a powerful and cooperative ally. Second, they both met with OAU approval, as well as with the approval of many of the neighboring states, because the Soviet Union was clearly enforcing the declaration of the Organization for African Unity supporting the territorial integrity of existing states. In addition, in the Angolan case, the Soviet Union benefited from the fact that its major competitors, China and the United States, both supported the same side as South Africa and were thus condemned by many African states.

In sum, during the 1970s the Soviet Union utilized two strategies in sub-Saharan Africa. With Marxist regimes or movements it utilized a model strategy; with non-Marxist regimes the Soviet Union utilized an ally strategy, which based relationships on shared international positions. As noted at the outset of this chapter, in both cases the Soviet Union was quite successful. Our next task is to examine how the Soviet Union has fared in the 1980s in these two areas.

SOVIET TIES TO MARXIST MOVEMENTS AND REGIMES

By 1980 it appeared to many that the Soviet strategy of support for national liberation movements that had already yielded such impressive gains would also provide significant future gains. Although in South Africa and Namibia the African National Congress (ANC) and the Southwest African Peoples' Organization (SWAPO) were still, even according to Soviet assessments, in the early stages of a national liberation struggle, they were moving more and more toward an armed struggle. In that struggle the Soviet Union became a willing arms supplier and provider of military training, just as it had earlier in other African liberation struggles. While neither the ANC nor SWAPO is Marxist in official program, both have significant factions which are and which would be likely to increase in size during a long military struggle as further radicalization would occur. Yet, it was in Rhodesia (contemporary Zimbabwe) where Soviet prospects for immediate gains looked brightest at the end of the 1970s. Since the early 1960s the Soviet Union had been a major supplier of the Zimbabwe African People's Union (ZAPU), at the time Rhodesia's major revolutionary organization. In 1963 when a number of ZAPU members, dissatisfied with Joshua Nkomo's leadership, left ZAPU and formed the Zimbabwe African National Union (ZANU), in keeping with earlier precedents elsewhere the Soviet Union remained true to its chosen liberation movement. Despite the fact that ZANU soon emerged as a more militant and radical liberation movement, the Soviet Union repeatedly rebuffed ZANU's requests for military assistance. While ZAPU was well-armed with modern Soviet conventional weaponry, ZANU carried on the brunt of the war effort supplied with smaller amounts of arms from China, the more maverick Eastern European states, and second-hand Soviet weaponry provided by Ethiopia and Mozambique. Even after ZANU and ZAPU formed a joint military command in 1976, the Soviet Union largely ignored ZANU's existence.

Soviet hopes of an outright ZAPU victory were destroyed in 1979 when the two liberation movements jointly negotiated under British auspices a peaceful transition to black rule. However, Soviet leaders still expected ZAPU to win the elections of March 1980, or at least to play a major role in the resulting government. When ZANU, under the leadership of Robert Mugabe, won an outright majority in the elections the decade-long Soviet efforts were shattered. Almost immediately the Soviet Union attempted to reverse its policy and develop ties to ZANU. This time, however, it was the Soviets who were bluntly rebuffed. Despite Soviet efforts to establish formal ties to Mugabe's new regime, diplomatic relations were not established until February 1981. Mugabe's coldness toward the Soviets is only partially attributable to the Soviet policy toward ZANU during the liberation struggle. More importantly, the tenuous alliance between ZANU and ZAPU began eroding even prior to the 1980 elections. Thus, Mugabe undoubtedly realized that if a ZAPU uprising or coup attempt developed, Soviet military might could conceivably be used against ZANU.[26]

Since the establishment of diplomatic relations the Soviet Union has apparently abandoned its ties to ZAPU; as a result there has been a gradual improvement in Soviet-Zimbabwean relations since 1981. In 1983, after three trips to Beijing, Mugabe visited Moscow for the first time. Yet although Zimbabwe had received $32 million in economic credits and grants from Eastern Europe as of 1984, it had not signed a major aid package with the Soviet Union.[27] Furthermore, there are no Soviet economic or military advisors in Zimbabwe.[28] Finally, despite Mugabe's clearly stated commitment to Marxism-Leninism as a long-term objective, his domestic policies and attitudes toward the West have both proven to be pragmatic. Thus what promised to be another major victory for the Soviet Union in 1979 has proven to be nothing of the sort.

At the same time Soviet ties to two former national liberation movements, the MPLA in Angola and Frelimo (the Front for the Liberation of Mozambique) in Mozambique, have visibly declined since their peak in the late 1970s. In the 1980s the Angolan government (the MPLA) has faced three interconnected problems. First, in the early 1980s South Africa exponentially increased its military assistance to the Union for the Total Independence of Angola (UNITA) which resulted in a dramatic escalation of the civil war; moreover, between 1981 and 1983, South African regular troops made major incursions into southern Angola. Second, Angola's economy has deteriorated sharply; factors contributing to the economic decline include damage incurred from UNITA troops, Western pressures, the general decline in the price of oil and simple economic mismanagement. Between 1980 and 1984 the Soviet Union helped to alleviate the problem by providing $500 million in economic credits and grants.[29] But, despite its receiving the second largest amount of Soviet assistance of any state in sub-Saharan Africa, Angolan officials frequently complain about the inadequacy of Soviet aid, virtually all of which is in the form of credits rather than outright grants.

Ironically, the third problem which the Angolan government faces results from the extremely large contingent of Soviet-bloc advisors and Cuban troops that it hosts. Although Cuban troops and Soviet-bloc arms have been vital to Angola's security, their cost is a tremendous drain on the economy. According to one recent account the Angolan government pays between $14,000 and $22,000 per year for each Soviet advisor and Cuban soldier, for a daily cost of about $4 million.[30] When the tab for Cuban troops, Soviet-bloc arms and advisors and Angola's own military are added together, it consumes nearly two-thirds of Angola's total revenues. Furthermore, the Angolan government resents the fact that the Cuban troops it supports have report-edly assumed a defensive posture and are reluctant to engage the enemy.[31]

Not coincidentally, in the 1980s Mozambique has faced an almost identical set of problems—a growing threat from a South African backed revolutionary movement, economic stag-nation, and the high costs of Soviet-bloc assistance which it receives. Mozambique sought to resolve its problems by join-ing the Council for Mutual Economic Assistance (CMEA), but was firmly rejected by the established communist powers.[32] In fact, between 1980 and 1985 Mozambique received only $155 million in Soviet economic credits and grants, or less than one-third those provided to Angola over the same period.[33]

For both Angola and Mozambique the immediate effect of these problems stimulated a fundamental adjustment in their foreign policies. First, both Angola and Mozambique have sought to improve relations with the West in an effort to ob-tain the level of economic assistance which the Soviet Union is either unwilling or incapable of providing. Second, in recog-nition of South Africa's military power and its ability to destabilize the black regimes in southern Africa by supporting movements committed to their overthrow, both Angola and Mozambique followed the examples of their smaller neighbors and reached military accommodations with South Africa. In January 1984 Angola signed the Lusaka Accord, in which it pledged to prevent SWAPO use of its territory in exchange for the withdrawal of South African forces from southern Angola. In March 1984 Mozambique followed suit by signing a non-aggression pact with South Africa popularly known as the Nkomati Accord. In effect, Mozambique was to cease its assis-tance to the ANC in exchange for a cessation of South African support for RENAMO, a Mozambican counter-revolutionary movement opposed to Frelimo. Although the Soviet Union reluctantly accepted the necessity of some sort of detente with South Africa, it was clearly displeased with developments. Apparently most disconcerting for the Soviet Union is in the case of Angola, where the Soviet Union had the most invested, Moscow had not been consulted in advance.[34]

In sum, the 1980s have seen a significant erosion in Soviet ties to both Angola and Mozambique. It is not yet clear what effect the death of Mozambican President Machel might have on the development of his country's future policies. What is most surprising about the trend is that it directly contradicts what appears to be Gorbachev's emerging policy toward the developing world. Gorbachev, as previous Soviet leaders, realizes that in order to rejuvenate the Soviet economy, overseas expenses must be held in check. But the Soviets invested so much prestige in the acquisition of new allies in the 1970s that any policy reassessments are more likely to result in prohibiting new commitments, rather than in cutting back on previous ones. Mozambique appears to be an exception, while in Angola's case even the relative increase in Soviet commitment cannot keep up with Angola's needs.[35] Although the Soviet Union is likely to remain the paramount foreign supporter for both Angola and Mozambique, it probably enjoyed its maximum influence in those countries in the years immediately following independence. More recent developments have further undermined Soviet objectives in the region by denying critical base facilities to SWAPO and the ANC on which the Soviet Union places much of its future hope. Thus, the emergence of South Africa as the dominant regional power has severely reduced the Soviet role in southern Africa. However, there is still room for Soviet optimism; when the erosion of South Africa's domestic balance eventually reaches critical proportions, the Soviet Union hopes to gain throughout the region.

The final regime to be considered is Ethiopia, probably the Soviet Union's most valued client in sub-Saharan Africa. Since 1978 the Soviet Union has invested more economic assistance and provided more arms to Ethiopia than to any other regime in sub-Saharan Africa. Unlike developments in southern

Africa, these investments, at least on the surface, appear to be still paying off. As noted above, Ethiopia has now launched a vanguard Marxist-Leninist party, a development long sought by the Soviet Union. In 1984 the evolution of this party was proceeding at a rapid enough pace for one analyst to comment that Africa was now on the verge of seeing its first true "communist" state.[36] Although this conclusion is still somewhat premature, in fact the Soviet-bloc presence has clearly been institutionalized in Ethiopia to a greater extent than elsewhere. Soviet-bloc advisors and troops not only help maintain Ethiopia's defenses vis-a-vis Somalia and a half-dozen ethnic liberation movements, but assist in day-to-day education, police work, and bureaucratic administration. As of 1984 Ethiopia served as host to 2,500 Soviet and East European "technicians" and 2,600 economic "technicians," again the most in a sub-Saharan African country.[37]

Despite the closeness of the Soviet-Ethiopian relationship, a number of problems, albeit minor ones, have developed. First, despite the relative size of its economic aid package, Ethiopians have frequently joined the chorus of complaints over Soviet aid. During the recent famine Ethiopia was forced to turn grudgingly to the West for aid. Second, in 1984 Mengistu partially alleviated the high cost of Cuban assistance by sending 6,000 of the 10,000 troops packing, at an estimated savings of $6 million annually.[38] On a lesser note Mengistu, also in 1984, expelled two Soviet diplomats who were accused of spying. Finally, in February 1986 Ethiopia openly challenged Soviet wishes. When the Soviet Union and the new government in Aden demanded the extradition of Ali Nabir, the pre-coup president of South Yemen, Mengistu reportedly personally challenged Soviet and South Yemeni wishes.[39] Ethiopian-South Yemeni relations are clearly improving, and Soviet-Ethiopian relations do not appear to have suffered noticeably. But Mengistu, by now a domestically well-entrenched leader, is beginning to show a degree of foreign policy assertiveness that must be of concern to Moscow.

THE SOVIET UNION AND AFRICA: PROSPECTS FOR THE FUTURE

When Brezhnev died in the fall of 1982, Soviet policy toward the Third World had already entered a period of reassessment. Soviet analysts had begun to question the optimism of the prior decade concerning likely developments in the Third World.[40] The importance of the reassessment is most visible in the Party Program of the CPSU approved at the twenty-seventh Party Congress in March 1986. While the 1961 program had spoken with great optimism about prospects for liberation and the role of the USSR in supporting the liberation struggle, the new program discusses in some detail the revitalized role of neo-colonialism and imperialism in the Third World and not only that the "CPSU supports the just struggle waged by the countries of Asia, Africa, and Latin America against imperialism..." and that the "Soviet Union is on the side of the states and peoples repulsing the attacks of the aggressive forces of imperialism and upholding their freedom, independence, and national dignity." Progressive states are informed that the tasks of building a new society are primarily their own responsibility.[41] Another example of the more modest level of Soviet commitment to national liberation can be seen in General Secretary Gorbachev's referring merely to Soviet "sympathies" for the aspirations of people who are attempting to overthrow the yoke of neo-colonialism in his first speech as new leader of the CPSU, rather than making any specific Soviet commitment of major support.[42]

What emerges from the recent discussions among Soviet analysts concerning the Third World and even more from the authoritative pronouncements from the top of the party is the fact that the Third World is no longer given the central position in overall Soviet foreign policy that it received under Brezhnev. The results of expanded Soviet activism in the Third World in the 1970s have been disappointing from a Soviet perspective. Moreover, the economic and political costs of that activism have become evident. The Soviets have now entered a period in which they are emphasizing the consolidation of the positions that they gained in the 1970s in countries such as Afghanistan, Angola, Ethiopia, and Vietnam. They are apparently not prepared to take on significant and costly new initiatives in the foreseeable future. On the other hand, they have not indicated that they are likely to consider withdrawing direct or indirect support for client regimes such as those in Angola and Ethiopia.

Soviet activism in the Third World in the latter stages of the Brezhnev era resulted in a large part from a coincidence of several factors: the acquisition of strategic nuclear parity with the United States, the extension of Soviet power-projection capabilities, the opportunities presented to the USSR by the collapse of the Portuguese empire in Africa and the radicalization of a number of other developing countries, and the malaise that engulfed the United States in the wake of Vietnam and Watergate. The Soviets took advantage of these factors to extend significantly their involvement in various Third World conflict situations where their ability to provide military support was crucial for the successful acquisition or retention of power by their new-found clients. This was all part of the much heralded "changing international correlation of forces" in favor of socialism and the Soviet Union which was referred to in virtually all Soviet assessments of global developments in the 1970s.[43]

As a result of their support for revolutionary movements and governments the Soviets obtained important advantages through access to military facilities in strategically significant regions of Africa, the Middle East, and Southeast Asia. However, most of their new clients were small, weak, and dependent upon continued Soviet support for their existence. While this weakness represented an asset for the Soviets' ability to exert influence, it also meant that these countries soon became a substantial drain on Soviet resources. Even prior to the death of Brezhnev, Soviet commentators and analysts began to recognize that the benefits that the USSR had gained from the "successes" in the Third

World were counterbalanced, in part at least, by a new series of problems.

The first of these problems derives from the growing cost of supporting clients. It has been estimated that the costs of Soviet empire—including Eastern Europe and the growing subsidies to Cuba and Vietnam—had reached somewhere between \$35 and \$46 billion dollars annually by 1980.[44] More recent estimates place direct economic aid from the Soviet Union and East Europe (with about 80 percent coming from the former) for 1984 at about \$700 million for Cuba, \$1.2 billion for Vietnam, and \$600 million for Mongolia. In addition, price subsidies for Cuba were worth more than \$4.2 billion in 1984.[45] Added to this were the costs of military and economic support provided to countries such as Ethiopia and Afghanistan, neither of which is able to cover the costs of Soviet supplies with their own exports. It is essential to recall that the growing costs of overseas commitments occurred precisely at the time that the Soviet economy was suffering from falling economic growth rates, complicated more recently by the precipitous falling export price of petroleum (the single most important Soviet hard currency earner).

During his brief tenure as CPSU General Secretary Yuri, Andropov made a number of statements that questioned the benefits for the USSR of extensive involvement in the Third World. He made most clear that under his leadership the Soviet Union would not likely expand its economic commitments to socialist-oriented developing states when he noted: "We contribute also, to the extent of our ability, to economic development. But on the whole their economic development, just as the entire social progress of those countries, can be, of course, only the result of the work of their peoples and of a correct policy of their leadership."[46] As we have already seen this view has been incorporated into the Party Program approved at the first Congress held under Gorbachev's leadership.

Besides the growing concern about the drain on the Soviet economy resulting from commitments to Third World clients,

Soviet analysts have recognized the fact that the successes of national liberation movements in coming to power in the 1970s have not been matched by successful efforts to create viable political-economic systems. In most of these countries economic production has fallen off since the mid-1970s, the governments face continuing indigenous challenges to their authority (in part, as in Angola, Afghanistan, Ethiopia, and Nicaragua, supported from the outside). As recent Western surveys of Soviet literature on the Third World have demonstrated, the Soviets have been quite frank in recognizing the difficulties facing vanguard parties that have come to power with Soviet assistance.

A third set of problems that face the Soviets, in part as a result of their Third World "successes" of the 1970s, derives from the role that Soviet activism played in the deterioration of their relations with the United States. The new Party Program, for example, notes with concern the interrelationship between the renewed "aggressiveness" of the West in the Third World and the contradictions between the socialist and capitalist states.

The message that emerges from recent Soviet discussions about the Third World is that the Soviets are concerned about the staggering costs that the maintenance of their "empire" presents and about the inability of their weaker clients to achieve political and economic stability. They have already initiated efforts to divert some of the economic burden to their East European allies—with only limited success, given the problems facing most of these countries. Moreover, they have become increasingly selective in the amounts and types of support that they are willing to provide to existing clients—e.g., Mozambique and Angola. As one US analyst recently argued:

> The bottom line of the broad-ranging Soviet reassessment of the early 1980s is clear: the Soviet leadership would like to reduce the costs of its Third World empire in favor of the development of its own economy; within its empire, it would like to shift emphasis away from weak, narrowly based regimes to larger, more

influential ones, even if this means cultivating capitalist-oriented states in place of Marxist-Leninist regimes.[47]

In short, they would like to emphasize an ally-based strategy, as we have defined it, because of the increasingly prohibitive costs associated with expanding support for Marxist-Leninist regimes.

The major difficulty in implementing this strategy, as far as Africa is concerned, stems from the fact that there are relatively few wealthy, influential (or potentially influential) regimes in sub-Saharan Africa. As we have already argued, the emergence in southern Africa of South Africa as a regional "superpower" has resulted in a relative decline in Soviet influence. This decline has held for non-Marxist as well as for Marxist regimes. This has been most clearly evident in the case of tiny Lesotho, where Prime Minister Jonathan's ouster by a South African-backed coup in early 1986 resulted in a dramatic shift from improving relations with the USSR to a deterioration of those relations.

In many respects future developments in Africa present the Soviet leadership with a major dilemma. On the one hand, support for radical revolutionary movements and regimes is likely to bring certain benefits, as it has in the past. Yet, as we have seen, those benefits will be achieved at a cost that the USSR cannot or will not bear over the long run. On the other hand, Africa offers few prospects for long-term beneficial relationships based on what we have called an ally strategy. Moreover, as African leaders move from a situation where their primary concern is with economic development rather than with security (including the acquisition or retention of power), the inherent weaknesses of the Soviet Union as a global power become most evident. They simply have not been able to respond adequately to the economic needs of most developing countries, including those in Africa.

Whether the Soviets will pursue a policy of limited new commitments in Africa over the medium term, as implied in both recent authoritative Soviet statements and in recent behavior, will obviously depend upon a variety of factors. Most important will be the estimates in Moscow of the risks and costs involved, when balanced against the potential gains. From a Soviet perspective, the collapse of the current system in South Africa, which would most likely benefit the Soviet-oriented African National Congress, would be the type of development worth the commitment of substantial new resources. A Soviet-oriented South Africa—whether as an ally or "model" regime—would eliminate the single most important regional impediment to Soviet policy elsewhere in southern Africa. Moreover, it could become the focus of the type of relationship that the Soviet leadership is seeking throughout the Third World—strong ties to a large, influential state.

Table 6-1
SOVIET AND EAST EUROPEAN CREDITS AND GRANTS
EXTENDED TO SUB-SAHARAN AFRICAN COUNTRIES
(In millions of current US dollars)

	1954-84		1980		1981		1982		1983		1984	
	USSR	EEur	USSR	EEur	USSR	EEur	USSR	EEur	USSR	EEur	USSR	EEur
All Countries	30,305	14,915	2,605	1,320	600	725	1,015	560	3,360	415	2,350	1,750
Sub-Saharan Africa	4,645	2,360	330	285	155	105	745	115	310	100	545	80
Angola	560	100					450				50	2
Benin	15				5							
Burkina	5										n	
Burundi		50				n						
Cameroon	10											
Cape Verde	10	5			n	1						
Centr.Afr.Rep.	5									n		
Chad	5											
Congo	75	65		5	30							
Equa.Guinea	2	2	n				1					
Ethiopia	1,255	410	190	20	60	5	230		250	2	250	20
Gabon		2										
Gambia	2											
Ghana	110	160			1		10	n	n	10	5	
Guinea	400	130	5			n		20			165	
Guinea-Bissau	35	5			n		15					
Kenya	50	10								10		
Lesotho		5								5		
Madagascar	85	40	50				5				10	
Mali	135	20	1	35	5		20				15	
Mauritius	10										10	
Mozambique	220	195	85	2	45	80	5	10	15	10	5	
Niger	2											10

Table 6-1
SOVIET AND EAST EUROPEAN CREDITS AND GRANTS
EXTENDED TO SUB-SAHARAN AFRICAN COUNTRIES
(In millions of current US dollars)

	1954-84		1980		1981		1982		1983		1984	
	USSR	EEur	USSR	EEur	USSR	EEur	USSR	EEur	USSR	EEur	USSR	EEur
Nigeria	1,205	505		160		20		70		5		45
Rwanda	1											
Sao Tome & Prin		5										
Senegal	10	35										
Seychelles	30										20	
Sierra Leone	35				1							
Somalia	165	40		30						35		
Sudan	65	270										
Tanzania	45	85					5	10				
Uganda	35	25							10			
Zambia	30	165		30	5				10			
Zimbabwe		30						2		30		
Other	35								15		20	

Note: "N" signifies credits valued at less than one million dollars. These figures are merely estimates.
Source: US Department of State, *Warsaw Pact Economic Aid to Non-Communist LDCs, 1984* (May 1986), pp. 12-14.

Table 6-2
SOVIET TRADE WITH SUB-SAHARAN AFRICA
(In millions of Rubles)

	1980		1985	
	Exports	Imports	Exports	Imports
Total Trade	49,634.5	44,462.8	72,463.7	69,101.9
Of Which, Developing				
Countries	6,869.6	5,092.0	9,600.9	7,624.2
Total Africa	336.8	350.4	724.7	360.7
Angola	69.1	15.8	94.0	2.5
Cameroon	5.2	5.2	8.2	31.4
Congo	9.7	4.6	5.8	4.1
Ethiopia	120.8	25.7	280.1	34.6
Ghana	0.3	122.3	1.0	38.4
Guinea	13.2	50.8	40.5	58.0
Ivory Coast	2.9	76.8	4.6	125.6
Madagascar	6.0	3.1	37.8	6.0
Mali			6.6	0.5
Mozambique	17.9	1.7	83.9	1.5
Nigeria	80.2	19.4	149.1	41.0
Sudan	5.6	11.9	5.7	4.2
Sierra Leone	5.1	3.2	2.7	10.7
Tanzania	0.8	9.9	4.7	2.2

Source: Ministerstvo Vneshnei, Torgovlia SSR v 1985 g.: Statisticheskii Sbornik Moscow:
"Finansy i Statistika," 1986), pp. 8, 12-14.

Table 6-3
SOVIET AND EAST EUROPEAN
MILITARY RELATIONS WITH SUB-SAHARAN AFRICA

	Soviet-East European Military Technicians in Africa, 1984	African Military Personnel in Soviet Union-Eastern Europe, 1955-84
Total, All Developing Countries	21,335	78,445
Of Which, Sub-Saharan Africa	6,585	14,895
Angola	1,700	380
Burundi		105
Cape Verde		160
Chad		170
Congo	350	660
Equatorial Guinea		200
Ethiopia	2,600	2,120
Ghana		245
Guinea	60	1,025
Guinea-Bissau		125
Madagascar	125	285
Mali	50	855
Mozambique	1200	530
Sao Tome and Principe	170	
Somalia		2,605
Sudan		350
Tanzania	65	2,205
Uganda		990
Zaire		140
Zambia	50	625
Other	115	1,105

Source: US Department of State, *Warsaw Pact Economic Aid to Non Communist LDCs, 1984* (May 1986), pp.20-21.

Table 6-4

SOVIET MILITARY RELATIONS WITH DEVELOPING COUNTRIES
BY REGION, 1955-1985

(In millions of US dollars)

	Total 1955-79	1955-74	1975-79	1980	1981	1982	1983	1984	Total 1955-1984
Agreements (Total)	48,440	18,905	29,520	13,915	6,060 **	11,765	2,995	9,155	94,470
North Africa	10,960	2,805	8,155		0				
Sub-Saharan Africa	4,635	715	3,920		1,910				
East Asia	890	890	0		0				
Latin America	970	205	765		105				
Middle East	24,445	11,980	12,492		3,505				
South Asia	5,410	2,330	3,030		535				
Deliveries (Total)	361,680	12,495	23,190	6,290	8,105	8,065	7,130	7,135	49,415
North Africa	7,165	695	7,185						
Sub-Saharan Africa	3,530	410	2,625						
East Asia	885	885	0						
Latin America	675	30	645						
Middle East	18,675	9,375	9,300						
South Asia	4,410	2,130	1,930						

* Values are based on estimated Soviet prices in rubles converted into dollars. Since they are taken from different sources, they do not total.

** Values for 1981 given in the 1986 source are $6,505; these are retained, however, for they are the last estimates to provide a geographic breakdown.

Note: The recent sources do not provide any breakdown by region for 1980 and following nor a regional breakdown for new agreements in 1981. The totals for all agreements and deliveries come from the 1986 source and do not agree exactly with the total given in the 1980 CIA data nor the 1983 State Department data.

Sources: CIA, *Communist Aid Activities in Non-Communist Less Developed Countries, 1979 and 1954-79: A research Paper* ER 80-10318U, October 1980, p. 14. US Department of State, *Soviet and East European Aid to the Third World, 1981*, February 1983, p.2. US Department of State, *Warsaw Pact Economic Aid to Non-Communist LDCs, 1984*, May 1986, p. 19.

NOTES

1. The government of Alphonse Massemba Debat, which was overthrown in July 1968, was itself the oldest self-declared Marxist-Leninist regime in Africa, having exercised its so-called Marxist-Leninist option in 1963. See Michael S. Radu, "Congo," in *1984 Yearbook on International Communist Affairs*, ed. by Richard F. Staar (Stanford, CA: Hoover Institution Press, 1984), pp. 15-17.

2. For more extensive accounts of Soviet involvement in the Angolan Civil War and the Ogaden War respectively see Arthur Jay Klinghoffer, *The Angolan War: A Study in Soviet Policy in the Third World* (Boulder, CO: Westview Press, 1980) and Marina Ottaway, *Soviet and American Influence in the Horn of Africa* (New York: Praeger Publishers, 1982).

3. For a similar periodization of Soviet policy in the Third World see the excellent recent study by Rajan Menon entitled *Soviet Power and the Third World* (New Haven/London: Yale University Press, 1986), pp. 1-18. For lack of a better alternative, the terms "Third World" and "developing countries" are used here to refer to all noncommunist countries of Asia, Africa, and Latin America except Japan, South Africa, and Israel. The authors are well aware of the lack of precision of the term and that it includes countries with a wide range of political and economic characteristics—rapidly industrializing states of East Asia and Latin America, the rich oil-producing states, countries making only modest progress in expanding their economies, and those that are, in fact, regressing.

4. For a discussion of Soviet policy in this period see Roger E. Kanet, "The Soviet Union and the Colonial Question, 1917-1953," in *The Soviet Union and the Developing Na-*

tions, ed. Roger E. Kanet (Baltimore: Johns Hopkins University Press, 1972), pp. 16-26.

5. For a discussion of these points see Carl G. Jacobsen, *Soviet Strategic Initiatives: Challenge and Response* (New York: Praeger, 1979), pp. 1-8.

6. See Norman Polmar, *Soviet Naval Power: Challenge for the 1970s*, rev. edn. (New York: Crane, Russak, for National Strategy Information Center, 1974), pp. 40-45.

7. For a number of studies of the use of the Soviet fleet in international conflict situations see Michael MccGwire, Ken Booth, and John McDonnell, eds. *Soviet Naval Policy: Objectives and Constraints* (New York: Praeger, 1975); Michael MccGwire and John McDonnell, eds. *Soviet Naval Influence: Domestic and Foreign Dimensions* (New York: Praeger, 1977); Bradford Dismukes and James M. McConnell, eds., *Soviet Naval Diplomacy* (New York: Pergamon Press, 1979); and Bruce W. Watson and Susan M. Watson, eds., *The Soviet Navy: Strengths and Liabilities* (Boulder, CO: Westview Press, 1986). For an excellent analysis of the political role of Soviet military power see Stephen S. Kaplan et al., *Diplomacy of Power: Soviet Armed Forces as a Political Instrument* (Washington: The Brookings Institutions, 1981).

8. For discussions of the new Soviet capabilities see Thompson, *Power Projections*, and Jacobsen, *Soviet Strategic Initiatives*, esp. pp. 51-72. For a reasoned argument that one must be careful not to exaggerate the facilities that have been made available to the Soviets, see Richard Remnek's appendix in *Soviet Naval Diplomacy*, ed. by Dismukes and McConnell.

9. For an assessment of the importance of basing rights in Soviet Third World Policy see Robert E. Harkavy, *Great Power Competition for Overseas Bases: The Geopolitics of Access Diplomacy* (New York: Pergamon, 1982), esp. pp. 173-204, 233-239.

10. See Roger E. Kanet, "Soviet Military Assistance to the Third World," in *Communist Nations' Military Assistance*, ed. by John F. Copper and Daniel S. Papp (Boulder, CO: Westview Press, 1983), pp. 39-71. For data on Soviet economic and military relations with Sub-Saharan Africa see the tables in the appendix.

11. Several recently published books examine Soviet involvement in Third World conflicts in some detail. See, for example, Stephen T. Hosmer and Thomas W. Wolfe, *Soviet Policy and Practice toward Third World Conflicts* (Lexington, MA: B Lexington Books, D.C. Heath and Co., 1983); Joachim Krause, *Sowjetische Militarhilfepolitik gegenuber Entwicklungslandern* (Baden-Baden: Nomos Verlagsgesellschaft, 1985); and Bruce D. Porter, *The USSR in Third World Conflicts: Soviet Arms and Diplomacy in Local Wars 1945-1980* (Cambridge-London-New York: Cambridge University Press, 1984).

12. On Soviet objectives, for example, see David E. Albright, *The USSR and Sub-Saharan Africa in the 1980s* (New York: Praeger Publishers, 1983); Robert Legvold, "The Soviet Threat to Southern Africa," in *South Africa and Its Neighbors: Regional Security and Self Interest*, ed. by Robert I. Rotberg, et al. (Lexington, MA: Lexington Books, D.C. Heath and Co., 1985); and Robert F. Collins, "Soviet Influence in sub-Saharan Africa," *Military Review*, LXV (1985), pp. 46-67.

13. Robert D. Grey, "The Soviet Presence in Africa: An Analysis of Goals," *The Journal of Modern African Studies*, XXII (1984), pp. 11-27.

14. The delineation between model and ally "objectives" in Soviet policy toward the developing world originates in Richard Lowenthal, *Model or Ally? The Communist Powers and the Developing Countries* (New York: Columbia University Press, 1977).

15. See Mark N. Katz, *The Third World in Soviet Military*

Thought (Baltimore: The Johns Hopkins University Press, 1982), pp. 158-67.

16. In fact there have been numerous claims by revolutionary cadres in the developing world that their Russian advisors are condescending, racist, and refuse to partake in the hardships of life in the developing world. See, for example, George Volsky, "Cuba," in Thomas H. Hendriksen, ed. *Communist Powers and Sub-Saharan Africa* (Stanford, CA: Hoover Institution Press, 1981), pp. 57-84.

17. S. Neil MacFarlane, *Superpower Rivalry and Third World Radicalism: The Idea of National Liberation* (Baltimore: Johns Hopkins Press, 1985), p. 53.

18. Kenneth Jowitt, "Scientific Socialist Regimes in Africa: Political Differentiation, Avoidance, and Unawareness," in Carl G. Rosberg and Thomas M. Callaghy, eds. *Socialism in Sub-Saharan Africa: A New Assessment* (Berkeley: Institute of International Studies, 1979), p. 137.

19. See Jerry F. Hough, *The Struggle for the Third World: Soviet Debates and American Options* (Washington: The Brookings Institute, 1986), pp. 221-230, and Peter Zwick, *National Communism* (Boulder, CO: Westview Press, 1983), p. 77.

20. Ibid., p. 229.

21. See Roger E. Kanet, "East-West Political Relations: The Challenge of Detente," in *Soviet Foreign Policy and East-West Relations*, ed. by Roger E. Kanet (New York: Pergamon Press, 1982), pp. 39-55.

22. Ottaway, *Soviet and American Influence*, pp. 104-105.

23. See Daniel S. Papp, *Soviet Perceptions of the Developing World in the 1980s: The Ideological Bases* (Lexington, MA: Lexington Books, D.C. Heath and Co., 1985), pp. 74-75.

24. For a discussion of Soviet policy in Africa in the 1960s see Roger E. Kanet, "Soviet Attitudes Toward the Search for National Identity and Material Advancement in Africa,"

Vierteljahresberichte des Forschungsinstituts der Friedrich-Ebert-Stiftung, no. 36 (1969), pp. 143-156.

25. Katz, *The Third World in Soviet Military Thought*, p. 184.
26. For an excellent summary of Soviet involvement in the Zimbabwean liberation struggle see Keith Somerville, "The Soviet Union and Zimbabwe: The Liberation Struggle and After," in ed. by Craig Nation and Mark V. Kauppi, *The Soviet Impact in Africa* (Lexington, MA: Lexington Books, D.C. Heath and CO., 1984), pp. 195-220.
27. United States Department of State, *Warsaw Pact Aid to Non-communist LDCs*, 1984 (Washington: US Government Printing Office, revised May 1986), pp. 12-15.
28. Ibid., pp. 16-20.
29. Ibid., p. 12.
30. *Christian Science Monitor*, January 20, 1984, cited in Robert I. Rotberg, "Africa, the Soviet Union and the West," in *East-West Rivalry in the Third World: Security Issues and Regional Perspectives*, ed. by Robert W. Clawson (Wilmington, DE: Scholarly Resources, 1986), pp. 225-239.
31. See Peter Clement, "Moscow and Southern Africa," *Problems of Communism* XXXIV (1985), pp. 29-50.
32. One of the stipulated purposes of the CMEA is the gradual equalization of participant economies which in practical terms would have meant heavy subsidization of the Mozambican economy by the other members.
33. Department of State, *Warsaw Pact Aid*, p. 12.
34. Clement, "Moscow and Southern Africa," p. 36.
35. Francis Fukuyama, "Gorbachev and the Third World," *Foreign Affairs*, LXIV (1986), pp. 715-731.
36. "Ethiopia," *African Contemporary Record*, 1983-84, p. 36. Despite the agreements signed between South Africa and both Angola and Mozambique, South Africa has continued to support anti-government rebels in both countries. See Karl Maier, "Angolan Civil War: Air Power

is Key," *The Christian Science Monitor*, August 19, 1986, pp. 9,14.

37. It should be added, however, that if the number of Cuban advisors were included in these figures, Angola, which hosted 6,000 Cuban economic advisors in 1984, would surpass Ethiopia as hosting the most Communist advisors. See Department of State, *Warsaw Pact Economic Aid*, pp. 16-20.

38. *Washington Post*, January 25, 1984, cited in R. Rotberg, "Africa, the Soviet Union and the West," p. 230.

39. See David Pollack, "Moscow and Aden: Coping with a Coup," *Problems of Communism*, XXXV (1986), pp. 50-70.

40. Among the most comprehensive recent treatments of changing Soviet interpretations of the Third World are Hough, *The Struggle for the Third World*; Papp, *Soviet Perceptions*; Thomas J. Zamostny, "Moscow and the Third World: Recent Trends in Soviet Thinking," in *Soviet Studies*, XXXVI (1984), pp. 223-235; and Sally W. Stoecker, *R.A. Ulianovsky's Writings on Soviet Third World Politics, 1960-1985* (Santa Monica, CA: The Rand Corporation, 1986).

41. "Programma Kommunisticheskoi Partii Sovetskogo Soiuza. Novaia Redaktsiia," *Pravda*, March 7, 1986, p. 7; translated in *New Times*, no. 12 March 31, 1986, p. 43. The previous party program, published in 1961, had spoken of "a mighty wave of national liberation revolutions" that were "sweeping away the colonial system and undermining the foundations of imperialism." *Pravda*, November 2, 1961.

42. *Pravda*, March 11, 1985.

43. For an overview of the Soviet view of "correlation of forces" see Michael J. Deane, "The Correlation of World Forces," *Orbis*, 20 (1976), pp. 625-637; for a Soviet discussion of the meaning of the term see Sh. Sanakoyev,

"The World Today: Problems of the Correlation of Forces," *International Affairs*, no.11 (1974), p. 40-50.

44. See Charles Wolf et al., *The Costs of the Soviet Empire* (Santa Monica, CA: The Rand Corporation, No. R-3073/1-NA, September 1983) p. 19.

45. Foreign and Commonwealth Office, London, "Aid to the Developing World," *Background Brief* (April 1986), p. 3.

46. "Speech of the General Secretary of the Central Committee of the CPSU Comrade Iu. V. Andropov," *Kommunist*, no. 9 (1983). See, also, Andropov's earlier article entitled "Under the Banner of Lenin, Under the Party's Leadership," *Izvestia*, (February 23, 1979). The Party program approved in 1986 used virtually the same wording as that of Andropov when it noted that "every people creates, mostly by its own efforts, the material and technical base necessary for the building of a new society, and seeks to improve the well-being and cultural standards of the masses." "Programma Kommunisticheskoi Partii," p. 7.

47. Fukuyama, "Gorbachev and the Third World," p. 722.

SUGGESTED READINGS

Albright, David E. *The USSR and Sub-Saharan Africa in the 1980s* (New York: Praeger Publishers [*The Washington Papers/101*], 1983).

Coker, Christopher. *NATO, the Warsaw Pact and Africa* (New York: St. Martin's Press, 1985).

Grey, Robert D. "The Soviet Presence in Africa: An Analysis of Goals," *The Journal of Modern African Studies*, XXII (1984).

Kanet, Roger E. "Military Relations Between Eastern Europe and Africa," in *Arms for Africa: Military Assistance and Foreign Policy in the Developing World*, ed. Bruce E. Arlinghaus (Lexington, MA-Toronto: Lexington Books, D.C. Heath and Co., 1983).

Laurance, Edward J. "Soviet Arms Transfers in the 1980s: Declining Influence in Sub-Saharan Africa," in *Arms for Africa: Military Assistance and Foreign Policy in the Developing World*, ed. Bruce E. Arlinghaus (Lexington, MA-Toronto: Lexington Books, D.C. Heath and Co., 1983).

Nation, R. Craig and Mark V. Kauppi, eds., *The Soviet Impact in Africa* (Lexington, MA/Toronto: Lexington Books, D.C. Heath and Co., 1984).

Nolutshungu, Sam C. "Soviet-African Relations: Promise and Limitations," in *Soviet Interests in the Third World*, ed. Robert Cassen (London-Beverly Hills-New Delhi: SAGE Publications, 1985).

Porter, Bruce D. *The USSR in Third World Conflicts: Soviet Arms and Diplomacy in Local Wars 1945-1980* (Cambridge-London-New York: Cambridge University Press, 1984).

Skak, Mette. "CMEA Relations with Africa: A Case of Disparity in Foreign Policy Instruments," *Cooperation and Conflict*, XXI (1986).

Steele, Jonathan. "Soviet Relations with Angola and Mozambique," in *Soviet Interests in the Third World*, ed. Robert Cassen (London-Beverly Hills-New Delhi: SAGE Publications, 1985).

SEVEN

SOVIET POLICY IN THE MIDDLE EAST

Alvin Z. Rubinstein

Moscow has long been interested in the Middle East. Generations of Muscovite rulers expanded their empire for a combination of strategic, political, economic, and ideological reasons. From the latter part of the seventeenth century to World War I, the Russian and Ottoman Empires fought each other thirteen times, with Moscow emerging the dominant force along the Black Sea littoral, in the Balkans, and in the Caucasus. In the early eighteenth century, under Czar Peter the Great, Russia also spread eastward into Central Asia and southward toward Iran. It conquered diverse peoples and cultures, absorbed them into its vast empire, and in the process became a major threat to the Muslim lands situated along its southern border.

By the beginning of the nineteenth century, the only bar to Russia's supremacy in these regions was Great Britain. Determined to prevent Russia from dominating the land route from the Mediterranean Sea to the Persian Gulf and thereby threatening its lifeline to India, Britain propped up a succession of weak Ottoman rulers, thus enabling them to maintain their control of the Bosporus and the Dardanelles (the Straits connecting the Black Sea to the Mediterranean) and keep the Russian Fleet bottled up in the Black Sea. Britain also deployed its naval power to exclude Russian influence from southern Iran and the Persian Gulf; and it meddled in Afghanistan to prevent Russia's moving south of the Oxus River (the boundary between Russia and Afghanistan). This imperial rivalry, sometimes referred to as "The Great Game," was shelved prior to World War I; uncertainty in Europe and the Far East mandated stability along the Central Asian rimland. Russia and Britain found it expedient to improve relations in the face of a shared threat from Germany.

World War I brought a decline in Russia's position and a dramatic change in its leadership. In 1917 the overthrow of the Romanov dynasty and the seizure of power by the Bolsheviks (communists) under V. I. Lenin temporarily ended Russian pressure on Turkey, Iran, and Afghanistan. Absorbed with problems of survival, consolidation of power, internal struggles, and security threats in Europe and the Far East, the Soviet leadership was satisfied to ensure stability and the status quo along its southern periphery. Not until 1945 did Moscow again manifest expansionist ambitions in the area.

At the end of World War II, Moscow sought to extend its power southward. Stalin pressured Turkey to grant the USSR a naval base on the Straits and return the provinces of Kars and Ardahan in northeastern Turkey; supported separatist movements in the Kurdish and Azerbaijanian areas of northwestern Iran that had been occupied by Soviet troops in August 1941; and tried to obtain part of the former Italian colonies, particularly the Dodecanese Islands in the Aegean Sea and a trusteeship over Libya. But the Western powers held firm, defending Turkey's sovereignty; backed Iran, whose prime minister used the prospect of US support to induce the Soviets to withdraw without, as matters turned out, having to give away anything tangible in return; and rebuffed Stalin's maneuvering in the United Nations for a possession in Africa.

Only on the Palestine issue could Stalin derive some satisfaction. To weaken the British position in the Middle East, he supported the UN's partition of Palestine and the consequent creation of the state of Israel, because from his perspective the Zionist struggle for a Jewish state was objectively anti-imperialist—in this instance, anti-British. Moreover, in addition to forcing Britain to relinquish a major stronghold in the eastern Mediterranean, Stalin had reason to hope that the left-socialist outlook of the heavily Russian and East European Jewish leadership in Palestine would result in close relations with the Soviet Union.

Stalin's assistance was crucial. Soviet bloc votes in the UN General Assembly ensured adoption by the required two-thirds majority of the resolution to partition Palestine. Moreover, without Stalin's sanctioning the sale of Czech arms to Israel and permitting the emigration of Jews from Soviet-controlled Eastern Europe, Israel would most probably not have survived the initial assault by the Arab states. As a result of siding with Israel, the USSR's standing in the Arab world plummeted, so that by the time of Stalin's death in March 1953, the Middle East was a wasteland for Soviet diplomacy.

THE USSR's "FORWARD POLICY"

One of the first steps taken by Stalin's successors was to revamp policy toward the Third World. Nowhere was this new look more evident than in Moscow's policy toward the Middle East. Within a few years, Moscow succeeded in shedding Stalin's flawed policies, normalizing diplomatic relations with key regional actors, and leapfrogging over the network of military alliances that the United States had nurtured in an effort to contain the Soviet Union. It pushed itself into the mainstream of regional developments and wrought a major transformation in the region's alignments.

Looking at the way in which Soviet policy in the Middle East has evolved, one can distinguish different approaches to four subregions, which for analytical and policy-relevant reasons may be divided as follows: first, the non-Arab Muslim tier of countries situated along the USSR's southern border, namely, Turkey, Iran, and Afghanistan; second, the Arab-Israeli sector of the Arab world, with particular focus on Egypt, Syria, Jordan, Lebanon, and Israel; third, the Persian Gulf-Arabian Peninsula, which includes countries such as Saudi Arabia, Iraq, Kuwait, Oman, the United Arab Emirates, the People's Democratic Republic of Yemen (PDRY), and the Yemen Arab Republic (YAR); and fourth, the Maghreb, which includes Libya, Tunisia, Algeria, Mauritania, Morocco, and Mali. The USSR's policy toward each region has developed independently in response to a changing combination of concerns, opportunities, and calculations.

The 1980s, in contrast to the 1950s, are characterized by the following: (1) an enormous growth of Soviet military capability and commitments; (2) active involvement in all regions of the Middle East and a readiness to use force on behalf of prized clients; and 3) a far more promising strategic-diplomatic environment within which to promote its wide-ranging interest.

To better understand Soviet aims, how and why they have changed, and what have been the major successes and failures, an assessment of the Soviet Union's evolving policy toward each of the regions of the Middle East will be made, with special attention to the past two decades. From this perspective on past Soviet policy will emerge an appreciation of the most serious dilemmas that Soviet party leader Mikhail Gorbachev faces in the years ahead.

TURKEY, IRAN, AND AFGHANISTAN

Moscow's greatest strategic-political successes in the Middle East may well be the changed policies of the countries situated along its southern border. Relations with Turkey, Iran, and Afghanistan have developed in dramatic and unforeseen ways, troubled in the latter two cases, but strategically more promising at the end of the 1980s than they were three decades ago.

Turkey. After Stalin died in March 1953, the Soviet leadership moved quickly to repair the damage done by his heavy-handed pressure tactics and to restore the accommodation that had prevailed in the 1920s. Though the Turks were wary, they slowly reached for the Soviet olive branch and by the mid-1960s began to accept economic assistance. Ankara's readiness to explore economic cooperation and political accommodation with the colossus to the north developed initially from disillusionment with the United States over the removal of US intermediate range missiles from Turkey, in what it saw as part of a deal between Kennedy and Khrushchev to settle the Cuban missile crisis of October 1962; this disappointment was then intensified by President Lyndon B. Johnson's unfriendly attitude during the 1964 Cyprus crisis, when the Turks felt the US behaved more as an adversary than an ally.

The Soviets handled the Turks skillfully. They extended large scale economic assistance for industrial projects without political strings (Turkey is one of the largest recipients of Soviet economic credits in the Third World); maintained a low military profile along the border; and took advantage of Turkey's persistent tensions with the United States over the Cyprus issue, military assistance, and Greek-Turkish policy. In return, Moscow obtained unimpeded and easy access through the Straits, restraints on US military activities at bases on Turkish soil, and expanded trade and economic ties.

Gorbachev has continued his predecessors' policy of peaceful coexistence, but constraints on closer Soviet-Turkish ties are strong. Though traditional Turkish fears of Moscow's territorial ambitions have been allayed for the time being, Soviet support for illegal communist activities and terrorism serves as a reminder of Russia's age-old ambitions, as do periodic calls for legalization of the Turkish Communist Party. Centuries of hostility cannot be forgotten in a decade or two, while the shadow of Soviet military power looms large over the entire region.[1]

Iran. Throughout the nineteenth century, successive Czars expanded at the expense of a weak Iran, and on the eve of World War I northern Iran was a Russian sphere of influence. The revolution in Russia enabled Iran to regain its independence. During World War II the Soviet Union and Great Britain temporarily occupied Iran to forestall its drift to the German side and to assure a safe transit for shipments of war material to the USSR. After the war, Stalin tried unsuccessfully to hold on to the Kurdish and Azerbaijanian provinces of Iran, eventually withdrawing in mid-1946.

Soviet-Iranian relations remained poor until September 1962, when the Shah announced that no US military bases or missiles would be permitted on Iranian soil, even though Iran was a military ally of the United States. Pleased with this decision, which removed Iran as a potential source of direct military threat to the USSR, Soviet leaders pushed a full-fledged rapprochement: they moderated their criticisms of the Shah's regime, exchanged high-level visits, expanded trade, and constructed a wide array of industrial projects, including a steel complex at Isfahan and a natural gas pipeline that enabled Iran to sell the Soviets all its surplus natural gas. During the halcyon period of 1968 to 1978, Moscow even helped Iran build up its arms industry, a development that was to serve Iran well after the Iraqi invasion of September 1980.

There were some frictions, primarily because of competing foreign policy objectives in the Persian Gulf, the Soviet Union's military buildup of Iraq (Iran's rival in the region), Iran's role in suppressing a Soviet-armed insurgency in Oman, and the Shah's friendship with China. But none of these were serious enough to upset their illusionless detente. With its own security assured, Moscow hoped that, despite differences, good relations would eventually lead Iran to loosen its military links to the United States.

In January 1979 Ayatollah Khomeini's Islamic Revolution toppled the Shah and ushered in a difficult and troubled era in Soviet-Iranian relations. At first Moscow was elated. It welcomed the end of the Shah's policy of alignment with the United States and the intense anti-American animus that dominated Khomeini's militant Islamic regime. Indeed, Khomeini even permitted the communists to operate openly for a time. Soviet expectations of a rapid normalization of diplomatic relations and continuation of the good state-to-state relations that had existed with the Shah were dashed by a combination of unforeseen and disruptive developments: the communist takeover of Afghanistan in April 1978; the challenge to Khomeini from the Iranian left, which in May 1983 brought a crackdown on the communists, among others; the USSR's refusal to meet Iran's demands for a stiff increase in the price it charged for natural gas exports; and the outbreak of the Iran-Iraq War in September 1980.

Moscow has been unable to overcome Tehran's ideological antipathy and deep-rooted suspicion. The situation is complex. Notwithstanding occasional exchanges of delegations and modest increases in trade since 1984, Moscow seems resigned to strained relations and sporadic anti-Soviet outbursts until Khomeini dies. It also warns Tehran against aiding the Afghan freedom fighters. For the time being, the Soviet approach is to seek expansion of bilateral economic relations,[2] adopt a public posture of neutrality toward the Iran-Iraq War while covertly selling arms to both sides, denounce US "imperialism" and encourage Iran's anti-Americanism, and wait upon developments. There are factions in the Iranian government that favor better relations with the Soviet Union, as witnessed by the help Tehran provided in November 1985 in securing the release of three kidnapped officials of the Soviet Embassy in Beirut; Moscow is prepared to be patient.[3]

Afghanistan. Czarist Russia's expansion in Central Asia reached Afghanistan in the late 1860s, at about the same time that Great Britain was expanding its Indian Empire northwest to the Khyber Pass. After endless intriguing and several near-confrontations, the two imperial powers agreed in 1907 to maintain Afghanistan as a buffer state between them. However, with the end of World War II and the partition of India, the politics of the region underwent a profound change. Of particular significance was Afghanistan's decision to seek arms from the Soviet Union in order to incite the Pushtun tribes of neighboring Pakistan's North West Frontier Province (NWFP) to revolt, creating an independent Pushtunistan, and eventually becoming part of a Greater Afghanistan.

Under Khrushchev, the Soviet Union became Afghanistan's main patron. From 1953 to 1978, Afghanistan's economic development depended on Soviet credits and equipment; its military was Soviet-trained and Soviet-equipped. The military infrastructure that was created after 1956 would, in time, service a Soviet army of occupation. It was from among the officers trained in the Soviet Union that Moscow recruited the communist agents who toppled the regime in April 1978. For a generation, Moscow's relationship with Afghanistan had ensured Soviet security interests, economic domination, and political preeminence. Its response to the communist coup demonstrates its desire to turn Afghanistan into a compliant communist puppet and, in time, to see it as a springboard for playing a major role in South and Southwest Asia.

The new communist government, headed by Nur Muhamad Taraki, signed a twenty-year-friendship treaty with the Soviet Union on December 5, 1978. Soviet assistance and advisory personnel poured into the country, and Afghanistan was drawn even more intimately into the Soviet orbit. Very soon dissatisfaction with communist rule erupted into open rebellion. By early 1979 the regime was hard-pressed and required increasing Soviet help. In September, Taraki was killed in a showdown with his deputy prime minister, Hafizullah Amin, who pursued a hard-line policy in an attempt to destroy the Mujahideen ("Holy Warriors"), as the Afghan resistance fighters are called. Fearing the growing strength of the resistance, Moscow grew impatient with Amin's unwillingness to make temporary tactical shifts to placate the tribes. On December 27, 1979, it intervened in force, murdering him and installing Babrak Karmal as its man in Kabul.

Babrak Karmal headed a faction of the People's Democratic Party of Afghanistan (PDPA) known as Parcham; his predecessors had been affiliated with the Khalq. He tried to institutionalize communist rule, with little success. In May 1986, Karmal was replaced as general secretary of the party by Najibullah, a Soviet-trained former head of the secret police.

But Gorbachev wanted out. An agreement was forged under the auspices of the United Nations, and a Soviet withdrawal started in May 1988. With an estimated 120,000 troops, the USSR had undertaken numerous military campaigns, but none had succeeded in pacifying any area for long. It appeared to be pursuing a three-pronged strategy to break the resistance and Sovietize Afghanistan in much the same way it did Mongolia: a military drive to extirpate the opposition, using depopulation, terror, starvation, and destruction of traditional rural communities as adjuncts of coercive Sovietization; a political investment in cadres and institutions that would enable the Soviet-backed PDPA regime in Kabul to broaden its base of support and convince the population of the futility of resistance and the benefits of cooperation; and an effort to control the cities and key lines of communication, either by the sword or by the purse. Intensification of the fighting after Gorbachev came to power suggested that Moscow would not soon agree to a formula that called for the withdrawal of its forces from Afghanistan. Apparently, though, the human and military cost of the war became too great, political expediency won out over the urge not to be embarrassed, and Soviet troops did indeed begin to pull out of Afghanistan. It remains to be seen what the Soviets will leave behind them, however, and whether Afghanistan will return to a situation approximating the one that existed in 1978.

THE ARAB-ISRAELI SECTOR

Soon after Moscow leapfrogged into the center of the Arab stage with arms for Egypt in 1955, it discovered that the Arab-Israeli conflict could be used to advance many goals: the establishing of close relations with Arab regimes who wanted a military option; weakening of US influence by linking it to partisan support for Israel; acquisition of military facilities; and enhancement of Soviet prestige. This policy unfolded gradually, in part because the USSR lacked the capability to intervene effectively on behalf of Arab clients until the end of the 1960s; and in part because the polarization caused by the Arab-Israeli conflict did not become pronounced until the June 1967 War.

The Arab defeat in that conflict proved a boon for Moscow, paving the way for a massive intrusion of aid and advisers to Egypt and Syria. Total dependency led Nasser to grant the facilities that the Soviet military had sought since 1961: naval access and depots at Alexandria and Sollum and airfields to reconnoiter the movements of the US Sixth Fleet in the Mediterranean and the Red Sea region. In return, Moscow restored Egypt's combat capability and intervened in force to save Nasser (who died in September 1970) from another defeat in the 1969-1970 War of Attrition. The ensuing cooperation with Anwar Sadat (winner in the struggle to succeed Nasser) encountered serious difficulties, including Sadat's expulsion of most Soviet military personnel in July 1972. Nevertheless, Moscow came to the rescue of Egypt and Syria in the 1973 October War, during which the USSR acted the generous and protective patron, shielding both countries from defeat and enabling them to emerge from the war with strategic and political gains. Sadat, far from grateful, turned to Washington for assistance in regaining Egyptian territory controlled by Israel. In the process, he eliminated the Soviet military foothold in Egypt. By 1976 Moscow had nothing tangible to show for almost two decades of diplomatic, military, and economic assistance to Egypt.

To offset its setback in Egypt, Moscow shored up its position in this sector of the Arab world by arming Syria, Libya, the PLO, and all who were opposed to US-sponsored efforts to negotiate a partial settlement. Increasingly, the Soviet Union used arms transfers to solidify the new polarization in the Arab world that emerged as a result of Sadat's decision to sign a peace treaty with Israel in March 1979.

Moscow takes its cues from Arab opponents of the United States. Its opposition to the peace process continues to be a mixture of opportunism, commitment to keeping key clients in power, instigation of anti-Americanism, and reliance on guns to retain friends.

In the 1980s Soviet options have been limited, but Moscow is persistently wedded to an approach that believes in the utility of incremental gains to produce, over time, a strategic environment conducive to the advancement of its objectives. First, it encourages Arab actors (Syria, Libya, the PDRY, Algeria, and the PLO) committed to unrelenting war against Israel and opposed to any piecemeal US-sponsored peace process. Second, it upholds the PLO's international position, following the Arab states' lead in calling for the establishment of an independent Palestinian state, and supports pro-Palestinian and anti-Israeli resolutions in international forums, the aim being the diplomatic isolation of Israel and the United States. Since December 1983, when a Syrian-backed faction challenged Yasir Arafat's leadership in the wake of PLO setbacks in Lebanon, Moscow has urged reconciliation, but is unwilling to jeopardize its relationship with Syrian President Hafez Assad by taking sides in the internecine Palestinian struggle for power. Third, and perhaps most important, Moscow has made Syria the centerpiece of its policy in the Arab-Israeli sector, the position which was Egypt's until Sadat's turnabout after the October War. Assad has shown himself to be a skillful political strategist. Secure under the protection of the Soviet military umbrella in Lebanon, he out-intrigued Israel and outmaneuvered the United States; in Palestinian affairs, he has made sure that no moderate faction emerges to negotiate a settlement without his approval; as godfather of diverse terrorist organizations, he undermines US policy and interests.

THE PERSIAN GULF-ARABIAN PENINSULA REGION

Soviet attempts to establish firm footholds in this region, the significance of which stems from its various reserves of oil, lagged because the less explosive regional animosities enabled the local Arab actors to maintain their distance from the USSR. The breakthroughs for Soviet diplomacy came in the Yemens and Iraq. In October 1955, Moscow made its first tentative inroad by way of a treaty with (North) Yemen signed in Cairo; but not until 1968, when South Yemen (PDRY) gained its independence from Britain, did the USSR acquire a solid position in the Yemeni part of the peninsula. In Iraq, a revolution in July 1958 overthrew the pro-Western monarch and brought in a succession of militant, anti-American regimes prepared to deal with the USSR. Soviet-Iraq relations reached their apogee in the early 1970s, with the signing of a friendship treaty on April 9, 1972, and cooperation in 1974-1975 to prevent a possible Iraqi-Iranian war over the Kurds and competing territorial claims. However, since the outbreak of the Iran-Iraq War in September, 1980, the Soviet position has deteriorated, and the Ba'athist regime of Saddam Hussain has improved relations with the United States.

Moscow's principal military asset on the Arabian Peninsula is access to naval and air facilities in the PDRY, whose port of Aden is the best in the region. With relatively small outlays of military and economic assistance and with little risk, Moscow has drawn handsome strategic dividends from its PDRY investments. Its position with this Marxist regime is apparently still strong, despite the subtle damage, not easily evident, done by the brief and bloody civil war in January 1986. Saudi Arabia is really Moscow's prime target, and in focusing on the Yemens it pursues an indirect strategy, with which it shrewdly tries to change the center by radicalizing the periphery.

However, elsewhere on the peninsula Moscow has little to show despite an assiduous courtship. Diplomatic relations with Saudi Arabia continue to elude it. Despite periodic reports of Riyadh's imminent move toward normalization of relations with the Soviet Union, the Saudis have not taken the step. Fear of Khomeini's purist position on Afghanistan is a powerful restraint; that is, because he has accused the Saudis of not being devout Muslims, they must be wary of appearing friendly to the Soviet Union as long as it wages war on Muslim Afghanistan.

The USSR's relations with Kuwait since 1963 are a function of that oil-rich mini-Sheikhdom's assumption that, situated as it is in the shadow of covetous Iraq and Iran, possible help should be sought in all quarters. Over the years Kuwait has purchased small quantities of weapons from the Soviet Union to keep ties tangible enough to be attractive to Moscow, and has worked to persuade other mini-states in the Gulf to normalize their relations with Moscow. In the fall of 1985, for reasons of their own, Oman and the United Arab Emirates followed Kuwait's example. But Moscow's presence remains minimal: Soviet ambassadors stationed elsewhere are being accredited, suggesting that neither country is keen on too close a relationship.

The limitations on Soviet advances in the region are heavily political and ideological.[4] Moscow is checked by the widespread hostility to communism, by suspicion of communist involvement in dissident activities, by its arms and intervention in the Yemens, and by the prevailing belief that its long-term ambitions are antithetical to the survival and stability of the Islamic, monarchical, conservative oligarchies that rule in the region.

A new development in the Gulf is the introduction of a Soviet naval presence. In response to a Kuwaiti request in December 1986 for protection of its ships against Iranian attack, Moscow has undertaken to escort some Kuwaiti-chartered Soviet tankers. Though relegated to a lesser role (Kuwait has preferred that the

United States assume the greater burden for protecting its tankers), Gorbachev has seized the opportunity to intrude the USSR into the mainstream of the region's politics and to demonstrate its credibility as a patron.

THE MAGHREB

Algeria was the first of the five North African countries (Algeria, Libya, Mauritania, Morocco, and Tunisia) to establish a major economic and military relationship with the USSR, doing so in the mid-1960s when it sought an alternative to dependence on France, from which it had recently gained independence after a bitter eight-year struggle. However, the main impetus behind greater Soviet involvement came in the 1970s, with regional rivalries setting the stage. The undeclared war between Algeria and Morocco over the former Spanish Sahara heightened the need for Soviet weapons and led each to cultivate a Soviet connection. As always, Moscow was ready to supply massive amounts of arms—especially for hard currency—irrespective of the consequent aggravation of local tensions and instability.

The main Soviet impact in the area, however, has come as a result of an extensive, complex relationship with Libyan leader Colonel Muammar Qaddafi. The Soviet-Libyan relationship developed gradually after Qaddafi seized power on September 1, 1969. At the urging of Egyptian President Anwar Sadat, Qaddafi began to buy Soviet weapons in 1972-1973.[5] His arms purchases and ties to Moscow grew after the October 1973 War, when he quarreled with Sadat over the conduct of the war and Egypt's subsequent abrupt turn to the United States.

In May 1974, a delegation headed by Major Abdel Salaam Jalloud, the number two man on Libya's ruling Revolutionary Command Council, concluded a major arms agreement in Moscow. The joint communique declared that Libya and the Soviet Union shared an interest in opposing "imperialism, Zionism, and reaction," code words signifying hostility to the United States and to all efforts to negotiate a political settlement of the Arab-Israeli conflict.

Since then, Moscow has sold upwards of $15 billion worth of advanced weaponry to Libya, and with this have come large numbers of Soviet and East European advisors, technicians, and security forces (like the East Germans who serve in Qaddafi's Praetorian Guard). A number of considerations entered into Moscow's calculations. First, as a result of soaring OPEC oil prices in the 1970s, Libya could pay for its arms in hard currency, which the Soviet Union needs to help finance imports of technology and grain from the West. Second, Soviet arms sales required a sizable Soviet presence. In time, this brought limited access to port facilities for the Soviet navy, which sought to compensate for the termination of their foothold in Egypt after March 1976. Third, Libya's hostility to US peace initiatives in the Middle East aligned Moscow with the anti-Western coalition of Arab states and gave it a role in Arab world politics. Moreover, Qaddafi's intrigues in the Sudan, Chad, and Tunisia, and his patronage of international terrorism, suit the USSR's aims of exacerbating regional rivalries, destabilizing pro-Western governments, and sowing discord between the Arab world and the West. Finally, Moscow is careful to keep Qaddafi at arm's length, refusing to sign a friendship treaty lest he involve the Soviet Union in an unwanted confrontation with the United States. For the moment, it is content with Libya's dependence on Soviet arms and advisers and with the problems Libya creates for the United States.

GORBACHEV'S POLICIES AND DILEMMAS

Since coming to power in March 1985, General Secretary Mikhail Gorbachev's foreign policy initiatives have centered on improving relations with the United States, Western Europe, and Japan; on arms control issues; and on China. With one exception—Afghanistan—he has said little about the Middle East or even the Third World as a whole. For example, at the twenty-seventh Congress of the CPSU on February 26, 1986, in the part of his report devoted to foreign policy, a mere 150 words dealt with Third World issues, and two-thirds of these spoke of

Afghanistan. Since Stalin's death and Moscow's adoption of a forward policy in the Third World, no Soviet leader has, on such an occasion, spent so little time on the "zone of peace," the national liberation struggles, and the various regional conflicts that have occasioned Soviet commitment and concern. Except in referring to Afghanistan, Gorbachev gave no hint of difficulties, dilemmas, or new directions.

Without a doubt, the war in Afghanistan was the most pressing and difficult problem that Gorbachev faced in the Middle East. At the party congress, he called it a "a bleeding wound."[6] He became prepared to make meaningful concessions to obtain a peaceful settlement, and Soviet troops began to withdraw. Upwards of 120,000 Soviet troops were fighting in a contiguous country ruled by a puppet communist regime opposed by a substantial proportion of its citizens; the war, in its ninth year, at its end has been a terrible drain on Soviet resources, an international embarrassment, and a mote in the eye of the Soviet people, who became increasingly aware of the struggle due to expanded coverage by the Soviet news media. Clearly, Gorbachev had to address the issue directly and define the official position.[7]

Gorbachev's comment on Afghanistan at the party congress was his longest on a Third World issue:

> For example, counterrevolution and imperialism have turned Afghanistan into a bleeding wound. The Soviet Union supports this country's efforts, which are directed at the defense of its own sovereignty. We would like in the near future to bring the Soviet forces—situated in Afghanistan at the request of its government—back to their homeland. The time scale of their step-by-step withdrawal has been worked out with the Afghan side [this withdrawal to take place] as soon as a political settlement has been achieved that will provide for a real end to and reliably guarantee a non-renewal of the outside armed interference in the internal affairs of the DRA [Democratic Republic of Afghanistan]. Our vital national interest lies in unfailingly good and peaceful relations with all states bordering on the Soviet Union.

A close examination of the passage suggests that it was crafted with a lawyer's eye for assuring the upper hand in any bargaining over details and conditions. While indicating a desire to withdraw Soviet forces, Gorbachev stressed that they had been introduced into the country at the request of the Afghan government and hence were there, by implication, legally and appropriately. The conditions he set for a withdrawal of Soviet troops were as rigid and demanding as ever: agreement on a political settlement that would provide "for a real end to—and *reliably* guarantee a non-renewal of—*outside* armed interference in the internal affairs of the DRA" (italics added).

For all of his seeming obdurateness, Gorbachev was clearly dissatisfied with the status quo. On May 4, 1986, he replaced Babrak Karmal as general-secretary of the PDPA with Najibullah, the head of the secret police and a leader he hoped could reconcile the Parcham and Khalq factions, suppress the Mujahideen insurgency and establish a government of "national reconciliation." At the end of October, 8,000 Soviet troops were pulled out, in what was hailed by Moscow as evidence of its desire for a peaceful solution. Diplomatically, Gorbachev made new overtures to Pakistan and courted nonaligned leaders, in the hope of easing international pressure and the annual condemnation of the Soviet intervention by the UN General Assembly.

A crucial consideration in Gorbachev's decision to withdraw from Afghanistan was the introduction of the Stinger missile, a 35-pound, shoulder-fired surface-to-air missile that denied the Soviets control of the air—the one great military advantage they had heretofore possessed. The supply of stingers to the Mujahideen at the end of 1986 brought a quick turnabout in their military situation. Realizing that it was now unable to win the war by military means, Moscow devoted more attention to the conference room.

UN-sponsored efforts to reach a political settlement had been ongoing since June 1982. Diego Cordovez, UN Under-

Secretary General for Special Political Affairs and personal representative of the UN's secretary general, had been holding periodic rounds of "proximity talks" with Pakistani and Afghan officials. In one room each side conducted separate talks with the UN interlocutor; this formula was insisted on by Pakistan, to which direct negotiations with the Afghan government were unacceptable since they implied recognition of the communist regime as the legitimate government of Afghanistan.

On February 8, 1988, on the eve of a new round of talks in Geneva, Gorbachev announced that the Soviet Union was prepared to begin the removal of Soviet troops on May 15, 1988, "and to complete their withdrawal within ten months." Of equal significance was his statement that he would be only too happy to have as a neighbor "an independent, nonaligned, and neutral" Afghanistan.

On April 14, 1988, a series of agreements were signed in Geneva, the most important of which calls for the withdrawal of Soviet troops from Afghanistan by February 1989. The withdrawal started on May 15 and, as of the end of August, was generally proceeding on schedule; there is no reason to believe that Gorbachev will reverse himself on this issue. The Soviet Union has paid a stiff price for its imperialist venture in Afghanistan.

Gorbachev's decision to pull out of Afghanistan is significant, and we need to keep it clearly in mind when speculating about the future of the USSR's policy elsewhere in the Middle East. But we must also not adduce too much from this one issue because, overall, Gorbachev's Middle East policy has so far demonstrated an activism that belies any fundamental retrenchment of interest or involvement.

SETTLING THE ARAB-ISRAELI CONFLICT

Is Gorbachev interested in contributing to a political settlement of the Arab-Israeli conflict and thereby removing a major source of tension from the US-Soviet relationship that has existed since the late 1960s? Or is he bent on continuing to use the conflict to weaken US influence and promote Soviet ambitions in the Arab world? To date, he has done little of substance on the issues. At the twenty-seventh Party Congress, he gave no intimations of any rethinking of Soviet policy toward the Arab-Israeli conflict, or of the problems that support for the Arab confrontation states entail for his efforts to improve relations with the United States.

A great deal has been written on this aspect of Soviet policy. However, the absence of authoritative information on the thinking underlying the policies of Soviet and Arab leaders leaves us dependent on an approach that deduces Soviet aims from Soviet behavior. For such an approach, which seems reasonable under the circumstances, there is substantial evidence, the bulk of which suggests a basic continuity in Soviet policy during the past two decades.

A pattern is discernible in which the Soviet Union will constantly espouse a more pro-Arab position than that supported by the United States. In November 1967, for example, after Resolution 242 was adopted by the UN Security Council, the Soviets "quickly identified themselves with the Arab interpretation of the deliberately ambiguous language of the Resolution, emphasizing maximum Israeli withdrawal from occupied territories and minimum Arab commitments to peace, and opposing any process of face-to-face, direct negotiations."[8] In the ensuing years, this Soviet propensity for upholding maximalist Arab demands may even have contributed to the impasse that existed until the 1973 War.

Moscow has been unwilling to pressure its clients to make concessions. Those of its proposals that do not obtain Arab support are quickly dropped. At no time was it prepared to risk jeopardizing good relations with Nasser in order to advance the prospect of peaceful settlement. This unwillingness to pressure Arab clients all the way to the negotiating table is acknowledged even by Western analysts, who believe that Moscow is interested in a political settlement based on superpower collaboration, albeit not at any price.[9] The fact is that Moscow has never made a major diplomatic effort to fashion a settlement that would be acceptable to all parties. When push comes to shove, it backs off from using its leverage on Arab clients and accepting the consequences of subordinating its regional interests to its global interests.

An examination of past Soviet peace proposals shows them to be close facsimiles of Arab proposals. None ventures beyond what the Arab consensus is prepared to accept. A brief comparison of the Arab plan proposed at Fez, Morocco on September 9, 1982, with the Soviet proposals of July 29, 1984, is instructive: the Arab plan did not mention UN Security Council Resolution 242, and neither did Moscow's; on issues such as the withdrawal of Israel from all territory occupied in 1967, the establishment of a Palestinian state, the return of East Jerusalem, and the transition mechanism, there is complete agreement between the two plans. Soviet proposals seem designed to serve propagandistic purposes, and to demonstrate their support for the Arab cause.

Gorbachev's adherence to the Arab confrontation position is also evident in his clever handling of the issue of a possible restoration of diplomatic relations with Israel, broken off in June 1967. Over the years steady attention has been paid to Soviet actions and "signals" that affect Israel. At times, the heavy traffic of signals and unofficial contacts has resulted in recurring predictions of a diplomatic breakthrough—of a return to the situation that existed prior to the June War.

Since coming to power, Gorbachev's handling of Israel has been a shrewd mix of openness and disinformation; so far, he has promised more than he has delivered, but there have been signs of flexibility to warrant a measure of guarded optimism.

The first sign that the Soviet government was rethinking its policy towards Israel was *Izvestia*'s publishing, on May 12, 1985, a telegram from Israeli President Chaim Herzog on the occasion of the fortieth anniversary of the Allied victory in Europe. By printing the Israeli message in the commemorative celebration, Moscow gave rare diplomatic affirmation of Israel's right to exist. This hint of a thaw was followed up by a publicly acknowledged meeting in July between the Soviet and Israeli ambassadors in France. By the time then Prime Minister Shimon Peres met Soviet Foreign Minister Eduard Shevardnadze at the United Nations in New York on October 26, 1985, the Soviet-Israeli dialogue had become front-page news.

Indeed, in the period prior to the first summit meeting between Gorbachev and Reagan in Geneva in November 1985 and the CPSU Congress in late February 1986, hints of an imminent Soviet restoration of diplomatic relations with Israel were heard with increasing frequency. But both the summit and the Party Congress came and went with no change in Soviet policy. For several months, there was virtual silence. Then, in early August 1986, the Soviets proposed a meeting to discuss "consular" affairs. On August 18, amid high hopes abroad, Soviet and Israeli officials met in Helsinki for their first official contact since the rupture of relations in 1967. The first meeting lasted for only ninety minutes, and no second one was held. For a year there were other brief meetings, but no tangible progress. In July 1987, a Soviet consular delegation visited Israel, ostensibly to check on the status of Russian Orthodox Church property and Soviet passport holders living in Israel; more likely, it is another step toward more systematic relations between the two countries, especially after Foreign Minister Peres indicated his support for convening an international conference, favored by Moscow, to discuss remaining issues in the Arab-Israeli conflict. (Prime Minister Yitzhak Shamir, however, is cool to the idea, and as long as the offices of prime minister and foreign minister are rotated between the Labor Party Peres and the Likud Party, due to their stalemated electoral position in the Knesset, no satisfactory outcome is in prospect.)

Still, Gorbachev has made clear his interest in an international conference on the Arab-Israeli conflict. Underlying this interest are multiple aims—to demonstrate the USSR's ability to advance Arab political aims and reassure moderate Arabs; to reverse the US's preeminence in the Arab-Israeli sector since the 1973 October War; and to enhance Moscow's prestige by making it an integral part of the peace process. This search for a formula to bring the Soviet Union into the center of the Middle East peace process, coupled with halting moves towards improving relations with Israel and with moderate Arab states, raises hopes for a major change in Gorbachev's policy.

As he looks ahead, Gorbachev has five basic possibilities, each of which has very different policy implications.[10] First, the Soviet Union could continue its present policy of placing particular emphasis on strengthening ties with Syria, arming other opponents of the peace process, and awaiting regional developments for new opportunities. In the absence of any major US initiative, Moscow may well believe that time is likely to bring the Arabs closer to the Soviet Union than to the United States. Second, Moscow could again, as after the October War, end up being odd capital out. It could, for example, find itself looking for a new role to play, in the event that Syrian President Assad suddenly decided to emulate Sadat and offer Israel a peace treaty in return for territory occupied since 1967 and "justice" for the Palestinians; or if PLO leader Yasir Arafat was prepared to recognize the existence of the state of Israel and negotiate in accordance with the principles set forth in UN Security Council Resolutions 242 and 338. Neither situation is apt to occur, but both are worrisome contingencies, which Moscow hopes to forestall by giving full support to Assad's hardline policy.

Third, if the United States decided to impose a settlement on Israel, Moscow might have to reconsider its opposition to the peace process, in order not to be left out of the negotiations. Fourth, if there were a return to an international conference co-chaired by the United States and the Soviet Union (one was convened briefly after the October War), Soviet policy would be vindicated, but Gorbachev would have to decide if a settlement was really in the USSR's interest and, if so, how far he could go in working for one without angering his Arab clients. Finally, and least likely, Moscow might independently decide to force its clients to make concessions and agree to a negotiated settlement that would remove the Arab-Israeli conflict as a source of tension in US-Soviet relations.

In all likelihood, Gorbachev will adhere to the essential consensus that has shaped Soviet policy since the 1960s. He has reason to see in the present configuration of actors and underlying cleavages sufficient basis for optimism about Moscow's long term prospects and about US difficulties ranging from rising anti-Americanism to spreading socioeconomic discontent and political instability. Confirmation of this assessment can be seen in his continued funneling of arms, still Moscow's trump card, to keep the USSR's Arab clients as aggressive players in the Middle East power game.

ARMS TRANSFERS AND POLITICAL WARFARE

According to psychologists, we tend to see what we expect or desire to find, and we overlook what does not accord with our expectations or hopes. Since Gorbachev took power, many Western analysts have glimpsed signs of long overdue Soviet domestic reforms that would tackle the country's severe economic and social problems. Usually implicit in such assessments is the assumption that Gorbachev would want to retrench, to cut Soviet commitments to clients in the Middle East and elsewhere in the Third World, if only to be better able to concentrate on internal issues:

> Gorbachev, like his predecessors, seeks detente as a corollary of superpower equality. Given his more sober appraisal of Soviet vulnerabilities, both at home and abroad, his conception of detente has a defensive ring, in sharp contrast to its offensive ring in the 1970s. Gorbachev is also not likely to hazard new foreign adven-

tures because he realizes that the Soviet Union is already overextended, that the risks of new military adventures will far exceed those of the 1970s, that his foreign policy resources are severely limited.

Soviet publications convey a serious loss of confidence in the effectiveness of Soviet policies in the Third World and in the expectation that the internal political dynamics in these countries will make them "natural allies" of the Soviet Union. They convey growing recognition that influence in the Third World depends significantly on economic instruments that the Soviets have in short supply.[11]

So argue some Western analysts. Though Gorbachev's decision to withdraw from Afghanistan lends support to the theory that he wants to focus his energy primarily on troublesome domestic issues and on improving relations with the United States, his policy elsewhere in the Middle East suggests a different mood that can best be described as activist, tough-minded, and ambitious. His highly skillful probes in new areas of opportunity have been particularly impressive in the Gulf. Introducing a naval presence, he undertook new commitments on behalf of Kuwait and risked alienating Iran, thus showing his determination not to be outbid by Washington. Now that the Iran-Iraq War seems to be drawing to a close, Moscow seeks to position itself as a potential mediator and to demonstrate to the moderate Arab regimes of the Gulf its interest in promoting regional stability—even while its massive arms shipments to Syria and Libya serve to stoke tensions in the Mediterranean.

The Soviet military buildup of Syria is particularly ominous given the explosiveness of the Syrian-Israeli relationship—and puzzling if one assumes the Soviet leadership wants to avoid triggering another Middle East war, which could easily draw the superpowers into a dangerously confrontational situation.

Gorbachev's arming of Syria exceeds the levels needed to ensure Syria's security and give it a credible deterrent posture; it represents a new escalation of the Syrian-Israeli arms race. Moscow's commitment to the defense of the Assad regime has never been an unknown in the military equation. After Syria lost 90 aircraft to Israel in fighting over the Bekaa Valley region of eastern Lebanon during Israel's invasion of Lebanon in June 1982, Moscow replaced Syrian losses and significantly upgraded Syria's military capability, providing a thickened air defense system, modern tanks and artillery, and new surface-to-surface missiles (SS-21s), which have a 75-mile range and are capable of hitting targets in Israel. More recently, Israeli intelligence reported the impending arrival of Soviet SS-23s, which have an estimated range of 350 miles and are thought to be of greater accuracy than the SS-21s.[12] Moscow's modernization and upgrading of Syria's military capability gives Assad the option of starting a (limited) war. The construction of fortifications capable of housing a combat division close to Israel's security line in Lebanon, the increase in size of the Syrian army by 100,000 men since 1982 (a 50 percent expansion of its regular forces), and the spate of Syrian-sponsored terrorist acts, all fuel speculation that Assad may be preparing to unleash a limited war on the Golan Heights. Not only is his military position vis-a-vis Israel as strong now as it is apt to be at any time in the foreseeable future but, a shrewd strategist, he knows Israel's internal weaknesses and may calculate that the Israelis will not respond to a local thrust by undertaking a major war.

Gorbachev's use of regional tensions to complicate US policy is also evident in the Libyan sector of the Mediterranean. He does not appear to have second thoughts about the paradox of seeking better relations with the United States while having egged on Libya's Qaddafi with sophisticated weapons that served only to worsen an already tense US-Libyan relationship. Thus far, the infusion of "Americanists" (Soviet specialists on the United States, like Anatoly Dobrynin, Moscow's ambassador in Washington from 1962 to 1986) into the foreign policy decision-making hierarchy has brought few new approaches or policies to Middle East aspects of the US-Soviet relationship.

To Washington's surprise, the Soviets sold Qaddafi a new weapons system, the SAM-5, a surface-to-air missile of limited effectiveness, but possessing a 75-mile range. In late 1985, the US government protested the sale, arguing that this upgrading of Libya's military potential could have serious consequences.[13] With prophetic accuracy, it emphasized that unlike the SAM-5s supplied to Syria in late 1982 for protection against air attacks by Israel, the ones provided to Qaddafi would be directed against US forces and, in the hands of so unpredictable and reckless a leader, would have dangerous consequences. Unconvinced, indifferent, or perhaps even cunning in his calculations, Gorbachev proceeded, installing the missiles in early 1986. At the end of March, Qaddafi fired off a number of missiles at US aircraft on maneuvers in the Gulf of Sidra, which he claims as Libyan territorial waters, albeit without any basis in international law of the sea. US aircraft returned fire. The situation worsened a month later, when US planes bombed Libyan military installations in Tripoli and Benghazi in retaliation for Qaddafi's alleged masterminding of terrorism against American servicemen in West Berlin. Gorbachev went out of his way to demonstrate political support for Libya—providing intelligence information, sending naval ships to "show the flag," cancelling a scheduled visit to Washington by Foreign Minister Eduard Shevardnadze, and denouncing US "imperialism." But he did not take any steps to back up Qaddafi militarily. In keeping with the approach followed by his predecessors, he uses arms to aggravate regional tensions for multiple purposes—strategic, political, military, economic, and ideological.

In adapting to changing circumstances, Gorbachev is pursuing objectives that demonstrate an essential continuity in the USSR's Middle East policy. At this juncture, the signs suggest that while he may be more prudent than his predecessors in projecting Soviet military power, he will be no less determined than they to advance Moscow's imperial ambitions.

NOTES

1. For a detailed assessment of Soviet-Turkish relations, see Alvin Z. Rubinstein, *Soviet Policy Toward Turkey, Iran and Afghanistan* (New York: Praeger, 1982), Chapter 2.
2. For example, in early February 1986, First Deputy Foreign Minister Georgii Korniyenko became the highest ranking Soviet official to visit Tehran since Khomeini came to power. *FBIS/USSR*, February 5, 1986.
3. *Radio Liberty*, RL 385/85, November 15, 1985, p. 3.
4. For example, Keith A. Dunn, "Constraints on the USSR in Southwest Asia: A Military Analysis," *Orbis*, Vol. 25, No. 3 (Fall 1981), pp. 628-629.
5. Mohamed Heikal, *The Road to Ramadan* (London: Collins, 1975), p. 159.
6. *Pravda*, February 26, 1986, p. 8.
7. Alvin Z. Rubinstein, "A Third World Policy Waits for Gorbachev," *Orbis*, Vol. 30, No. 2 (Summer 1986), pp. 355-360.
8. Alfred L. Atherton, Jr., "The Soviet Role in the Middle East: An American View," *Middle East Journal*, Vol. 39, No. 4 (Autumn 1985), p. 692.
9. For example, George W. Breslauer, "Soviet Policy in the Middle East: Unalterable Antagonism or Collaborative Competition?" in Alexander L. George (ed.), *Managing US-Soviet Rivalry* (Boulder, CO: Westview Press, 1983) pp. 66-67, 96-98.
10. These options are examined in greater detail in Alvin Z. Rubinstein, "The Soviet Union and the Peace Process Since Camp David," *The Washington Quarterly*, Vol. 8, No. 1 (Winter 1985), pp. 53-54.
11. Seweryn Bialer and Joan Afferica, "The Genesis of Gorbachev's World," *Foreign Affairs: America and the World 1985*, Vol. 65, No. 3 (1985), pp. 641-642.
12. *The New York Times*, May 25, 1986.

13. *The New York Times*, December 22, 1985.

SUGGESTED READINGS

Bradsher, Henry S. *Afghanistan and the Soviet Union*, new and expanded edition. Durham, NC: Duke University Press Policy Studies, 1985.

Collins, Joseph J. *The Soviet Invasion of Afghanistan*. Lexington, MA: Lexington Books, 1986.

Dawisha, Adeed and Karen Dawisha, eds. *The Soviet Union in the Middle East*. London: Heinemann, 1982.

Dawisha, Karen, *Soviet Foreign Policy Towards Egypt*. London: Macmillan, 1979.

Freedman, Robert O. *Soviet Policy Towards the Middle East Since 1970*. 3rd ed. New York: Praeger, 1981.

Golan, Galia. *Yom Kippur and After: The Soviet Union and the Middle East Crisis*. Cambridge: Cambridge University Press, 1977.

Golan, Galia. *The Soviet Union and the Palestine Liberation Organization*. New York: Praeger, 1980.

Heikal, Mohamed. *The Road to Ramadan*. London: Collins, 1975.

Katz, Mark N. *Russia and Arabia: Soviet Foreign Policy Toward the Arabian Peninsula*. Baltimore: The Johns Hopkins University Press, 1986.

Laqueur, Walter Z. *The Struggle for the Middle East: The Soviet Union in the Mediterranean, 1958-1968*. New York: Macmillan, 1969.

Malik, Hafeez, ed. *Soviet-American Relations with Pakistan, Iran, and Afghanistan*. New York: St. Martin's Press, 1987.

Page, Stephen. *The Soviet Union and the Yemens*. New York: Praeger, 1985.

Ro'i, Yaacov, ed. *From Encroachment to Involvement: A Documentary Study of Soviet Policy in the Middle East, 1945-1973*. New York: John Wiley, 1974.

Ro'i Yaacov, ed. *The Limits to Power: Soviet Policy in the Middle East*. New York: St. Martin's Press, 1979.

Rubinstein, Alvin Z. *Red Star on the Nile: The Soviet-Egyptian Influence Relationship Since the June War*. Princeton: Princeton University Press, 1977.

Rubinstein, Alvin Z. *Soviet Policy Toward Turkey, Iran, and Afghanistan*. New York: Praeger, 1982.

Sella, Amnon. *Soviet Political and Military Conduct in the Middle East*. New York: St. Martin's Press, 1981.

Yodfat, Aryeh. *The Soviet Union and the Arab Peninsula*. New York: St. Martin's Press, 1983.

EIGHT

THE SOVIET UNION AND SOUTH ASIA UNDER GORBACHEV

Šumit Ganguly

While most analyses of Soviet conduct in the nonindustrialized world tend to emphasize Soviet imperatives and the concerns of the regional actors, in this paper we will dwell on another variable at considerable length: namely, the past actions and the present behavior of the other superpower, the United States, in influencing not only Soviet behavior but also the regional actors. The paper considers Soviet-South Asian relations in the Gorbachev era. As far as South Asia is concerned, the paper will primarily emphasize Soviet relations with India, Afghanistan, and Pakistan—in that order of importance. We will not deal with the other South Asian states (Bangladesh, Bhutan, Nepal, and

Sri Lanka) because their foreign policies are largely inconsequential to the Soviet Union.

HISTORICAL BACKGROUND

Any discussion of Soviet relations with South Asia must necessarily begin with India, despite the Soviet invasion and occupation of Afghanistan since 1979. Afghanistan's importance to the Soviet Union does not equal that of India. Most commentators on Indo-Soviet relations have correctly focused on "the coincidence of interests"[1] to explain the enduring quality of the Indo-Soviet relationship. This "coincidence of interests" derives in part from the common distrust of the PRC (People's Republic of China) and in recent years from an expanded trade and arms transfer nexus. However, this explanation does not fully address the evolution and continuance of the Indo-Soviet link. To fully unravel the ties that bind India with the Soviet Union we need to delve briefly into the real and perceived historical background of this relationship. Three points are pertinent. First, a long-standing distrust of the United States exists among Indian elites, stemming chiefly from India's colonial experience. This attitude may change in the not-too-distant future as a new elite begins to establish itself, one that has little or no memory of the Western colonial experience. Yet any erosion of historic mistrust appears premature; while a new generation may not have the direct experience of living under colonialism, they nevertheless have an "historical" memory of colonialism.

Second, these selfsame Indian elites engage in a selective reading of the United States, particularly US involvement with a range of reactionary and despotic regimes during the 1950s, while Washington simultaneously professed commitment to democracy and freedom.

Third, and derivative of this reading of postwar diplomatic history, are the memories of specific actions taken (and not taken) by the United States as they affected India. Indian elites often recall events such as the following: the willingness of the US to supply arms to Pakistan under the Eisenhower administration; the failure of the US to endorse India's planning efforts, particularly to develop an indigenous steel industry; the US "hands-off" policy during the 1965 Indo-Pakistani conflict; the Johnson administration's economic pressures on India in 1966-1967, (specifically the so-called "short-tether" food aid policy); and finally, Nixon's tilt towards Pakistan during the 1971 Bangladesh crisis.

The Soviets in turn have capitalized on these breaches and the consequent disharmony in Indo-US relations. In the 1950s they built post-independence India's first steel plant, helped expand India's public sector, mediated the 1965 Indo-Pakistani conflict in Tashkent, and steadfastly (albeit unwillingly) stood by India during the 1971 Bangladesh crisis. They also were muted in their criticism of India's 1974 nuclear explosion. Thus, owing to the real and perceived grievances of the Indian elites against the United States, and the Soviet ability to capitalize on a large number of them, the USSR has been able to obtain a favored position in India's global outlook.

However, these reasons alone do not explain the Indo-Soviet nexus. India needs the Soviet Union because the former has a border dispute of many years' standing with Pakistan over Kashmir. The Indo-Soviet relationship is linked to India's dependence on Soviet veto power in the UN Security Council in the event of the Kashmir question being raised once again. In an indirect way, India sought this protection under the aegis of the Treaty of Peace, Friendship and Cooperation that it signed with the Soviets in 1971. The treaty obligated the Soviets to stand by India during the subsequent Bangladesh crisis. It made it incumbent on the Soviets to veto UN Security Council resolutions that sought to censure India for its actions in East Pakistan. Thus, the Bangladesh crisis and India's previous experience over the Kashmir question in the Security Council has taught India the vital importance of having the support of a veto-wielding power in that body.

From the Soviet standpoint, in turn, India is important—first, because it serves as a counterweight to Chinese influence in Asia.

Second, India's historic role in the struggle for independence provides it with a degree of legitimacy in the newly industrializing world. Third, and derivative of the second factor, India can (for the most part) be counted on to stand behind the Soviet Union at crucial moments in the UN and other multilateral fora. Fourth, India in particular, and South Asia in general, are important in terms of extending Soviet influence and, to the extent possible, of eroding US and Chinese influence. This concern obviously has assumed far greater significance since the Soviet invasion and occupation of Afghanistan and the subsequent US involvement in Pakistan. It is against this backdrop that we must analyze the evolution of Soviet policies towards the South Asian region in the Gorbachev era.

LEADERSHIP CHANGES AND FOREIGN POLICY

Despite the change in India's ruling elites (Rajiv Gandhi and a number of the individuals that he brought into high office with him do represent a virtual generational change in Indian national politics), it is not immediately apparent that any dramatic shifts in Indo-Soviet relations are imminent. The reasons for this are not difficult to identify. Though the new Prime Minister and his men have been described as "pragmatic" and "less ideological" in their outlook and appear to be more oriented towards the so-called "magic of the marketplace," it does not necessarily follow that they will precipitously change the fundamental foreign policy orientation of the country. As we stated at the outset, while the new elite has no firsthand memory of living under the onus of British colonialism, the other two historical factors mentioned do influence their thinking.

Despite the elite turnovers in both India and the Soviet Union, there have not been significant shifts in the foreign policies of

either state toward the other. For example, shortly after consolidating power at home, the first foreign trip that Rajiv Gandhi
took was to the Soviet Union. On the eve of his visit to the
Soviet Union in late May 1985, TASS quoted the Prime Minister as saying, "The economic and commercial relations between
our two countries have registered spectacular growth in recent
years. India attaches great importance to them."[2] Gorbachev
echoed those sentiments in Moscow. Indeed there was a good
deal of truth to these claims. Despite Western hopes to the contrary, the official communiques that emerged from Moscow after
his visit did not indicate a significant shift in either Indian perceptions or policies on the continuing crisis in Afghanistan. The
trip did yield substantial gains for India, particularly in terms of
the extension of Soviet credits and aid for the development of
crucial sectors of the Indian economy, including power generation, coal, oil, and machine building.[3] Apart from the lack of
Indian criticism of Soviet policy towards Afghanistan, the gains
from this meeting were essentially one-sided. Soviet credits were
once again made available on exceedingly favorable terms (about
two percent interest over an extended period of time) and were
directed towards the sectors of the Indian economy that have
serious bottlenecks. That the Soviets were willing to continue
extending trade credits and aid on such terms at a time of domestic contraction and stringency indicated the continuing
importance they attach to their ties with India.

COSTS AND BENEFITS OF THE
SOVIET-INDIAN NEXUS

The reasons for this continued Soviet largess are not difficult
to ascertain. The Soviets were not oblivious to the shifts and
changes in economic policy that Rajiv Gandhi and his government had set in motion.[4] Consequently they had to be concerned
about the longer-term ramifications of an increasingly open
economy more hospitable to foreign (especially American) multinational investment and a declining role for the behemoth

public sector industries. Furthermore, they no doubt realized that their abilities to participate in India's continued economic growth and development were shrinking because of two important reasons. First, while India did have bottlenecks in key infrastructural industries and services (notably power and transportation), the overall economy benefitted from increased investment in such areas as electronics, telecommunications, and computer technology. Second, Rajiv Gandhi appeared particularly interested in promoting those industries and continuing the policy of opening the Indian economy to foreign investment, a policy initiated by his mother during her last years in office. Here the Soviets would find increasingly fewer opportunities for providing assistance. As Salamat Ali has written:

> ... despite continuing collaboration in the development of industries and infrastructure, there is a growing realization that the Soviets and their allied countries are good only at helping in building basically nineteenth-century industrial plants, and incapable of significant assistance in the contemporary vital sectors such as electronics, biotechnology, technology for automotive and chemical industries.[5]

To underscore Ali's contentions, it needs to be mentioned that during Rajiv Gandhi's visit to the United States, he signed a Memorandum of Understanding (MoU) which opened the way for Indian purchases of American dual-use technology. Shortly thereafter India reached an agreement with Control Data Corporation for the sale of $500 million worth of computer technology. These developments did not escape Soviet comment, however muted. For example, in a wide-ranging interview with the editor of a prominent Pakistani paper, *The Muslim*, Soviet Deputy Foreign Minister Mikhail Kapitsa stated the following about Indo-American relations under the Rajiv Gandhi regime:

> We have an old and durable relationship with India. We are glad they have been able to resolve (their) problems following Mrs. Gandhi's assassination. Rajiv Gandhi is an able and talented per-

son. He wants to modernize India. Having solved their food problem he now wants technology for its development. The Americans are very foolish. They think they can make India pro-US while at the same time providing sophisticated arms to Pakistan. These positions are irreconcilable. Of course, India is a big country and the United States has interests there. We are not against Indian-American cooperation. India needs us and we need India. India knows we are reliable friends.[6]

That India deems the Soviets reliable friends is evident from certain remarks by Rajiv Gandhi in an interview with Pierre Lellouche of *Newsweek International*.[7] Responding to a question about India becoming too dependent on the Soviet Union for weaponry (70 percent of India's arsenal is of Soviet origin), the Prime Minister stated:

We have a lot of French and British weaponry. Almost all our weapons are made in India—not just manufactured under licence but actually designed and developed by us. As for the Soviets, we feel fairly secure that they will not let us down at a critical moment.

Yet the Indo-Soviet relationship is not without its problems. Even prior to Gorbachev's assuming office, critical decision makers in India had become distressed with the continued Soviet occupation of Afghanistan. Though few explicit statements were made to that end, privately Indian officials pointed out that the Soviet invasion and occupation of Afghanistan had serious security implications for India. Unlike the US, they did not see the Soviet presence there as an intrinsic threat to the security of the subcontinent, but they were concerned about the steady stream of armaments that poured into Pakistan as a consequence of the Soviet invasion. (The initial shipment was a package of direct grants and loans to the amount of $3.2 billion over five years. A new package of $4.02 billion, over a period of six years, is now under consideration.) To this extent, the Afghan crisis impinged directly on India's security.

Today there is greater unhappiness in policy-making circles in New Delhi because the US is planning to provide Pakistan weaponry to some degree independent of the Soviet threat. Furthermore, in the Indian view, the Pakistani regime has been able to steal a march on its nuclear program because US enforcement of its nonproliferation policy has been lax, due to Pakistan's role as a conduit for weaponry to the Afghan resistance. In the Indian view this unhappy situation would not have occurred had the Soviets not invaded Afghanistan and thereby triggered this chain of events. Yet no government in New Delhi wishes to risk the possible costs of alienating the Soviets, though it is by no means clear that India needs the Soviets at the cost of official silence on the Afghanistan issue.[8]

THE INDO-AMERICAN RELATIONSHIP

While the present Soviet regime has little to fear from the prospects of a substantial expansion of Indo-US ties, some developments in Indo-US relations since Gorbachev assumed power cannot be of great comfort. We have already alluded to the MoU that was signed during Rajiv Gandhi's visit to the United States. Despite the generosity of the Soviets, Rajiv Gandhi emphasized India's continuing quest for technology during his visit to the United States in June 1985. This was occasioned with considerable fanfare both in the US and India. It yielded substantial gains for India as the United States proved willing to provide India with various forms of sensitive (and dual-use) computer and electronics technology (made available under the aegis of the MoU), both of which were high on Gandhi's agenda. Furthermore, this MoU may have paved the way for further cooperation not only in matters of trade and investment but also in the development of military technology. Currently discussions are under way between US and Indian government officials for the development of an Indian Light Combat Aircraft (LCA).[9]

Despite these developments and whatever good that they portend for Indo-US relations, a number of problems continue.

First, as we have mentioned earlier, there exists a bitter legacy of policy differences which vitiates the chances of rapprochement. Second, India and the US do not share a political-strategic consensus. As a consequence of past differences, India gravitated towards the Soviet Union. Furthermore, US commitments to Pakistan (especially in the wake of the Soviet invasion of Afghanistan) and an expanding relationship with the PRC makes India wary of undertaking any precipitous actions in terms of its time-honored links with the Soviet Union.

In turn, the Soviets remain quite aware of India's hesitation in making any rash or drastic decisions that would impact the relationship. They periodically remind their Indian counterparts that there are dangers in taking the Soviets for granted. Soviet support for India has waxed and waned on the critical issue of disputed territory near the Indo-Pakistani border along the Siachen glacier in Karkoram Range. This area is of particular concern to both countries despite its inhospitable physical conditions. Its significance lies in that the glacier borders Pakistani- and Chinese-claimed territory and if taken over by either country could mean a substantial disadvantage to India in a future conflict in this region. According to well-placed Indian diplomatic sources, Soviet vacillation on the respective Indian and Pakistani claims to the Siachen glacier has caused considerable concern in New Delhi.[10]

SOVIET RELATIONS WITH AFGHANISTAN AND PAKISTAN

Another possible area for eventual divergence of Indian and Soviet interests involves South Asian regional issues. Some of the difficulties stem from the recent efforts of the South Asian states to push for a degree of regional cooperation under the aegis of the SAARC (South Asian Association for Regional Cooperation) forum. Part of the thrust taken by India in this forum involves limiting superpower intrusion in resolving outstanding bilateral issues. There is, of course, a not-so-hidden agenda that India harbors under the guise of this principle: India's continuing dispute with Pakistan over the state of Kashmir and the US arming of Pakistan. Unfortunately, from the Soviet standpoint this also could influence the Indo-Soviet arms transfer relationship and thereby could lead to a wayward drift on India's part. Thus, last year when Prime Minister Rajiv Gandhi was about to embark on the SAARC meeting, the Soviets abruptly disclosed that an unprecedented arms deal with India was under consideration. If this deal went through, India would receive technology to manufacture nuclear submarines, obtain a new generation of all-weather tanks and V/STOL aircraft for India's new aircraft carrier, and have access to Soviet spy satellite information.[11] Deals of this nature certainly will not help India's cause with its neighbors.

The other regional issue that plagues Soviet relations with the subcontinent is the Afghanistan crisis. Despite the indirect tripartite talks (involving the Pakistanis, the Afghan regime's representatives, and the Soviets) in Geneva and a number of blighted hopes of a possible resolution to the conflict, the crisis continued. Late in 1987, Gorbachev announced that Soviet withdrawal of military forces would occur in the first half of 1988, and troop withdrawals began in May of this year. Meanwhile Soviet attempts to indoctrinate younger Afghans have continued. To this end, substantial numbers of Afghan college-aged men and women have been sent to the Soviet Union.[12] The question remains whether or not this effort to socialize a segment of the Afghan youth into developing supportive attitudes towards the Najibullah regime and the Soviets has met with any success.

In addition to sending Afghan youth to the Soviet Union, the Soviets have resorted to other means to try and win the "hearts and minds" of the Afghan population. Inducements in the forms of cash and arms to fight rival groups have been proffered to minority ethnic groups, usually with little success. Furthermore, recently the regime has made offers to return confiscated property, to extend a general amnesty, and even to allow a degree of local self-government. These gestures have met a similar fate. The failure of many of these measures can be attributed essentially to three sources: first, the common hatred of the presence of a foreign and repressive power; second, the continuing Parcham/Khalq (the two factions of Afghanistan's communist party) schism which the Soviets seem unable to bridge; and third, the important role played by an alternative ideology, that of Islam and the notion of "jihad" (holy war against infidels) which animates several of the resistance groups.

Not only have these efforts to build a sociopolitical base for the regime proved difficult both for Moscow and Kabul but, owing to the continuing war with the Afghan resistance, the Soviets have had to subsidize the Afghan economy by as much as $420 million a year in 1984.[13] Indicative of the increasing costs that this war imposed on the Soviet Union were the stories of the costs of "counterrevolutionary activity" carried in the Soviet press.[14]

In response to increased Mujahideen activity, the Soviets adopted a variety of measures over the course of the past several years before agreeing to troop withdrawal. First, they increased troop strength to around 115,000 from the approximately 80,000 troops that they had deployed at the time of the invasion.[15] Second, they had to come to grips with the fact that the Democratic Republic of Afghanistan (DRA) army is notoriously unreliable, plagued with frequent desertions. While its official strength is placed around 80,000, its actual deployable strength is no more than 30,000. These numbers obtain despite repeated efforts to dragoon men into the armed forces. Third, the Soviets resorted to increased use of firepower—extensive use of gunships, tanks (where the terrain permits) and various forms of anti-personnel mines. Still, military success was never achieved.

It was perhaps the very elusiveness of military victory and a more general desire to disengage from third world involvements that led the Gorbachev regime to sign an accord for withdrawal from Afghanistan. The accord which was signed in Geneva on April 14, 1988, involved the United States, the Soviet Union, Pakistan and Afghanistan. Under the terms of the accord the Soviet Union started to withdraw its troops from Afghanistan beginning May 15, 1988. The withdrawal should be completed within nine months from that date.[16] By mid-August the Soviets had withdrawn close to half of their 115,000 troops.[17]

Though the accord calls for all parties to desist from interfering in the internal affairs of Afghanistan, the United States has insisted that it reserves the right to aid the Mujahideen as long as the Soviets continue to assist the Najibullah regime. Despite this American commitment to the Mujahideen, the future of the American military assistance program is in some doubt due to the death of General Zi-ul-Haq. With the demise of General Zia Pakistan's role in supporting the Mujahideen may well change depending on the complexion of the government that emerges after the projected November elections.

PAKISTAN IN SOVIET STRATEGY

A related element in Soviet politico-military strategy has been to put increasing military (and diplomatic) pressure on Pakistan, to prevent that country from providing a sanctuary to the resistance and from remaining a conduit of weaponry. To this end the DRA air force has repeatedly bombed refugee encampments on the Pakistani border. Denying sustenance to the Afghan resistance is crucial to the DRA/Soviet strategy, and intimidating the Pakistanis would best accomplish this. Yet the Soviets have not gone very far in this direction. One reason they may have not chosen to carry the war into Pakistan is because this might result in greater US involvement in the subcontinent and the Persian Gulf. Yet the Soviets have warned Pakistan about the latter's support for the Afghan resistance. In particular, Soviet Deputy Foreign Minister Kapitsa, in an interview with Mushahid Hussain, the editor of the prominent Pakistani newspaper, *The Muslim*, stated:

"Your country is at war with the Soviet Union ... There is an un-declared war launched from your territory against Afghanistan."[18]

In the same interview he made some obvious references to the possibility that the Soviets may incite restive Pathans in Pakistan who currently harbor irredentist claims on portions of that country. He also warned Pakistan about the dangers of pursuing its nuclear option, reminding his interviewer that his concern was shared by the Indians, whom he hoped would not take action against Pakistan's nuclear facilities. The Soviets have recently returned to this theme. While the Pakistani Prime Minister, Mohammed Khan Junejo, was visiting Washington in July 1986, the Soviets issued a particularly stiff warning to the Pakistanis about the dangers of pursuing their nuclear weapons program. They stated that the Pakistani program posed a threat to "the southern part of the USSR."[19] The timing of this admonition was significant because the indirect talks on Afghanistan were about to resume at the end of July 1986. It might also have reflected a Soviet attempt to convey to the Pakistanis a rising Indian concern about their nuclear weapons program.

THE INTERACTION OF SOVIET AND SUBCONTINENTAL INTERESTS

Based on the foregoing analysis, it can be argued that the Soviets' interest in Pakistan is largely derivative of their concerns about India and Afghanistan. They have little or no intrinsic interest in Pakistan because in and of itself it cannot significantly further or inhibit the pursuit of Soviet goals in the subcontinent or beyond. The American presence in Pakistan, however, is of concern to the Soviets in two different ways. First, in immediate terms the American commitment to Pakistan creates problems for the Soviets in Afghanistan. After all, it is under the aegis of the US-Pakistani relationship that the Pakistanis continue to provide military assistance and sanctuaries to the Afghan resistance. If the US commitment to Pakistan were to markedly erode, it remains an open question whether or not the Pakistanis would continue to support the Afghan resistance. Second, the Soviets also are concerned about the continuing US commitment to Pakistan in terms of the threat it poses to their own security. A renewed American presence in Pakistan after a resolution of the Afghan crisis clearly bodes ill for Soviet interests in the region, for the US conceivably may emplace appropriate reconnaissance and intelligence-gathering facilities in Pakistan.

CONCLUSIONS

The Soviets' position in the South Asian subcontinent is at a most interesting juncture. They cannot expect to win the war in Afghanistan unless there is a cessation of outside aid or they are willing to dramatically escalate the level of conflict. Even if they were to win the war it would amount to little more than a Pyrrhic victory. The reasons for this are clear. Owing to the brutality of their war effort and the near-complete illegitimacy of their position both within and outside Afghanistan, there is little hope they could emplace a regime that could survive long on its own. Given these conditions, the only reasonable option that they have would be the virtually permanent placement of a Soviet garrison in Afghanistan. Afghan Foreign Minister Shah Mohammed Dost stated as much in January 1985.[20] Despite persistent cries from certain quarters, primarily in the US, about the proclivity of the international community to appease the Soviets, there is little evidence that the world community will readily accept a government of this order and acquiesce in the Soviet satellitization of Afghanistan. While hardly any government broke diplomatic relations with the Soviets following the invasion of Afghanistan, it does need to be remembered that the vast majority of the states in the UN General Assembly continue to vote against the USSR on the Afghanistan resolution. In fact, the number of countries voting against the Soviets has increased with each passing year. As long as the Afghan resistance continues to receive support from abroad and the issue of the Soviet presence in Afghanistan is kept alive in international fora, their consolidation of authority in Afghanistan will remain elusive. Given these conditions the best the Soviets can hope for is some form of multilateral guarantee (possibly underwritten under UN auspices) of noninterference in the internal affairs of Afghanistan and a government that is not actively hostile to their interests.

Long-term Soviet relations with India and Pakistan will depend in large measure on three important factors. First, the nature and thrust of American policy toward the subcontinent influences the choices of regional actors. If there is a continuing US commitment to Pakistan well after a resolution of the Afghan conflict, India will continue to rely on the Soviets for political and military support, despite its economic needs and increased economic ties with the United States. Under these conditions the Soviets would continue to have poor relations with Pakistan and would continue to walk the tightrope that they tread with India: continuing their support for India while occasionally reminding the Indians that Soviet support cannot be taken for granted. If, however, the US substantially alters its South Asia policy (an unlikely scenario from today's vantage point), diminishing its ties with Pakistan and actively wooing India, one may see a marked shift of superpower alignments in the region.

The second factor influencing Indo-Soviet relations involves Indian domestic politics. From the vantage point of the mid-1980s, it seems unlikely that the Congress Party will lose its ability to govern the nation (despite a host of pressing problems); however, it is not inconceivable that a new regime might emerge after the next general elections. A non-Congress (possibly a coalition) government at the center could very well loosen Indo-Soviet ties in an effort to move closer to the United States or simply to assume a more nonaligned posture. There is historical precedent for this line of speculation. During the Janata interregnum (1977-1979), the government did shift from its pro-Soviet orientation. A similar shift cannot be written off, though as we have argued earlier it would in all probability be gradual.

Third, a shift may come about because of an Indo-Pakistani rapprochement. Again, from the standpoint of the mid-1980s this scenario appears dubious. Yet there are reasons why such a detente may be desirable for both parties. Owing to the Soviet invasion and continued occupation of Afghanistan, India has acquired a stake in Pakistan's integrity and stability. Though some elements in India still harbor visions of destabilizing Pakistan, there is a realization in New Delhi that Pakistan's balkanization would not be to India's benefit. A fragmented Pakistan would be composed of a set of inherently unstable states which external powers could easily manipulate. Furthermore, such small unstable states could well become safe havens for insurrectionary activity against India. From Pakistan's standpoint a rapprochement with India is desirable as well. With the Soviet presence on one border and a potentially hostile India on the other, it makes sense to woo India. If indeed such a reconciliation does come about, India's dependence on the Soviet Union could well be reduced because its need for Soviet support on the Kashmir question would be markedly diminished.

NOTES

1. See Robert Horn, *Soviet-Indian Relations: Issues and Influence*. (New York: Praeger, 1982).
2. Steven R. Weisman, "Gandhi, Due in Soviet, Goes as Friend." *The New York Times*, May 21, 1985.
3. Seth Mydans, "Gandhi in Soviet on First Official Visit." *The New York Times*, May 22, 1985.
4. Grigor G. Kotovsky, "Certain Trends in India's Socioeconomic and Socio-Political Development," *Asian Survey*, Vol. XXIV, No. 11 (November 1984), pp. 1131-1142.
5. Salamat Ali, "The Soviet Connection," *Far Eastern Economic Review* (March 7, 1985), pp. 34-37.
6. Mushahid Hussain, "Superpowers Summit not to Focus on Afghanistan—Soviets Rule Out Time-Frame for Withdrawal," *The Muslim*, October 11, 1985.
7. Pierre Lellouche, "Interview with Rajiv Gandhi," *Newsweek International*, October 7, 1985, p. 16.
8. Alexander I. Chicherov, "South Asia and the Indian Ocean in the 1980s: Some Trends Toward Changes in International Relations," *Asian Survey*, Vol. XXXIV, No. 11 (November, 1984), pp. 1117-1130.
9. Inderjit Badhwar, "Discovery of India," *India Today*, May 31, 1985.
10. Taranjit Singh Sandhu, "Conflict in Siachen," *Hindustan Times*, (December 27, 1985).
11. Salamat Ali, "The Soviet Connection" (see note 5 above) pp. 34-37.
12. Nicholas Daniloff, "Afghan War Finally Hits Soviet Home Front," *US News and World Report*, December 16, 1985, pp. 41-42.
13. US Department of State, *Warsaw Pact Economic Aid to Non-communist LDCs, 1984*. Washington, D.C.: GPO, 1986, p. 7.

14. M. Nepesov, "Surmounting the Difficulties," *Sotsialis-ticheskaya Industriya*, April 19, 1985. (Translated and reproduced in *FBIS*, April 23, 1985.)
15. "Russians in a Rut," *The Economist* May 19, 1984, p. 39.
16. Paul Lewis, "Four Nations Sign Accords For Soviet Afghan Pullout," *The New York Times* April 15, 1988.
17. Unattributed article. "Half of Soviet Troops Leave Afghanistan," *The Times of India* August 15, 1988.
18. Hussain, "Superpowers Summit ...." (See note 6 above).
19. Don Oberdorfer, "US, Pakistan Puzzled Over Soviet Move," *The Washington Post* July 21, 1986.
20. Tom Heneghan, "Soviet Advisers Would Stay if Peace Came, Afghan Says," *The Washington Post* January 23, 1986.

SUGGESTED READINGS

Banerjee, Jyotirmoy. *India in Soviet Global Strategy*. Calcutta: South Asia Books, 1977.

Barnds, William J. *India, Pakistan and the Great Powers*. New York: Praeger, 1972.

Donaldson, Robert. *Soviet Policy Towards India: Ideology and Stategy*. Cambridge: Harvard University Press, 1974.

Ganguly, Sumit. *The Origins of War in South Asia*. Boulder: Westview Press, 1986.

Horn, Robert C. *Soviet-Indian Relations: Issues and Influence*. New York: Praeger, 1982.

Sen Gupta, Bhabani. *The Fulcrum of Asia: Relations Between China, India, Pakistan and the USSR*. New York: Pegasus, 1970.

NINE

SOVIET-CHINESE RIVALRY OVER THE KOREAN PENINSULA

Ilpyong J. Kim

The emergence of new leadership in the Soviet Union under Mikhail S. Gorbachev, General Secretary of the Communist Party of the Soviet Union (CPSU), has ushered in a new relationship between the Soviet Union and the Democratic Peoples' Republic of Korea (DPRK) in recent years. An official visit of DPRK President Kim Il Sung to the Soviet Union October 22-27, 1986 created the perception in East Asia as well as in the West that Soviet-North Korean relations have been further consolidated while Chinese-North Korean relations have cooled. Thus, the North Korean tilt toward the Soviet Union in the 1980s was caused, according to some Western observers, by the declining relationship between China and North Korea.

The main thrust of this paper is to analyze recent developments in Soviet-North Korean relations within the context of changing triangular relations among the Soviet Union, China and North Korea. It is the thesis of this paper that North Korea's tilt to the Soviet Union is not necessarily a shift in the pattern of Sino-North Korean relations but rather indicates improvement in Sino-Soviet-North Korean relations, since the leadership change in Moscow and China's adoption of an independent foreign policy position at the twelfth congress of the Chinese Communist Party (CCP) in March 1982. Thus, Sino-North Korean relations remain intact despite the dramatic improvement in relations between Moscow and Pyongyang, thereby creating a new pattern of relationships in the Northern Triangle among Moscow, Beijing, and Pyongyang.

CHANGES IN THE NORTHERN TRIANGLE

Changes in the triangular relationship among the Soviet Union, China, and North Korea took place in the first half of the 1980s as the result of a shift in Soviet policy toward China and North Korea. The March 24, 1982 Tashkent proposal by the late Leonid Brezhnev, then General Secretary of the CPSU, for the improvement of Sino-Soviet relations provided an impetus to reduce tensions in the Sino-Soviet border areas and to accelerate the process toward resumption of negotiations between Chinese and Soviet leaders for normalization of relations. The Vice Foreign Ministers of China and the Soviet Union met in late 1982, the first such conference since the fall of 1979, when negotiations between the Chinese and Soviet Foreign Ministry officials were terminated as a consequence of the Soviet invasion of Afghanistan.

The resumption of negotiations for normalization of relations between China and the Soviet Union in 1982 might be characterized as a shift in China's posture toward the Soviet Union, a result of China's adoption of an "independent foreign policy" in March 1982. At the same time, stresses and strains in the Sino-American relationship emerged in 1981 over the issues of US arms sales to Taiwan and US technology transfer to China. Thus, China has moved away from its close relationship with the United States and tilted somewhat toward the Soviet Union thereby

274

changing the nature of the triangular relationship to one of greater equidistance among the three powers.

The development of adversarial relations between the United States and China over the issues of arms sales to Taiwan and technology transfer in 1981-1982 prompted China to move toward a minimization of the Sino-Soviet conflict, since it cannot afford to maintain a hostile posture toward both superpowers. Beijing thus no longer considers the Soviet Union as its principal enemy and seeks to establish and maintain an equidistant relationship with the two superpowers; this process seems to have created a new structure in the US-Soviet-Chinese triangle.[1]

While Sino-Soviet relations have improved from an adversarial relationship to one of mutual accommodation, Soviet-North Korean relations have improved dramatically during the same period. Rapprochement between the Soviet Union and North Korea began with the visit of North Korean Premier Li Chong-ok to Moscow in August 1981 on his way to Syria, thereby paving the way for North Korean President Kim Il Sung's visit to the Soviet Union and Eastern Europe in May 1984. The improvement in relations between the two states was greatly enhanced by the 1981-1985 agreement on mutual delivery of commodities and payments, which was signed on July 12, 1981, in Pyongyang. It was further consolidated by the summit meetings and frequent exchange of high level visits between the two countries in the first half of the 1980s, which led to the conclusion of a Soviet-North Korean agreement on economic and military cooperation.

North Korea's tilt toward the Soviet Union is not due to Soviet efforts in winning North Korea over to its side but rather is a consequence of North Korea's shift in policy toward its two communist-ruled neighbors. In the formulation of new policies vis-a-vis China and the Soviet Union, the North Korean leadership seemed to have taken into consideration the emerging new strategic environment of the Korean peninsula. North Korea was

not convinced by the Chinese argument (though it closely followed the Chinese policy line in the 1978-1981 period) that
Pyongyang's foreign policy objectives of peaceful unification of
the two Koreas would be achieved if it initiated a dialogue with
the South. Such a dialogue would inevitablty lead to direct
negotiations with the United States, thereby helping to conclude
the peace treaty which North Korea has sought since the 1950s.
What the DPRK wanted was to convert the armistice agreement
of the Korean War into a peace treaty in order to establish
diplomatic relations with the US and Japan. However, despite
North Korea's effort to develop direct contact with the US by
initiating North-South negotiations, as the Chinese advised, the
US was not willing to respond to North Korea's overtures as
the Chinese had expected. Thus, Chinese influence in Pyongyang
began to dwindle.

While Sino-Soviet relations were gradually improving in the
1982-1986 period, Soviet-North Korean relations changed
dramatically. "The positive changes that have come about in
Soviet-Chinese economic ties are well known," a Soviet commentary asserted in late 1986. "The two countries are concerned
with accelerating socioeconomic development and have similar
priorities in this sphere."[2] However, Sino-Soviet relations were
not improving as rapidly as relations between the Soviet Union
and North Korea. Their economies have long been mutually
complementary, but there were still some problems of
breakthrough in Soviet-Chinese relations. Speaking in Vladivostok in July 1986, Mikhail Gorbachev listed major areas of possible
cooperation between China and the Soviet Union, such as utilization of the water resources of the Amur River, assistance in
building a railway from the Xinjiang-Uigur Autonomous Region
to Kazakhstan, or joint research in outer space. "The problem
of extending relations between the two countries was discussed,"
according to a Soviet commentator, "during the recent visit of
Nikolai Talyzin, First Deputy Chairman of the USSR Council
of Ministers, to China," the highest ranking Soviet official to

visit China since the break in the Sino-Soviet relations.[3]

There still remain three obstacles to the normalization of relations between China and the Soviet Union, which China has insisted that the Soivet Union remove before normalization can occur. These include the withdrawal of the Soviet troops from Afghanistan, the reduction of troop strength along the Sino-Soviet border area and Mongolia, and the withdrawal of Soviet-backed Vietnamese troops from Kampuchea. However, Gorbachev's Vladivostok speech on Soviet domestic and foreign policy included a proposal for a series of measures to ease the tensions, including the withdrawal of some Soviet troops from Mongolia and Afghanistan, mutual reduction in forces at the border, and a Soviet-Chinese summit meeting. Chinese leader Deng Xiaoping responded that "if the Soviet Union can contribute to the withdrawal of Vietnamese troops from Cambodia," he would be ready to go any place in the Soviet Union to meet Gorbachev. Thus, the beginning of a Sino-Soviet detente developed in the 1982-1986 period.

SOVIET-NORTH KOREAN RELATIONS

North Korea's relations with the Soviet Union and China might best be analyzed and understood within the context of changing Sino-Soviet relations and the determined independence of North Korea vis-a-vis relations both with China and the Soviet Union. When World War II ended in August 1945, Korea was liberated after thirty-five years of Japanese colonial rule but was divided into two zones at the 38th parallel: the North found itself under Soviet occupation and the South was placed under a US military government. Two separate governments, the DPRK in the North and the Republic of Korea (ROK) in the South, were established in 1948 under the auspices of the USSR and the US, respectively. A series of diplomatic efforts were made in the late 1940s to unify the two parts of Korea but the Soviets and Americans were unable to agree on reunification terms because of ideological conflicts and the Cold War. Both the North and South depended heavily on the economic and military assistance provided by their respective allies. In the early 1950s, North Korea's staunch ally was the Soviet Union, which played the major role in shaping North Korea's political institutions and guiding its foreign relations.

North Korean relations with the USSR gradually evolved from a client state to one of interdependence by the late 1950s, following the twentieth congress of the CPSU in 1956. It was during the 1956-1960 period that the North Korean leader began to assert his independence and policy of self-reliance based on *Juche* (National Identity) in Soviet bloc affairs as well as a policy of neutrality in the Sino-Soviet conflict. However, during the height of that conflict in the early 1960s, North Korea began to tilt toward China and maintained close ties with Beijing. Therefore, Soviet-North Korean relations from 1945 to 1985 should not be characterized as close, as Soviet writers have attempted to make the outside world believe.[4]

It was in the 1962-1964 period that North Korea began to tilt toward China as a result of Nikita Khrushchev's heavy-handed policies, which included reduction of economic and military assistance to the DPRK. When the ideological disputes between China and the Soviet Union escalated further during this period, North Korea sided with China. However, it was in the 1965-1969 period when the Brezhnev-Kosygin leadership replaced Khrushchev and resumed an economic and military assistance program that relations between Moscow and Pyongyang were normalized. The cultural revolution in China during 1966-1969 contributed to the estrangement in Sino-North Korean relations, and there was no diplomatic exchange from the time the Chinese and North Korean ambassadors were recalled until they returned to their posts in 1970. North Korea sought to maintain an equidistant position toward China and the Soviet Union beginning in 1966, thereby adopting an independent foreign policy (although there was an occasional tilt toward China or the Soviet Union).

The dramatic change in Soviet-North Korean relations, however, began in the 1980s, with North Korean Premier Li Chong-ok's visit to Moscow in 1981. The DPRK delegation led by Premier Li stopped in Moscow on its way to Syria and had discussions with the Soviet Deputy Premier on the future of Soviet-North Korean relations. According to the press reports, Premier Li requested that the Soviet Union supply modern MIG-23 fighter planes so that North Korea might be in a position to counter the F-16s which the US was providing to South Korea. Moreover, the Treaty of Friendship, Cooperation, and Mutual Assistance that was signed July 6, 1961, was to expire after twenty years, but was renewed in 1981. "Attaching the greatest importance to this treaty as a major legal act regulating bilateral relations, the Soviet Union and the Democratic People's Republic of Korea prolonged it in 1981," the Soviet commentary asserted. "It was stressed that in today's world it continues to serve the cause of the development and enrichment of long-standing Soviet-Korean friendship and fruitful cooperation."[5]

The brief visit of Premier Li in August 1981 opened the way for a higher level exchange of visits between the Soviet Union and North Korea, which strengthened the solidarity and close ties between the two countries. Li's visit was followed by President Kim Il Sung's visit in May 1984; Kim's trip was characterized by the Soviet Union as a "major landmark in Soviet-North Korean relations in the 1980s...."[6]

What came out of Kim's visit to Moscow has been variously analyzed and interpreted by observers and specialists in Seoul, Tokyo, and Washington. A Soviet expert on Korean affairs at the Institute of the Far East, USSR Academy of Sciences, informed this writer during his visit to Moscow in July 1986 that Kim's visit to Moscow paved the way for further development of Soviet-North Korean relations through which economic and cultural exchanges were renewed and Soviet assistance programs resumed.

President Kim's visit to Moscow prompted Soviet Deputy

Foreign Minister Kapitsa's visit to Pyongyang in November 1984; Kapitsa negotiated border issues, discussed the bilateral trade and cultural exchange programs, and reportedly endorsed Kim Jong Il as the successor-designate to his father's leadership position. Kapitsa's unusually prolonged stay in Pyongyang from November 12-27 seemed to indicate that hard bargaining and tough negotiations were being conducted in Pyongyang. During Kapitsa's stay, Kim Il Sung was reported to have traveled briefly to China (November 26-28), for consultation with Deng Xiaoping and Hu Yaobang on critical issues of mutual concern. Kapitsa's visit was followed by the official visit of First Deputy Premier and Politburo member Geidar Aliev to Pyongyang in August 1985 and Premier Kang Sung-san's return visit to Moscow in December of that year, during which a formal economic and cultural exchange treaty was concluded and a military assistance program was initialed. The five-year agreement (1986-1990) for economic and technical assistance, the treaty for the construction of a nuclear energy plant, and a consular agreement, and one involving citizens' travel to each country were also finalized by the Soviet and North Korean authorities.

An aggressive Soviet policy toward Korea produced impressive results with a series of agreements, whereby the Soviet Union acquired overflight rights for its TU-95 bomber, the right of Soviet naval ships to call on the port of Nampo (across from the Chinese naval base Qingtao), and linking of the railway system between Vladivostok and the North Korean port of Najin. The Soviets also agreed to sell a number of MIG-23 fighter planes, six of which had already been delivered to Pyongyang, with forty more scheduled to arrive in the near future. The Soviet-North Korean relationship was further enhanced in 1986 when Soviet Foreign Minister Shevardnadze came to Pyongyang to implement close contact and establish a policy framework for Soviet-North Korean relations during the remainder of the 1980s.

REVIVAL OF THE MILITARY ALLIANCE

The twenty-fifth anniversary celebration of the signing of the Treaty of Friendship, Cooperation, and Mutual Assistance took place in Moscow, Beijing, and Pyongyang in July 1986. It was on July 6, 1961, that North Korean president Kim Il Sung signed the treaty in Moscow and five days later that he flew to China and signed a similar treaty in Beijing. On the occasion of the twenty-fifth anniversary, the North Korean delegation headed by Kim Hwan, a member of the Politburo and a KWP Secretary, went to Moscow while the Soviet delegation, led by Yuri Solovyov, candidate member of the Politburo and the First Secretary of the Leningrad regional party committee of the CPSU, came to Pyongyang to participate in the celebration. The Soviet delegation was received by President Kim Il Sung, while the North Korean delegation was received by President Andrei Gromyko, Chairman of the Presidium of the Supreme Soviet, in Moscow.

The North Korean delegation to China was led by Vice President Li Chong-ok and was received by Hu Yaobang, General Secretary of the CCP, while the Chinese delegation to North Korea was headed by Tian Jiyun, a member of the Politburo and Vice Premier of the People's Republic of China (PRC). The Chinese delegation was also received by President Kim during its stay in Pyongyang. Since the anniversary dates for the signing of both treaties were only five days apart and the high level exchanges took place between Moscow and Pyongyang on the one hand, and between Beijing and Pyongyang on the other, it is useful to contrast the contents of speeches each delegation head delivered at the banquet and reception in order to detect the changing perceptions of the leadership in Moscow, Beijing, and Pyongyang.

One of the important aspects of the twenty-fifth anniversary celebration in Pyongyang was the heavy representation of the Soviet military in the delegation. The Soviet Union demonstrated its military strength by sending a detachment of the Soviet Red Flag fleet, consisting of the large anti-submarine cruiser *Minsk*, the large anti-submarine ship *Admiral Spriridonov*, and the escort craft *Riyany* under the flag of Admiral V. V. Sidorov, Commander of the Soviet Red Flag Pacific Fleet. A flying corps of the Soviet Air Force led by Lieutenant General V. S. Bulankin, Air Force Commander of the Far Eastern Military District of the Soviet Army, was also part of the Soviet delegation.[7] A North Korean air force corps led by Major General Pak Hyon-uk, Deputy Commander of the Air Force, flew to the Soviet Union on the occasion of the twenty-fifth anniversary celebration. Thus, there was a strong military presence on both sides, which indicated the recent developments in military cooperation between Moscow and Pyongyang.

When we compare the exchange of high level visits and the content of speeches delivered at the banquet and reception in Moscow, Beijing, and Pyongyang, one is struck by the similarity in content of both the Soviet and Chinese high level officials' speeches in which policy positions toward the Korean peninsula were articulated. Though the Soviet government sent somewhat lower ranking officials than did the Chinese, the Soviets included strong military representation. In contrast, the Chinese did not include any military officers in its delegation, perhaps to reflect a peaceful approach to the Korean problem. The Soviet delegation pointedly addressed the security issues of the Korean peninsula, while the Chinese delegation emphasized the peaceful solution to the Korean problem, with special emphasis on North-South negotiations.

Addressing the mass rally at Wonsan on July 5th, Soviet Admiral Sidorov asserted, "We struck up fraternal friendship with blood in the common struggle against the Japanese aggressors and the US imperialists and have become comrades-in-arms in this struggle." Further, the admiral made a strong commitment when he stressed that "I can assure you, the working people of Kangwon Province present at this mass meeting, that the Pacific

Fleet is practically ready to come to help you at your first call, discharging its fraternal duty without fail." Because, he emphasized, "as Comrade M.S. Gorbachev said, we make every effort possible to firmly guarantee the security of the motherland and that of our friends and allies."[8]

The head of the Soviet party and government delegation Yuri Solovyov spoke at the banquet in Pyongyang on July 16 and asserted that the treaty signed on July 6, 1961 had tightened the friendly bonds of the Soviet and Korean peoples. But he seemed to ignore the history of Soviet-North Korean relations in the 1960s and 1970s when North Korea maintained an independent position during the height of the Sino-Soviet conflict. The Soviet Union at one point withdrew its military and technical assistance in order to induce the North Korean leadership to support the Soviet policy line in the Sino-Soviet dispute. North Korean leader Kim Il Sung sought to visit Moscow and patch up the differences, but he was not invited during the leadership of Leonid Brezhnev. Thus Kim was able to visit Mosow only after Brezhnev's death.

Yuri Solovyov asserted "the Soviet-Korean treaty is of peaceful character, aimed at strengthening friendship and cooperation between the Soviet Union and the DPRK, accords with the vital interests of the two countries, and most effectively contributes to the development of their economy and culture."[9] Reviewing the development of Soviet-North Korean relations for the past quarter century, Solovyov reiterated the "unswerving support" the Soviet Union had given to the DPRK's policy positions, such as the policy on Korean reunification, and the intergovernmental agreements on economic and technical cooperation, as well as support for the building of the first nuclear energy plant in North Korea, agreements for which were concluded in late 1985. He further stressed that Kim's visit to Moscow in 1984 had served "an important impetus to the development of Soviet-Korean relations in the 1980s." Apparently, close Moscow and Pyongyang ties developed only after the state visit of Kim Il Sung to Moscow in May 1984, which served as a foundation for the renewal of agreements and the revival of the alliance system.

With regard to the Asian security question, Solovyov asserted that the twenty-seventh congress of the CPSU has already emphasized the significance of the Asia-Pacific region in which the Soviet Union planned to expand its activities. "The Soviet proposal to take a complex attitude toward the Asian security problem was put in a concrete form in the Soviet government statement dated April 23, [1986]," he stressed. Therefore, "our country counters the policy of the US and Japanese militarist quarters for converting the Asia-Pacific region into an area of confrontation and competition with a line of rejecting the establishment of a bloc, an 'axis' and a three-way military alliance."[10] Thus, the Soviet Union recognized the strategic value of the Korean peninsula in countering the military alliance of the US, Japan, and South Korea. It also sought to establish itself as new competition for the US and Japan for hegemony over the Asia-Pacific region.

In contrast to the Soviet perception on the future of the Asia-Pacific region and the role North Korea should play in it, the Chinese delegation, led by Vice Premier Tian Jiyun, modestly asserted that "the Chinese Communist Party and Government has taken a consistent and unshakable stand regarding the Korean problem."[11] Therefore, "the Chinese hoped for an early relaxation of the Korean situation on the Korean peninsula and a peaceful reunification of Korea by her people themselves without foreign interference." Tian called on the United States and South Korea to "create by their deeds a favorable condition and climate for the peaceful reunification of Korea and the North-South dialogue."[12] China had consistently supported the North Korean policy of reunification in the 1970s and early 1980s when it was able to exercise more influence in Pyongyang than were the Soviets. However, the Chinese have now recognized the limits of their influence as they were unable to persuade the US to respond favorably to North Korea's open door policy by which North Korea attempted to convene the tripartite conference inviting the US and South Korea to participate in it. The DPRK also adopted legislation regarding foreign investment and joint ventures in North Korea.

Perhaps the Chinese leadership felt it had lost face and influence because of US unwillingness to negotiate with North Korea and thus had no choice but to acquiesce to Pyongyang's tilt toward the Soviet Union. A few days before Kim's departure for Moscow, CCP General Secretary Hu Yaobang paid a special visit to Pyongyang to consult with Kim about future relations with the Soviet Union. Despite North Korea's tilt toward Moscow, the Chinese leadership continued to support North Korea's policy initiatives. "The important initiatives for talks between the military authorities," Tian emphasized, "for converting the Korean peninsula into a nuclear-free peace zone put forward by the Workers' Party and Government of Korea some time ago are another important step toward easing the situation on the Korean peninsula and achieving a lasting peace in Korea."[13] Thus, China was more concerned with peace and stability, as another Korean War would wreck its modernization program, while the Soviet Union was more concerned with the building of military strength to achieve a balance of power on the Korean peninsula.

Both the Soviet and Chinese leaders in Moscow and Beijing respectively received the Korean delegations on the occasion of the twenty-fifth anniversary celebration. Soviet President Andrei Gromyko and Lev Zaikov, member of the Politburo and Secretary of the CPSU Central Committee, received the Korean delegation led by Kim Hwan on July 2 and they stressed that "the USSR was manifesting unswerving solidarity with the policy pursued by the Workers' Party of Korea and by the Government of the DPRK to secure the withdrawal of American troops from South Korea and the reunification of the country on a peaceful and democratic basis without outside interference."[14] Gromyko expressed his thanks on behalf of Mikhail Gorbachev when the

North Korean delegation conveyed warm greetings from President Kim and his son and successor-designate Kim Jong Il. In Pyongyang, on the other hand, the Soviet delegation led by Solovyov was received by President Kim on July 7, and a personal letter from Gorbachev was presented to Kim. The Soviet delegation also presented gifts to both Kims—father and son.

Chinese leader Hu Yaobang received the North Korean delegation led by Vice President Li Chong-ok on July 11, 1986 at Zhongnanhai. At the luncheon ceremony Hu stressed that "China will continue its efforts to develop friendly and cooperative relations between China and Korea." Obviously this was to alleviate reports in the Western media that relations between Beijing and Pyongyang were cooling off while Soviet-North Korean relations were dramatically improving. Furthermore, North Korean President Kim received the Chinese delegation headed by Vice Premier Tian Jiyun on July 12 and gave a dinner for its members. The Chinese delegation also presented a gift to Kim Il Sung and his son.

No one could detect any crucial difference between the Soviet and Chinese protocols on the occasion of the twenty-fifth anniversary celebration, except that the Soviet message portrayed more militant solidarity between the two countries while the Chinese message tended to emphasize a peaceful solution to Korean problems. The Soviet and Chinese leaders expressed their full agreement on such issues as the peaceful reunification of Korea through the North-South dialogue without any foreign interference, the withdrawal of US troops from Korea, and the establishment of a "nuclear-free and peace zone" in the Korean peninsula, all of which were put forward by North Korea, with the Soviet and Chinese leaders simply endorsing them. North Korea thus attempted to maintain a balancing act between the Soviet Union and China when it dispatched delegations to Moscow and Beijing and received the Soviet and Chinese delegations in Pyongyang.

In 1981 when the Soviet Union and North Korea celebrated

the twentieth anniversary of the signing of the same treaty, there was neither fanfare nor big ceremonies, although the treaty was renewed. Each side simply exchanged messages and the embassies gave receptions. Brezhnev and Kim Il Sung exchanged messages on July 6, 1981; the Soviet message simply noted "The last twenty years since the conclusion of the treaty have proved that the treaty plays an important role in developing friendship and cooperation between our two countries and ensuring peace and security in the Far East."[15] There was no delegation from Moscow to Pyongyang nor from Pyongyang to Moscow to honor the treaty's anniversary and renewal.

Five days later, on July 10, 1981, the Chinese and the North Korean leaders also exchanged messages on the occasion of the twentieth anniversary of the signing of the treaty; Hu Yaobang and Ye Jianying, Chairman of the Standing Committee of the National People's Congress (NPC), asserted "President Kim Il Sung has put forward the three principles for independent and peaceful reunification and the new program on the establishment of the Democratic Confederal Republic of Koryo showing the prominent road to the reunification of Korea."[16] Moreover, the Chinese people "resolutely support the Korean people," they stressed, "in their struggle for the withdrawal of US troops from South Korea and against the creation of 'two Koreas'...." While the Chinese leaders placed more emphasis on Kim's proposals for the reunification of Korea, the Soviet leaders simply gave lip service to friendship and cooperation between the two countries. This prompted some Western observers to conclude that the Chinese leaders supported Korean unification while the Soviet leaders preferred the status quo. However, the Soviet leaders emphasized their "solidarity with the Korean people in the struggle to make foreign troops withdraw from South Korea and reunify the country in a peaceful and democratic way free from foreign interference."[17] In contrast, celebration of the twenty-fifth anniversary took place in the post-Brezhnev period and was a much more important occasion for the Gorbachev leadership in view of increasing Soviet influence in North Korea and expanding economic and military cooperation between Moscow and Pyongyang.

THE GORBACHEV-KIM MEETING IN MOSCOW

North Korean President Kim Il Sung paid an official visit to the Soviet Union from October 22 to 27, 1986, the results of which have been closely analyzed and interpreted by both Japanese and Western observers. The Japanese press reported that the reason Kim had taken such an urgent trip to Moscow was due largely to economic pressures. In the process of formulating the seven-year economic development plan (1987-1993), North Korea needed Soviet assistance because of the shortage of foreign currency as well as a large foreign debt that has been estimated at $2 to $3 billion. Others analyzed the trip in terms of North Korea's urgent need for military hardware and security commitments because of the emerging military alliance between the United States, Japan, and South Korea. We may not know the real motivation and the reasons for Kim's trip to Moscow in the absence of hard facts, nor what was negotiated in secret. However, on the basis of press reports concerning the summit meeting, the speeches delivered by the two leaders, and Kim's own report to the Politburo meeting in late October 1986 upon his return to Pyongyang, we can draw certain conclusions about the results of the meeting.

Soviet leader Mikhail Gorbachev addressed two important issues in his speech at the banquet which the Soviet government and the CPSU Central Committee hosted at the Grand Kremlin Palace on October 24, 1986. One issue regarded the security question of the Korean peninsula and the Asian-Pacific region, and the other pertained to economic and technological assistance. It was reported in the Japanese press that the North Korean economy was on the verge of collapse because of the trade deficit and the foreign debt. Therefore, the Soviet Union had to provide massive economic assistance in order to bail North Korea out of its economic crisis by canceling repayment of a $700 million credit owed by the Pyongyang government. The situation prompted Gorbachev to state that "there still is ample room for growth in our cooperation" by which he meant room "to continue broadening and diversifying trade and economic relations, jointly look for new fields of scientific and technological cooperation, and interact more closely and vigorously on the international scene to ensure our peaceful interests and goals."

"The main thing," Gorbachev asserted, "is that there is a desire to raise the level of our cooperation markedly."[18]

Reviewing economic relations between the Soviet Union and North Korea, Soviet observers noted that the Soviet Union had provided North Korea a long term credit of 212 million rubles and a commercial credit of 47.7 million rubles in the 1950s. Thus, the North Korean economy was able to take off and achieve a high level of development. The Soviet Union subsequently provided additional assistance, totaling 1.3 billion rubles during the 1954-1960 period. In July 1960, the Soviet Union cancelled the repayment of a North Korean loan in the amount of 171 million rubles and converted the commercial credit to a long-term loan, thus providing a substantial grant to the North Koreans.[19] By the end of 1982, the enterprises constructed in North Korea with Soviet aid reached 62 plants, of which 34 were industrial plants; nine were still under construction, subsidized through a long-term loan.[20]

In the area of trade, Soviet exports to North Korea amounted to 287.9 million rubles in 1980, 278.9 million rubles in 1981, 318.5 million rubles in 1982, 347.2 million rubles in 1984, and 648.4 million rubles in 1985. Imports from North Korea amounted to 284.2 million rubles in 1980, 250.3 million rubles in 1981, 362.5 million rubles in 1982, 365.6 million rubles in 1984, and 402.8 million rubles in 1985. Thus, by 1985 trade between the two countries totaled 1.51 billion rubles. The Soviet Union exported 245.6 million rubles ($283.9 million) more to

North Korea than it imported from North Korea, thereby creating a trade deficit in Pyongyang. If we compare the volume of Soviet-North Korean and Chinese-North Korean trade, Soviet exports to North Korea in 1984-1985 increased 86.8 percent compared with the previous year, while Chinese exports increased only 29.4 percent. Soviet imports from North Korea in 1984-1985 increased only 10.2 percent (compared with 1983-1984) while Chinese imports during the same period increased 25.3 percent. Thus the Soviet Union was North Korea's major trade partner among the socialist countries, accounting for more than 37 percent of that country's foreign trade.[21]

On the security question, the communique issued on October 30, 1986 following the KWP Politburo meeting offered some evidence of what had been negotiated between the Soviet and North Korean leaders and what the Soviet Union had agreed to do. Kim's trip took place at Gorbachev's invitation and thus created "a new phase of development since the summit meeting of the two countries in Moscow in May 1984." The General Secretary and President Kim discussed, according to the communique, "the question of further developing in depth the traditional friendship and solidarity between the two countries and a series of questions of mutual concern on the basis of an analysis and appraisal of the present international situation and reached a complete unanimity of views."[22] The North Korean leader supported all the Soviet proposals, including prohibition of nuclear testing, nuclear disarmament, non-militarization of outer space, and abolition of nuclear and chemical weapons by the end of this century. With regard to the Asian situation, Kim also supported Gorbachev's proposal to "convert the Asian-Pacific region into a zone of peace and cooperation free from nuclear weapons and the danger of war."[23]

Concerning the Soviet commitment to Korea, the communique stressed that "he (Gorbachev) gave assurances that more active efforts would be made in the international arena for a peaceful settlement of the Korean question, declaring the strong

terms that the proposals of the KWP and the DPRK government to force US troops and nuclear weapons, the main obstacle
to Korean reunification, out of the South and turn the Korean
peninsula into a nuclear-free, peace zone without fail...."[24] Furthermore, by accepting Kim's invitation to visit North Korea,
General Secretary Gorbachev demonstrated Soviet support for
North Korean efforts to achieve Korean unification on Kim's
terms. The Gorbachev-Kim summit achieved Soviet acceptance
and endorsement of North Korea's policy on Korean reunification, economic and military cooperation, and the succession
question. In return, the Soviet Union was able to obtain North
Korea's full-fledged support for a Soviet-sponsored Asian
security conference, cooperation in the Asian-Pacific region, and
the use of North Korea as a military base for future operations
in countering greater US and Japanese influence in Asia and the
Pacific region.

Besides the economic and security commitment, the North
Korean leader was able to obtain complete endorsement of the
succession issue, which the Chernenko-Kim summit in May
1984 was not able to resolve. The recognition of Kim Jong Il
as the successor to his father has been perhaps the most controversial issue in Soviet-North Korean relations. It had been
suggested in the Western press that the Brezhnev leadership had
opposed the feudalistic arrangment of succession in North Korea.
However, since 1982 Soviet leaders began to adopt a different
position on the issue, noting that "it is rather the domestic affairs of North Korea and we don't wish to interfere with the
internal affairs of our fraternal party and government."[25] In May
1984, during Kim's trip to Moscow, the question of succession
by his eldest son was raised, but it was not fully resolved until
the leadership change came about in Moscow and the subsequent
Kim-Gorbachev Summit in October 1986. Soviet approval or
at least acquiescence in Kim Jong Il's succession was reported
by Kim Il Sung at the KWP Politburo meeting on October 30,
1986, after his return from Moscow. The communique of that

meeting stressed that "it is an unshakable policy of our party and the government of the Republic and the unanimous will of our people to constantly develop and strengthen generation after generation the traditional relations of Korean-Soviet friendship which has been forced in the protracted common struggle to accomplish the cause of the working class, the cause of Marxism-Leninism and withstood all the tests of history."[26] The code word for the endorsement of succession in Pyongyang has been "generation after generation" which means that the generation of Kim Il Sung will be succeeded by the generation of Kim Jong Il, thereby creating the so-called Kim Dynasty in North Korea.

CONCLUSION

Soviet policy toward Korea has been much more aggressive and dynamic than Chinese policy there in the 1980s. What North Korea needed most in the early 1980s was security, for the South was becoming a major power thanks to rapid economic progress and increasing military strength backed by the United States. In order to maintain the balance of power economically and militarily, the North Korean leadership perceived that it had to turn to the Soviet Union for economic and military assistance as China was not in a position to provide the assistance North Korea needed.

However, Chinese policy toward Korea in the 1970s and early 1980s has consistently supported North Korea's policy positions on the reunification of Korea by creating the Democratic Confederal Republic of Koryo, troop withdrawal from South Korea, and the creation of a nuclear-free peace zone in Northeast Asia. Relations between China and North Korea were close during the period when the North Korean leadership attempted to maintain an equidistant position between Moscow and Beijing.[27] The high level exchange visits and consultations between China and North Korea were more frequent than those between the Soviet Union and North Korea. Five days before Kim's departure for

Moscow in May 1984, CCP General Secretary Hu Yaobang was invited to Pyongyang for consultations, which indicated that Sino-North Korean relations remained intact. Two weeks before Kim's departure for Moscow in October 1986, Chinese President Li Xiannian was invited to Pyongyang from October 3-6 for consultations; during the visit, he emphasized "we have always held that the United States must stop meddling in the internal affairs of Korea, withdraw all its troops and military equipment from South Korea, and that the Korean people be left to solve the question of the country's peaceful reunification by themselves free from foreign interference."[28] Such frequent consultation and the endorsement of North Korea's policy position were expressions of a close relationship between the leaders of China and North Korea, thus contradicting the Western assumption that Sino-North Korean relations were cooling as Soviet-North Korean relations were warming up in the early 1980s.

China openly endorsed Kim Jong Il's succession by inviting him to China in June 1983 and according him treatment suitable to an heir apparent even before the Soviet Union reconsidered its position on the succession issue. The Soviets endorsed the succession after obtaining a strategic position in North Korea, including overflight rights and naval ships' call at the port of Nampo. The process of resolving the succession problems in North Korea began with Soviet Deputy Foreign Minister Kapitsa's visit to Pyongyang in November 1984 during which he called on Kim Jong Il, and ended with President Kim's trip to Moscow in October 1986 during which General Secretary Gorbachev presented him with a gift for Kim Jong Il, which was a clear indication of Soviet endorsement of Kim Jong Il's succession.

It should be noted that economic and military cooperation between China and North Korea has continued even after the North Korean tilt toward the Soviet Union. Therefore, it is apparent that there has been no serious rivalry between China and the Soviet Union over the Korean peninsula following the improvement of the triangular relationship among China, the Soviet Union, and North Korea during the 1982-1986 period.

The Soviet Union considers the geostrategic location of Korea as an important factor in serving its security interests. Therefore, Soviet policy makers attempted, at minimum, to prevent domination over the Korean peninsula by a single power and tried to keep North Korea within the Soviet sphere of influence. However, China had been a constant challenge during the height of the Sino-Soviet dispute because of its historic interest in Korea's geopolitical location. Thus, Beijing attempted to keep North Korea within its sphere of influence by encouraging the DPRK to negotiate with the United States in the early 1980s. The open door policy which North Korea adopted in the fall of 1983 at Chinese insistence, however, did not produce the desired results. Thus, North Korea had no choice but to turn to the Soviet Union for economic aid to assist its ailing economy and develop the third seven-year economic plan (1987-1993) and for military assistance to refurbish outmoded equipment, thereby serving Soviet security interests. North Korea will need to depend for a long time on Soviet economic and military assistance, but it cannot afford to distance itself from Chinese influence in Pyongyang because of its own security interests. Therefore, in order to maintain both neutrality and independence, North Korea must adopt an equidistant posture in the Sino-Soviet competition for influence on the Korean peninsula.

NOTES

1. Ilpyong J. Kim, ed. *The Strategic Triangle: China, the United States and the Soviet Union* (New York: Paragon House, 1987).
2. Genrikh Apalin, "Peace and Security for Asia and the Pacific," *International Affairs* (Moscow), November 1986, p. 30.
3. Ibid.
4. For recent Soviet writings on Korea, see A. Muratov, "The Friendship Will Grow Stronger" (40th Anniversary of the Liberation of Korea by the Soviet Army from Japanese Colonial Rule), *International Affairs* (Moscow), September 1985, pp. 22-28; V. Andreyev and V. Osipov, "The DPRK: Years of Struggle and Construction" (The 40th Anniversary of Korea's Liberation by the Soviet Army), *Far Eastern Affairs* (Moscow: Institute of the Far East, USSR Academy of Sciences), No. 4, 1985, pp. 4-45. Also see *Relations of the Soviet Union with People's Korea: 1945-1980, Documents and Materials* (Moscow: Foreign Languages Publishing House, 1981).
5. V. Andreyev and V. Osipov, "The DPRK: Years of Struggle and Construction," p. 51.
6. Ibid.
7. For this information, see *Korean Daily News of Korean Central News Agency* (Tokyo: Korea News Service), July 4, 1986. Hereafter *KCNA Daily News*.
8. *KCNA Daily News*, July 5, 1986.
9. For Solovyov's speech, see *KCNA Daily News*, July 8, 1986, pp. 28-31.
10. Ibid.
11. For Tian's speech, see *KCNA Daily News*, July 11, 1986, pp. 43-46. Emphasis added.
12. Ibid., pp. 37-38.
13. Ibid., p. 37.

14. *KCNA Daily News*, July 5, 1986, pp. 15-16.
15. *KCNA Daily News*, July 7, 1981, p. 8.
16. Ibid., July 11, 1981, pp. 20-21.
17. Ibid., July 7, 1981, p. 8.
18. For Mikhail Gorbachev's speech at the banquet on October 24, 1986, see *KCNA Daily News*, October 25, 1986, pp. 21-25.
19. For Soviet writings on Soviet-North Korean economic relations, see V. Andreyev and V. Osipov, "Directions for Mutual Interest and Cooperation Between the Soviet Union and the Democratic People's Republic of Korea," *Far Eastern Affairs*, Vol. 13, No. 1 (March 1984); and "The DPRK: Years of Struggle and Construction," op. cit., pp. 44-45.
20. For information on North Korea's trade with the Soviet Union, China, and other countries, see *Prospects for North Korea's Economy and Trade* (Tokyo: JETRO, 1986) (in Japanese).
21. For the full text of the Communique, see *KCNA Daily News*, October 31, 1986, pp. 11-16, emphasis added.
22. Ibid., p. 14.
23. Ibid., emphasis added.
24. Soviet specialists at the Institute of the Far East of the USSR Academy of Sciences expressed such a view during my discussions with them in July 1986.
25. See the Communique, *KCNA Daily News*, October 31, 1986, p. 15, emphasis added.
26. Ibid.
27. Ilpyong J. Kim, "The People's Republic of China and the Korean Reunification," *Korean Reunification: New Perspectives and Approaches* (Seoul: Kyungnam University Press, 1984), pp. 171-190. Ilpyong J. Kim, "China's Policy Toward the Two Koreas and its Implications for Inter-Korean Relations," *The Korea Observer*, Autumn, 1986. Ilpyong J. Kim, "The Major Powers and the Korean Tri-

angle," *Two Koreas—One Future* (University Press of America, 1986), Chapter 6, pp. 121-137.
28. For Li Xiannian's visit to North Korea, October 3-6, 1986 see *KCNA Daily News*, October 4-7, 1986.

SUGGESTED READINGS

Andreyev, V. and V. Osipov. "The DPRK: Years of Struggle and Construction (The 40th Anniversary of Korea's Liberation by the Soviet Army)" in *Far Eastern Affairs* (Moscow: Institute of the Far East of USSR Academy of Sciences), No. 4, 1985, pp. 44-55.

Chung, Cong Wook. *Triangular Diplomacy and the Inter-Korea Dialogue* (Claremont, California: The Keck Center for International Strategic Studies, Essays on Strategy and Diplomacy, No. 6, 1986).

Clough, Ralph N. "The Soviet Union and the Two Koreas" in *Soviet Policy in East Asia*, ed. by Donald S. Zagoria (New Haven: Yale University Press, 1982), pp. 175-199.

Gelman, Harry and Norman D. Levin. *The Future of Soviet-North Korean Relations* (Rand Report R-3159-AF) (Santa Monica: Rand, 1984).

Ha, Yong-Chool. "Soviet Perceptions of Soviet-North Korean Relations." *Asian Survey*, Vol. XXVI, No. 5, May 1986, pp. 573-590.

Kim, Ilpyong J. "The Major Powers and the Korean Triangle." in *Two Koreas—One Future* (Washington: University Press of America, 1986), pp. 121-137.

Kim, Young C. "Soviet Policies Toward Korea." Unpublished paper. The Japanese version is in *The Soviet Union in Transition* (Tokyo: Japan Institute of International Affairs, 1985), Vol. II.

Polomka, Peter. *The Two Koreas: Catalyst for Conflict in East Asia?* (Adelphi Papers 208) (London: International Institute for Strategic Studies, 1986).

Relations of the Soviet Union with People's Korea: 1945-1980, Documents and Materials. (Moscow: Foreign Languages Publishing House), 1981.

Williams, Michael C. "North Korea: Tilting Toward Moscow?" in *The World Today* (London: Royal Institute of International Affairs, 1984), October 1984, pp. 398-405.

US House of Representatives, Committee on Foreign Affairs. *The Korean Conundrum: A Conversation with Kim Il Sung* (Report of a Study Mission to South Korea, Japan, the People's Republic of China, and North Korea, July 12-21, 1980) (Washington: US Government Printing Office, August 1981).

US House of Representatives, Committee on Foreign Affairs. *North-South Relations on the Korean Peninsula* (Hearings Before the Subcommittee on Asian and Pacific Affairs, March 20, 1984) (Washington: US Government Printing Office, 1984).

TEN

SOVIET-JAPANESE RELATIONS
WHY NOTHING GETS SETTLED

Donald W. Klein

T he state of Soviet-Japanese relations is one of the main barometers by which we measure the pressure point of East Asian international affairs. That was true as the century began and it will be true when the century ends.

This paper offers an analysis of current Soviet-Japanese relations. It explores the factors that might maintain the positive aspects of these relations and those that might further disrupt the many negative sides. The framework for analysis centers on the positive and negative aspects of three types of relations— political-normative, military-strategic, and economic.

Before assessing contemporary Soviet-Japanese relations, some preliminary comments and historical reminders are in order. At first blush, we seem to be dealing with an overall superpower vs. an economic powerhouse: ICBMs vs. Toyotas. Old habits of thought die hard. It is probably more misleading than useful to label the Soviet Union a superpower, if by that term we mean the ability to project military, political, and economic power on a global basis.

The Soviets' ability to project military power globally is not contested, but Moscow's political power is much more problematic. For example, the Russians seemingly have China surrounded by formidable military power, yet China is today more able than ever to operate in the world's political and economic arenas with great success. In other words, Moscow's much-heralded military power has not translated into effective political power vis-a-vis China, and much the same can be said vis-a-vis Japan. In the economic sphere, few would contend that the USSR is a superpower, at least in the sense of being able to use trade, aid, and investments abroad as a highly effective foreign policy tool. If the USSR is a regional military giant in East Asia and Japan a military midget, then by the same token Japan is a regional economic giant and the Soviet Union is the midget.

On the Japanese side, so much attention is paid to Tokyo's ever-growing economic power that we may ignore the fact that this strength is increasingly being transformed into political influence. More and more nations of all types look admiringly at Japan. Initially (and this is only a few years back), all eyes gazed upon Japan's "economic miracle," but now the entire "Japanese system" is being intently studied for clues to success. (Notice that other successful Asian countries are often called "little Japans.")

Some historical reminders are also necessary to place Russo-Japanese relations in context. Modern history provides several instances in which two very significant nations have had longstanding hostilities, often punctuated by cataclysmic wars. For example, Franco-German relations between the 1870s and 1945, Russo-German relations from 1914 to date, and Sino-Japanese relations from the 1870s to the 1970s. Russo-Japanese relations, consistently hostile (be it Imperial Russia or Soviet Russia) since the 1890s, clearly fit into this unfortunate category. It is, in brief, one of the most enduringly hostile relationships in modern times.

The hostility dates back at least to the 1890s. A fitting birth date might be May 31, 1891, the day the Russian Empire formally concluded work on the Trans-Siberian Railway. The race for Northeast Asian supremacy had begun. In 1895, the Russians intervened with France and Germany to deny Japan what it felt were the just fruits of its impressive victory over China. Then came the Russo-Japanese War (1904-1905), won by Japan. If modern Japan has had a "good war," this was it. It marked the culmination of the Meiji Restoration and Japan's acceptance as a full-fledged modern international power. Not incidentally, the war against Imperial Russia also produced two of modern Japan's most legendary heroes—Admiral Togo and General Nogi, a twosome known to every Japanese school child.[1]

Prior to the end of World War II, Japan and the Soviet Union met twice more in battle. One incident occurred during the 1918-22 period when Japan occupied portions of the Maritime Province in an effort to strangle the infant Soviet regime, and the second during the so-called Nomonhan Incident of 1939 (along the Manchurian-Soviet border).

These battles are well known to educated Japanese through the normal educational and socialization processes. Yet even more telling are those events that took place within the adult lives of every senior contemporary Japanese leader. First is the 1945 Soviet stab-in-the-back, which is how Japanese perceive the Russian attack the day after Hiroshima in clear violation of the neutrality pact not due to expire until April 1946. Far, far worse was the capture and subsequent treatment of some 900,000 troops (plus about 400,000 civilians).[2] By August 1948, only 436,000 had been returned. Exact figures are not available, but something on the order of a third to a half-million men perished under slave-labor conditions in Siberian work camps. There is also the Russians' "illegal" occupation in 1945 of the so-called Northern Territories within sight of Hokkaido (a point to which we will return).

Today's Japanese leaders are also fully aware of the Soviet attempts to scuttle the generally benign American Occupation of Japan. And even before the Occupation ended, Japan was the one and only nation mentioned in the 1950 Sino-Soviet Treaty of Alliance, designed to prevent the "resumption of aggression and violation of peace on the part of Japan...." Even five years later, when the treaty was modified, the joint Sino-Soviet declaration crudely patronized Japan, which was dismissed as a "semi-colonial country." In the interim, in 1950, the Soviet-dominated Cominform tried unsuccessfully to foster uprisings in Japan; in 1951 the Russians tried (again in vain) to wreck the 1951 San Francisco Peace Treaty (restoring sovereignty to Japan), and from then until 1956 vetoed or threatened to veto Japan's admission to the United Nations.

It's easy to marshal the facts to show that prior to 1945 Japan sinned against Russia at least as much as the reverse. The Japanese, with some reluctance, would admit that. Not so after 1945. For the post-1945 period, all but a few (and dwindling) extremists on the political left feel that Japan is genuinely the aggrieved party.[3]

CURRENT SOVIET-JAPANESE RELATIONS

Political-Normative Relations

It would be simple but facile to dismiss Soviet-Japanese political and normative ties as all bad, and then move quickly to military and economic aspects. The situation is more complex. At the highest levels in Japan, both the importance of the Soviet Union and the difficulty of dealing with it run like a scarlet thread through Japanese documents. These themes are regularly spelled out in the Foreign Ministry's annual "diplomatic bluebook," as is the fact that Tokyo's foreign policy is predicated on its all-important links to the United States.

The most striking fact about the highest level contacts between Soviet and Japanese leaders is how seldom they have taken place. Since the advent of Khrushchev's many travels in the mid-1950s, there is scarcely a significant country not visited by the top Soviet leader. Japan is the notable exception, as illustrated in Table 10-1.

Table 10-1
TOP-LEVEL VISITS: USSR AND JAPAN (1956-DATE)

Year	To USSR	To Japan
1956	Prime Minister Hatoyama	(None)
1973	Prime Minister Tanaka	
1982	Prime Minister Suzuki	
1985	Prime Minister Nakasone	

The situation is not too different from the Japanese side. Beginning with the Japanese Peace Treaty signed in San Francisco in 1951, Japan's peripatetic prime ministers have traveled to over 150 countries.[4] Yet only four trips have been to Moscow; the last two, which were made to attend the funerals of Brezhnev and Chernenko, were symbolically important, but they didn't result in sustained, substantive discussions with Soviet leaders.

Moving down a notch to the foreign minister level, the paucity and one-sided nature of the nation-to-nation visits are again evident (see Table 10-2).

Table 10-2
FOREIGN MINISTER VISITS: USSR AND JAPAN (1956-DATE)

Year	To USSR	To Japan
1956	Shigemitsu	
1966	Shiina	Gromyko
1967	Miki	
1969	Aichi	
1972	Ohira	Gromyko
1973	Ohira	
1975	Miyazawa	
1976		Gromyko
1978	Sonoda	
1982	Sakurauchi	
1983	Abe	
1984	Abe (twice)	
1985	Abe	
1986	Abe	Shevardnadze

Again, it should be noted that half of the visits in the 1980s were for the funerals of Brezhnev, Andropov, and Chernenko.[5]

The relative paucity of direct, high-level visits is somewhat mitigated by the fairly frequent contacts by other officials and (on Japan's side) businessmen. For example, there has been a quite steady contact between the top foreign trade and fishery ministries, as well as labor union officials, Japanese opposition political party figures, cultural groups, and sports teams.

The sum of these contacts falls short of a fully institutionalized communications linkage between Moscow and Tokyo. Still, there are probably sufficient high-level contacts to handle any emergency or serious problems that arise. More concretely, one can also point to a significant number of official agreements between the two sides. For example, one compilation for the 1956-1980 period contained no less than 109 agreements—an impressive list even granting the fact that most of them concern economic issues and many of them are marginal in importance.[6] Beneath the often harsh rhetoric between Moscow and Tokyo there is at least an institutionalized functional relationship covering day-to-day relations.

There are no polls on the Russian public's view of Japan, but there seems to be a broad agreement that at both elite and popular levels there is little love lost for the Japanese. On the Japanese side, the situation is clear-cut. For the entire postwar period, Japanese citizens have shown a profound distaste for, and fear of, the Soviet Union. Table 10-3, based on a November 1983 Japanese poll, illustrates the point.

Table 10-3
JAPANESE PERCEPTIONS,
INTERESTS, AND TRUST OF THE SOVIET UNION

| | Like/Dislike | |
	Positive	Negative
Q: Indicate whether you like the Soviet Union very much, fairly much, not so much, or not at all.	6.2%	84.1%

| | Trust | |
	Positive	Negative
Q: Indicate whether the Soviet Union is very trustworthy, fairly trustworthy, not too trustworthy, or not at all trustworthy.	3.5%	84.7%

Note: Positive: "very" plus "fairly"
Negative: "not so" plus "not at all"
Adapted from: Masashi Nishihara, *East Asian Security and the Trilateral Countries* (New York: New York University Press, 1985).

Table 10-4, typical of scores of similar polls over the years, deals with Japan's fear of the USSR.

Table 10-4
THREATS TO JAPANESE SECURITY
(poll published in late 1984)

Question: Is there any country which you especially think of as a threat to Japan's security? From among the following, list as many as you like.

Country	Percentage of Responses
United States	7.8%
South Korea	2.9
North Korea	5.4
China	2.3
USSR	53.5
Others	0.1
Threat, but no specific threat	16.0
No threat	13.5
No answer	10.5

Source: William T. Tow, "Japan: Security Role and Continuing Policy Debates," in Young Whan Kihl and Lawrence E. Grinter, eds., *Asian-Pacific Security: Emerging Challenges and Responses* (Boulder, CO: Lynne Rienner Publishers, 1986).

This deeply felt distrust of the Soviet Union translates into an operative fact for Japanese leaders: they can be assured of near unanimous popular support for a firm bargaining posture when dealing with the Soviets. This stands in sharp contrast to Japan's relations with the People's Republic of China. Prior to the 1972 establishment of diplomatic relations between Beijing and Tokyo, Japanese leaders had to fight a constant rearguard action within Japan against the widespread view that Tokyo should have close ties to China. Put more simply, Tokyo's leaders must deal with what amounts to a "China Lobby" in Japan; no such "Soviet Lobby" exists.

Notwithstanding the absence of a Soviet lobby, Japan's leaders must deal with other important political and normative limitations. Three points stand out. First is the powerful current of neutralist sentiment in today's Japan which consistently questions the wisdom of too great a dependence upon the United States and which urges Japan's leaders to consider a more equidistant posture between the United States and the Soviet Union. Secondly, the vocal opposition with which political parties give voice to these neutralist sentiments within the halls of Japan's parliament. And third, the hyperactive press in Japan, while certainly not "pro-Soviet," quite often cautions against the strongly pro-US policies of the ruling conservatives.

Bilateral Russo-Japanese political relations might be far better were it not for a series of events of the late 1970s and early 1980s. Taken individually, none of these was extremely serious, but collectively they add up to a testy, strained relationship that inevitably spills over into strategic and economic issues. Briefly stated, here are a few of the issues:

1. Japan takes a dim view of Soviet aid to Vietnam, including the quasi-defense pact between Moscow and Hanoi (November 1978) and the use by Soviet ships and aircraft of Vietnamese military bases.

2. With prodding from the US, Japan reacted sharply against

the Soviet invasion of Afghanistan in 1979. Even the Japan Communist Party denounced the invasion. A variety of Soviet-Japanese visits and agreements were shelved because of Afghanistan, and it also led to Japan's boycott of the 1980 Moscow Olympics.

3. In early 1980, in the immediate wake of the Afghan problem, a retired Japanese major general was arrested on charges of spying for the USSR.

4. Later in 1980, a Soviet nuclear sub was crippled near Okinawa. In typically heavy-handed manner, the Soviets towed the sub through Japanese waters without informing the nuclear-sensitive Japanese.

5. In early 1982 Japan reacted sharply to real and potential Soviet interference in Poland, and took various steps (mainly economic) as sanctions against both the Soviet and Polish governments.

6. In September 1983, Soviet-Japanese relations were further strained when the Korean airliner was shot down immediately north of Japan—an act that took 269 lives, 28 of them Japanese. Japan suspended civil aviation flights between Tokyo and Moscow for two weeks as a punitive measure. When the Japanese Foreign Ministry tried to deliver a note demanding an apology, Moscow's ambassador in Tokyo refused to receive it.

Military-Strategic Relations

The previous discussion of political-normative relations obviously omits the crucial problem that has largely defined Soviet-Japanese relations for decades. The omission, of course, is Japan's security link to the United States. This highly durable treaty is now thirty five years old, and all signs point to a continuation well into the 1990s if indeed not into the twenty-first century. The US-Japan linkage is too familiar to require an analysis of US-Soviet-Japanese relations. But we should look carefully at the major manifestation insofar as it influences Soviet-Japanese relations. I refer to the thorny "Northern Territories" problem which, in turn, is the stumbling block that explains the absence of a Soviet-Japanese peace treaty. Initially, in the 1950s, the "Northern Territories" problem seemed to be a soluble bilateral political issue, but it is now more clearly a military-strategic matter.

The Northern Territories problem is complex in detail but fairly simple in rough outline. The islands, adding up to a mere 3,100 square miles (half again larger than Delaware), consist of two small islands within easy sight of Hokkaido, plus the two southernmost islands of the Kurile chain. The four islands are undeniably Japanese, and were recognized as such by Imperial Russia as far back as the 1855 Treaty of Shimoda. Nonetheless, in 1945 the Russians occupied the islands and simply expelled the 16,000 Japanese citizens to Hokkaido. When diplomatic relations were reestablished in 1956, Moscow promised to return two of the islands after a peace treaty was ratified. Then in 1960, Khrushchev piled on a new condition: that the two islands would be returned after a peace treaty plus the removal of all foreign (meaning American) troops from Japan. And still later the Russians simply claimed that all four islands were theirs, and that the issue was forever settled.

In recent years, the problem has become even more difficult because the Soviets have substantially built up their military fortifications on the islands. The formerly political issue has thus been unilaterally transformed into a strategic-military matter.

The Japanese have been almost uncharacteristically adamant on the problem. Their position is simple: no islands, no peace treaty. Tokyo has moved to institutionalize its position. For example, in recent years Japan's foreign minister always inserts the issue into his annual speech at the United Nations. Then in February 1981, Japan designated February 7 as "Northern Territories Day,"[7] a day typically featuring speeches by the prime minister and other top figures—not only from Japan's ruling party, but also from the opposition party chiefs. (In Japanese politics, such unanimity between ruling and opposition parties is a genuine rarity.) Japan has even stationed a Foreign Ministry official in Hokkaido since 1980. The ostensible purpose is to collect information about Russian activities in the Northern Territories; the real purpose seems to be a Japanese attempt to signal to Moscow their determined position on the basic problem.

Beyond the Northern Territories issue and the possibility of a peace treaty lies the heart of the issue: Japan's alliance with the United States. The alliance has been over some bumpy roads (especially during the Vietnam War), but somewhat ironically it is on a smoother path now than it has been in years. In part, this results from the Northeast Asian military buildup by the Soviets that has continued since the late 1960s. This buildup, of course, includes ground forces near the Chinese border (both within the USSR and Mongolia), as well as greatly increased naval and air strength, and an ever-increasing missile-delivery capability. The Soviets now deploy between a quarter and a third of their entire military strength in Asia.

Is all this increased Soviet firepower directed at Japan, or at others? Clearly, at the highest levels of strategy, it is aimed at the combination of the United States and China. Japan is certainly a lesser target.[8] With limited success, the Soviets try to play it both ways. When using the carrot, they reassure the Japanese by claiming that their major concerns are China and the United States. Yet, in Janus-like fashion, they are not averse to threatening gestures directed squarely at Japan—often laced with none-too-subtle references to Japan's great vulnerability or with veiled hints of another Hiroshima.

One result of this increased Soviet power is that the Japanese public (as measured in scores of polls) has grown steadily more accepting of Japan's need to maintain its own military force, in addition to a similarly increasing acceptance of the US-Japan Security Treaty. Both of these facts have, in effect, nudged the opposition parties away from a kind of knee-jerk anti-military and anti-American posture toward a more centrist position. The ruling Liberal Democratic Party, of course, has all along nurtured the idea of a reasonably strong military force as well as a steady military relationship with the US. If the Russians hoped that their military buildup would translate into clear-cut expression of anti-American sentiments, the mid-1986 election in Japan was a shattering blow. Prime Minister Nakasone Yasuhiro, well-known for his hawkish views, won by an avalanche, and the left-leaning parties suffered a disabling defeat. This election virtually assures that the Liberal Democrats will control Japanese politics into the 1990s (as they have since the 1950s).

Economic Relations

We will return to political and strategic issues, but first it is useful to round out a discussion of Soviet-Japanese relations by a brief analysis of economic ties.

The potential for close economic links between the Soviet Union and Japan seems unlimited. The basic formula: Japan's capital and technical know-how in exchange for Siberia's resources.[9] But life is seldom so simple when die-hard communists face cautious capitalists across the table, especially when one of the parties has American and Chinese officials looking over its shoulder. The US tends to be understanding of Japan's endless quest for resources and markets, yet Washington does not want too great a Japanese involvement with the Russians. The Chinese view tends to be more strategically oriented: Don't do anything that will build up Soviet strength in Asia.[10]

Whether seen from Moscow's or Tokyo's viewpoint, the economic ties have been useful but certainly not vital. Neither side is remotely capable, in purely economic terms, of gravely damaging the other's economy. During the past decade, from either Moscow's or Tokyo's vantage point, exports or imports as a percentage of total trade have been in the one to five percent range. This is illustrated in Table 10-5; the year 1977 was selected because it was before the substantial Soviet military buildup in the Northern Territories and also before the Russian invasion of Afghanistan.

Table 10-5
JAPAN-USSR TRADE IN PERCENTAGES

	1977	1984
Japan's Exports to USSR as % of Japan's Total Exports	2.4%	1.5%
Japan's Imports from USSR as % of Japan's Total Imports	2.0%	1.0%
USSR's Exports to Japan as % of USSR's Total Exports	2.6%	1.5%
USSR's Imports from Japan as % of USSR's Total Imports	4.8%	3.1%

It is worth recalling that, during the 1970s, Japan made a concerted effort to treat China and the Soviet Union as equally as possible. This Japanese policy of "equidistance" between Moscow and Peking held true in terms of trade. Through most of the 1970s, for example, Sino-Japanese and Soviet-Japanese trade was quite similar in dollar volume. Ultimately, the "equidistant" policy gave way to a decided Japanese tilt toward China—a situation brought on in part by the Soviet military buildup in the Northern Territories, closer Soviet-Vietnamese relations, and (most important) the Soviet invasion of Afghanistan. Table 10-6 illustrates how far the Soviets have fallen behind China as a Japanese trade partner. (Taiwan and South Korea, the two other major Japanese East Asian trade partners, are included in this table to give further perspective.) Taking into account the severe inflation of the 1970s and early 1980s, it is evident that USSR-Japan trade has reached a plateau. Indeed, virtually all Soviet-Japanese economic relations were put on hold by Japan in the wake of the Afghanistan situation.

Table 10-6
JAPAN'S TRADE WITH USSR, PRC, TAIWAN, AND SOUTH KOREA
(in US $ millions)

	USSR	PRC	Taiwan	South Korea
1973	1,560	2,010	2,540	3,000
1974	2,510	3,290	2,800	4,220
1975	2,790	3,790	2,630	3,560
1976	3,420	3,030	3,470	4,740
1977	3,360	3,490	3,840	6,190
1978	3,940	5,080	5,340	8,590
1979	4,370	6,650	6,840	9,610
1980	4,640	9,400	7,510	8,360
1981	5,280	10,390	7,930	9,050
1982	5,580	8,860	6,700	8,140
1983	4,280	10,000	7,710	9,370
1984	3,910	13,170	9,190	11,440
1985	4,200	16,600	7,360	11,190
1986	5,120	15,510	12,540	15,770
1987	4,960	15,820	18,520	21,520

Source: Japan Institute for Social and Economic Affairs, *Japan 1988: An International Comparison* (Tokyo, 1988), and earlier editions.

From Japan's view, still another survey shows the ranking of all of Japan's trading partners (see Table 10-7). This table adds further evidence to the point that the Soviet Union is an important but far from vital trading partner.

There is also the matter of how Japan is reorienting its economy. For more than a decade, Tokyo has been slowly but surely redirecting its economy away from resource-intensive manufactures and toward the information-intensive industries. And thus the well-worn cliche about Japan "needing" Siberian natural resources grows less salient. The world is currently awash in resources; indeed, prices are falling for many basic commodities. These facts should give Japan more leverage in dealing with Moscow. Or perhaps it is more accurate to say that Tokyo has less need and thus less desire to deal with the Soviets.

Still another angle of Japan's reorientation affects its economic

Table 10-7
JAPAN'S MAJOR TRADE PARTNERS

	1977	1978	1979	1980	1981	1982	1983	1984	1985
1st	US	US	US	US	US	US	US	US	US
2nd	S. Arabia	S. Arabia	S. Arabia	S. Arabia	S. Arabia	S.Arabia	S. Arabia	S. Arabia	China
3rd	Australia	S. Korea	Indonesia	Indonesia	Indonesia	Indonesia	Indonesia	Indonesia	S. Arabia
4th	Indonesia	Australia	S. Korea	Australia	Australia	Australia	Australia	China	Australia
5th	S. Korea	Indonesia	Australia	UAE*	China	UAE	China	Australia	Indonesia
6th	Iran	Iran	W. Germany	China	UAE	China	S. Korea	S.Korea	S. Korea
7th	Canada	W. Germany	Taiwan	S.Korea	S. Korea	S. Korea	UAE	W. Germany	UAE
8th	W. Germany	Taiwan	China	W. Germany	W. Germany	W. Germany	W. Germany	Canada	W. Germany
9th	Taiwan	China	Canada	Taiwan	Taiwan	Canada	Canada	Taiwan	Canada
10th	China	USSR	Kuwait	Canada	Canada	Taiwan	Taiwan	UAE	Taiwan
11th	UAE		Iran	Iraq	UK	UK	Iran	Hong Kong	Hong Kong
12th	Kuwait		UK	UK	Singapore	Singapore	UK	Malaysia	UK
13th	USSR		Malaysia	Iran	Hong Kong	USSR	Hong Kong	UK	Malaysia
14th			UAE	Malaysia	Malaysia		Singapore	Singapore	Singapore
15th			USSR	Singapore	USSR		Malaysia	Iran	USSR
16th				Hong Kong			USSR	USSR	
17th				Kuwait					
18th				USSR					

* - United Arab Emirates

links with the Soviet Union. Tokyo's quest for markets is becoming greater than its quest for resources. This has often sharply aggravated its relations with crucial trade partners, such as the United States and the Common Market. Japan has responded by massive overseas direct investments. These investments are often directly tied to a market situation—as, for example, building an auto factory in Ohio—which also has the financial capacity to buy these cars. The extremely sparse (and by no means rich) populace in Siberia is, in contrast, not much of an inducement. In short, Japan has found it far more lucrative and infinitely less cumbersome to invest in the West or relatively open developing nations. None of this augurs well for increased Japanese investments in the USSR.

THE FUTURE

Will Soviet-Japanese relations evolve along generally similar lines into the 1990s? A straight-line projection is a tempting prediction, especially since both sides have displayed such a broad consistency of policy during the post-war era. In this final section, we will raise points that seem to support the present trends, and some that suggest future changes.

Positive Aspects

The most positive elements in Soviet-Japanese relations tend to be bilateral issues in which third parties are not involved. For all the frustrations, annual trade in the $4-5 billion range is not to be sneezed at, and it provides a fairly regularized relationship between Soviet officials and their Japanese counterparts. Over the years there have been some stormy negotiations concerning disputed fishing grounds (Japan and the Soviet Union being the world's two largest fishing nations), but even these have been fairly routine and reasonable in recent years.

Both sides seem to recognize their basic economic complementarity. And, indeed, this has been acted upon for the past twenty years in Siberian development projects—Japanese capital and

314

technological know-how in exchange for Siberia's natural resources. Allen Whiting, who has interviewed scores of Japanese and Soviet officials, concluded that despite the various difficulties, the "net judgment on the desirability of continued economic cooperation is uniformly positive." He found varying degrees of enthusiasm, but "none of the individuals or groups involved expressed regret at the undertaking or advised against further joint efforts."[11]

Bilateral communications (through diplomatic channels, exchanges of delegations, routinized agreements) are at least reasonably good. Whiting found that Japanese government and business circles "involved in negotiations unanimously agree that Soviet specialists are well informed, and that they understand the Japanese scene quite well." (Unfortunately, he also found that these same Soviet specialists felt that "top Soviet officials, particularly at the Politburo level, lack this understanding and act independently of the experts.")[12] In any case, to put the best face on it, communications between Moscow and Tokyo seem sufficient to handle a crisis. Moreover, there are now strong signs that a Gorbachev-Takeshita meeting may be in the offing.

Because so many polls show Japanese dislike for and distrust of the Russians, it's useful to emphasize an oft-neglected aspect of these polls. The Japanese are devastatingly negative about the Soviet Union in response to subjective or emotionally-oriented questions. Yet these same people will usually reply quite differently to more "rational" questions. A November 1983 poll, for example, found that only three percent of the populace "trusted" the Russians. This same poll posed the following question: "To pursue our world interests, how important do you think it is for Japan to get along well with each of the following countries?" Interestingly, over half replied that it was "very" or "fairly" important for Japan to "get along well" with the Russians.[13]

Negative Aspects

If some elements of Soviet-Japanese relations sail along in fairly smooth waters, others flounder in choppy seas. First is the basic dislike and fear on Japan's part. At both elite and popular levels the Japanese see the Soviets as Japan's only enemy. There's very little to suggest this powerful undercurrent will change in the years ahead.

A more central issue is the security link with Washington, which in turn is connected to the Soviet unwillingness to return the Northern Territories. In Japan's view, a Russo-Japanese peace treaty rests squarely on the return of the islands—thus creating an impasse. Through all the Stalin, Khrushchev, and Brezhnev years there was no fundamental change. The tone of the Gorbachev period gives the appearance that Moscow might move on this issue. Yet balancing that point, and very likely precluding a policy change, is the fact that the Soviets have recently fortified these islands to such an extent that their abandonment seems most unlikely. Soviet strategic planners presumably see these islands as part of a chain of strongpoints that reaches from the Kamchatka Peninsula, through the Kurile Islands (including the Northern Territories), the base structure in and around Vladivostok, and now including bases in Vietnam. Allen Whiting's judgment (made in 1981) that the Northern Territories impasse "is likely to obstruct a formal Soviet-Japanese peace treaty throughout the 1980s" seems equally appropriate for the 1990s.[14]

Fortunately, the Northern Territories issue and the absence of a peace treaty are not the sort of issues that lead to war. Japan can get along quite well without either being settled. The Chinese insist "on principle" that the Russians must take certain steps to improve "basic" Sino-Soviet relations. Yet Sino-Soviet relations have obviously improved in the past few years without the Soviets budging on any basic point. In like fashion, Moscow can hold firm vis-a-vis Japan. More than a decade ago two American analysts, with tongues-in-cheek, noted that the state of Soviet-Japanese relations "might be described as no peace treaty, no oil, no islands, and less fish."[15] Not much has changed.

FINAL THOUGHTS

Those who feel that the Soviets are best dealt with at arm's length may feel that the present impasse is the best of all possible worlds. The reasoning could run as follows. East Asia, led by Japan, is in many ways the world's most dynamic region. It is so dynamic that China has virtually abandoned its cherished self-reliance doctrine and now has an active and growing involvement in this area. Thus the noncommunist, market economies, led by Japan (and including some Chinese involvement) are the wave of the present and, it seems, the future. Those omitted from the new adventure are all communist states—the Indochinese nations, North Korea, and, of course, the Soviet Union. The economic and technological gaps are already wide—and getting wider. If the Soviets don't become involved, the loss is theirs.

To date, and in rather typical style, the Soviets have entered the Pacific arena with a basic stress on the military-strategic factors. Their political influence is questionable, and their normative impact even more dubious. Moscow's economic involvement is quite minimal and is not growing.[16]

Yet there are recent signs that the Russians are shifting their policies. In January 1986, Soviet Foreign Minister (and Politburo member) Eduard A. Shevardnadze traveled to Tokyo—the first Soviet foreign minister to visit Japan in a decade. Unlike his dour-faced predecessor Gromyko, Shevardnadze was all smiles. The Soviets seemed to have budged a bit regarding the Northern Territories (the Japanese chose to interpret the final communique as an indication that the issue is at least on the agenda). The way was also cleared for a summit between Gorbachev and Takeshita (two men, incidentally, who have only recently become deeply involved in international relations). In addition, both sides saw fit to create a bit of momentum by signing trade and tax agreements, and talks were scheduled on scientific and technological cooperation.

A few months later, on July 28, Gorbachev made a remarkable speech indicating that some careful thinking about new policies is taking shape at Moscow's highest levels. First, it is notable that Gorbachev gave his speech in Vladivostok—a bit of geographic symbolism not lost on Tokyo's leaders (nor those in Peking and other Asian capitals).[17] On various occasions in the past four decades, Soviet leaders have held out olive branches to Asian nations. But never has the array of proposals—however tentative—been so comprehensive and aimed at so many audiences. Several of the proposals focus on disarmament measures, others center on economic cooperation. Gorbachev even declared his intention to open Vladivostok, probably the most militarized and closed major city in the world. We would like Vladivostok, he said, "to be our widely opened window to the East." Russian specialists noted the similarity to Peter the Great's building St. Petersburg as a "window to the West." Asian specialists might be more inclined to compare this to China's widely successful "opening" to the outside (i.e., noncommunist) world in recent years.

A few days after Gorbachev's possibly path-breaking speech, Soviet Deputy Foreign Minister (and one of the Foreign Ministry's leading Asian specialists) Mikhail Kapitsa said in conciliatory tones that Moscow was willing to make some border adjustments with China on the Amur and Ussuri Rivers—the latter being the scene of Sino-Soviet military skirmishes in 1969.[18] The possible parallel to the Northern Territories will not be lost on Japanese government analysts.

Yet optimists should beware. One can't ignore the Soviets' enduringly heavy-handed diplomacy toward Japan. We all know that people can act stupidly, and we also know that people run governments. Yet social scientists are uncomfortable with simple stupidity as a reason for bad diplomacy. We feel more comfortable ascribing diplomatic errors to "systemic" problems. But whatever the cause, the Soviet track record is pitiful. Veteran *Wall Street Journal* correspondent Robert Keatley wrote that "It might be possible for the Soviet Union to conduct its Japanese diplomacy with a higher degree of incompetence. But sometimes that seems hard to do." He concluded the same article by writing: "There may be some Soviet master plan for seeking world-wide dominance, as alarmists often claim. But if Japan is any guide, this plan needs repair."[19] Keatley wrote those lines in 1981, but they would fit equally well in 1971 or 1961. Only an optimist would predict that they won't be fitting in 1991.

NOTES

1. The Russo-Japanese War is described in a provocative way in Wada Haruki, "Japanese-Soviet Relations and East Asian Security," *Japan Quarterly*, Vol. XXX, No. 2, April-June 1983, pp. 188-92.

2. John Curtis Perry, *Beneath the Eagles' Wings* (New York: Dodd, Mead, 1980), p. 89.

3. For the Soviet view of these facts, see Paul F. Langer, "Soviet Military Power in Asia," in Donald S. Zagoria, ed., *Soviet Policy in East Asia* (New Haven: Yale University Press, 1982), pp. 260-261.

4. The reference to 150 countries includes nations visited more than once by Japanese prime ministers. For example, prime ministers have visited the United States on 26 different occasions.

5. As might be expected, Japan's foreign ministers go abroad even more frequently than the prime minister. By a rough calculation, Japan's foreign ministers have visited 170 countries from 1951 through mid-1986. As noted above, this includes nations visited more than once. For example, foreign ministers have traveled to the United States on 44 occasions.

6. Rajendra Kumar Jain, *The USSR and Japan, 1945-1980* (Brighton, Sussex, Great Britain: The Harvester Press, 1981), pp. 371-377.

7. February 7 was picked because that was the day in 1855 that the Russo-Japanese Trade and Friendship Treaty was signed in Shimoda, a small port city southwest of Yokohama.

8. In June 1975, a Japanese military planner said, presumably half in jest, that in case of a serious Soviet conventional attack, Japan's air force would last 4 hours, its navy 4 days, and its army 4 weeks. This was reported in the *New York Times*, June 5, 1975, and cited by Sheldon Simon in

Issues and Studies, August 1976, p. 4.

9. On Japan and Siberia, see Raymond S. Mathieson, *Japan's Role in Soviet Economic Growth: Transfer of Technology Since 1965* (New York: Praeger, 1979); and Allen S. Whiting, *Siberian Development and East Asia: Threat or Promise?* (Stanford: Stanford University Press, 1981).

10. Whiting (see note 9), pp. 144-145, notes that the Chinese have seldom articulated their objections to the Japanese. The latter, however, are sensitive to Chinese concerns.

11. Whiting (see note 9), p. 141.

12. Ibid., pp. 130-131.

13. Nishihara (see footnote, Table 10-3), p. 107.

14. Whiting (see note 9), p. 157.

15. P. Edward Haley and Harold W. Rood, "China's Major Trading Partner: Japan Dependent," in *Stanford Journal of International Studies,* Vol. X, Spring 1975, p. 200.

16. For a useful summary of recent events, see Takayama Satoshi, "The Soviet Union Smiles at Japan," *Japan Quarterly,* Vol. XXXIII, No. 2, April-June 1986, pp. 128-137.

17. Writing a few days after the Gorbachev speech, a *New York Times* correspondent noted that "Asians... have been intently discussing Mr. Gorbachev's Pacific overtures." *New York Times,* August 10, 1986.

18. *Boston Globe,* August 7, 1986.

19. *Wall Street Journal,* April 27, 1981.

SUGGESTED READINGS

Falkenheim, Peggy, "Some Determining Factors in Soviet-Japanese Relations," *Pacific Affairs,* Vol. 50, No. 4, Winter 1977-1978.

Kimura, Hiroshi, "Recent Japan-Soviet Relations: From Clouded to 'Somewhat Crystal,' " *Journal of Northeast Asian Studies,* Vol. 1, No. 1, March 1982.

Kimura, Hiroshi, "Soviet Policy Toward Asia Under Chernenko and Gorbachev: A Japanese Perspective," *Journal of Northeast Asian Studies*, Vol. 4, No. 4, Winter 1985.

Jain, Rajendra Kumar, *The USSR and Japan*, 1945-1980 (Brighton, England: The Harvester Press, 1981).

Mathieson, Raymond S., *Japan's Role in Soviet Economic Growth: Transfer of Technology Since 1965* (New York: Praeger Publishers, 1979).

Wada, Haruki, "Japanese-Soviet Relations and East Asian Security," *Japan Quarterly*, Vol. 30, No. 2, April-June 1983.

Whiting, Allen S., *Siberian Development and East Asia: Threat or Promise?* (Stanford: Stanford University Press, 1981).

ELEVEN

SOVIET POLICIES IN LATIN AMERICA

Morris Rothenberg with the assistance of
Robert K. Evanson*

T he use of the plural in the title is deliberate: the USSR has a wide spectrum of policies in Latin America to fit the wide variety of situations it faces in the region. At one end of the spectrum lies Cuba, formally a member of the "socialist community," and responsible for Latin America's transformation from an area of remote concern to Soviet policy-makers to one of considerable interest and involvement.

Next in line comes Nicaragua, where opportunity looms for establishing of a second long-term Soviet ally in the Western Hemisphere. From Moscow's perspective, the Sandinista victory constituted the third great revolutionary development in Latin America, after Castro's victory in Cuba and Allende's in Chile. Moscow also saw the Sandinista victory as a spur to further insurgencies in Central America, especially

* Due to Dr. Rothenberg's untimely death, he was unable to revise the original manuscript. We are grateful to Dr. Evanson for agreeing to review and revise the manuscript as needed.

in El Salvador, necessitating a new set of policies on Moscow's part to take advantage of newfound opportunities.

Finally, there are the remaining countries in the region where, in the words of a 1985 Congressional study, "the objective realities of stability dictate the pursuit of traditional diplomacy." Various Soviet discussions divide these countries according to size, political makeup and, most of all, anti-US potential.

The increasing importance of Latin America to the Soviet Union has been reinforced globally by the growth of the USSR as a world power, especially with respect to its military capabilities, and by the ongoing competition with the United States that has upgraded the value of Soviet or Soviet-supported gains in the US "strategic rear" and accomplished a reduction of US influence even without a commensurate Soviet gain. Soviet interest in Latin America has also been intensified by regional developments: perceived trends in US-Latin American relations, growing Latin American independence, and the demise of military rule in a number of countries.

At the same time, a number of constraints have caused Moscow to adopt a carefully circumscribed low-profile policy in the area: the United States' obvious geographic advantage and the importance given Latin America especially by the Reagan administration, the limits on Soviet military and economic resources available for the region, the weakness of pro-Soviet forces apart from Cuba and Nicaragua, the everpresent possibility that Latin American nationalism and ideological predilections can be turned against the Soviet Union, and the higher priority given by the USSR to other regions of the world.

THE CUBAN CORNERSTONE

The strengthening of the USSR's own position and that of the Castro regime in Cuba remains the cornerstone of Soviet policy in Latin America. It is in Cuba that the bulk of Soviet personnel and resources are concentrated, and the island remains Moscow's principal conduit to the rest of the region. Cuba, moreover, has an importance for Moscow transcending Latin America. Its survival as a socialist state is important to the Soviet leadership's claim to legitimacy on the basis of inevitable historical processes. Moscow's military position in Cuba strengthens the overall image of Soviet power, although Cuba's value as a launching pad for Soviet military operations in the face of superior US strength can be doubted. Cuba's general value as an adjunct of Soviet foreign policy, however, has been demonstrated militarily in Africa and politically throughout the Third World.

Cuba also represents a unique attempt to extend the Soviet sphere of influence overseas. Stalin had seen the Soviet writ limited to contiguous areas occupied by the Red Army. His successors have wrestled with the problem of how to handle Marxist-Leninist regimes separated from the Soviet Union or significantly different in their origins. Moscow welcomed Castro's acquiescence, after considerable resistance, in the institutionalization of his revolution along Soviet lines, initially to make better use of the Soviet economic investment but over the long run to justify Soviet doctrinal views and provide a means for the exercise of Soviet influence after Castro's departure.

Of utmost importance from the Soviet perspective has been the creation (in 1965) and strengthening of the Communist Party of Cuba. Its membership has grown from 55,000 in 1969 to 523,639 currently, and from 14,360 primary organizations in 1973 to 36,168 in 1986.[1] The Communist Party thus comprises about five percent of Cuba's total population as compared to seven percent for the Soviet Party, and seven to thirteen percent for the ruling parties of Eastern Europe.

The Soviet and Cuban parties have developed close ties at all levels. Castro headed delegations to Moscow for the twenty-sixth Soviet Party Congress in 1981, the funerals of Brezhnev and Andropov in 1982 and 1984, and the twenty-seventh Party Congress in 1986. Raul Castro and Carlos Rafael Rodriguez visit the USSR almost every year. Soviet Politburo member

Vorotnikov served as Ambassador to Cuba from 1979 to 1982, while other members—Solomentsev, Shevardnadze, and Ligachev—visited Cuba in July 1983, October 1985, and February 1986, respectively.

According to Cuban Politburo member Machado Ventura, over sixty Soviet Party delegations went to Cuba between 1981 and 1983, and over 100 Cuban Communist Party delegations visited the Soviet Union. Machado Ventura reported "close contacts" between the two countries' party schools, Central Committee departments, and media. The Cuban party, he concluded, has applied Soviet examples at all levels "from primary organizations to the Central Committee."[2] At the nonparty level, a steady stream of delegations flows between the two countries; in 1985, moreover, 10,000 Cubans were undergoing training in 60 Soviet cities.

A similar intertwining can be found between the Soviet and Cuban military, intelligence, economic, and propaganda establishments. According to a joint report by the US Departments of State and Defense in March 1985, "the Soviets now have in Cuba 7,000 civilian advisers, a 2,800-man combat brigade, another 2,800 military advisers, plus about 2,100 technicians at the Lourdes electronic intelligence facility."[3] Since 1969, the Soviet navy has deployed task forces to Cuba once or twice every year, while Soviet long-range naval reconnaissance aircraft use Cuba as a base of operations for shadowing US carrier battle groups and other US military forces and installations.

Conservative estimates place Soviet military aid to Cuba from 1961 to 1979 at $3.8 billion,[4] while the State-Defense Department report in 1985 asserted that during the preceding four years, the USSR had given Cuba almost $3 billion in military aid. Soviet weaponry, as well as Soviet advisers, provide the USSR with a powerful source of leverage, all the more so given the political importance of the Cuban military establishment.

Another key source of Soviet leverage is the virtually total dependence of the Cuban economy upon the Soviet Union.

Eighty-five percent of Cuban trade is carried out with the Soviet bloc. As candidly explained in one Soviet journal, the significance of Soviet oil shipments to Cuba is "hard to overestimate, since practically the entire functioning of Cuba's national economy is based on energy supplies from the Soviet Union."[5] The favorable terms for Cuban purchases of Soviet oil and the subsidy paid to Cuba for sugar contribute to an estimated $4 billion in annual Soviet aid for the Cuban economy.

From the Soviet perspective, one of the most portentous developments of the past two decades has been US acceptance not only of the existence of the Castro regime, but of its military relationship with the Soviet Union. Moscow has steadily built up its military presence, especially in response to Cuban fears of possible US actions, but has exercised care that this process does not generate such actions.

Castro's fears that Cuba might be left to US mercies as part of a US-USSR deal have clearly abated, but not his need for constant reassurance about the solidity of the Soviet commitment, especially since 1980, in response to US charges of Cuban aid to Central American insurgencies. In February 1981, Brezhnev at the twenty-sixth Party Congress for the first time explicitly listed Cuba as a member of the "socialist community." Later in 1981, the Defense Minister and other Soviet spokesmen issued a series of warnings to the US about the "serious consequences" of any US punitive actions against Cuba. These warnings were designed to reassure Havana, deter the US, and remind the rest of Latin America of the USSR's presence.

Nevertheless, since the 1962 missile crisis, Moscow has in fact accepted limitations on the nature of its military involvement in Cuba and has avoided any formal treaty commitment to Cuba even through observer status in the Warsaw Pact. Cuba's admission in 1972 to the Council for Mutual Economic Assistance (CMEA) is the closest the USSR has come juridically to such a commitment.

After a rocky start at the time of Gorbachev's accession in

March 1985, Soviet-Cuban relations appear to have settled into a groove satisfactory to both sides. Castro's failure to attend a June 1984 CMEA summit or the rites of succession after Chernenko's death in March 1985 had suggested that all was not rosy in Soviet-Cuban relations. Moreover, Raul Castro was not received by Gorbachev until almost one week after other "socialist community" leaders and well after such visiting luminaries as Imelda Marcos.

One year later, when Fidel Castro attended the Soviet Party Congress, he was received by Gorbachev in Cuba's "proper" hierarchical position after the Eastern European leaders, while TASS reported a "unity of views" between Castro and Gorbachev on "all questions under consideration."[6] In another show of amity, on his way home from North Korea, Castro was received once more by Gorbachev on March 12.

The emphasis in the Gorbachev-Castro meeting on "ways to improve the efficiency of economic cooperation between the two countries"[7] suggests that economic relations have been a major source of tension in Soviet-Cuban relations. In October 1984, agreements had been reached on long-term Soviet-Cuban economic ties as well as the deferral of Cuban debt payments to the USSR, scheduled to start in 1986, until 1990.

However, in December 1984 Castro admitted that Cuba had frequently failed to meet its obligations to the Soviet Union for sugar and other deliveries and in February 1986 revealed that, "making a huge sacrifice, our country bought in convertible exchange, 500,000 tons of sugar so we could meet our commitments to the USSR."[8] A Cuban National Bank account of the same transaction reported that the Cubans had used the proceeds from the purchase and re-export of oil,[9] possibly in competition with the Soviet Union. In April 1986, four new Soviet-Cuban agreements provided for the coordination of economic plans until 1990 and 2.5 million rubles in Soviet credit covering the same period.[10] The USSR also agreed to build Cuba's first nuclear power plant.[11]

In addition to differing Soviet and Cuban assessments about the extent of the US threat and the required amount of Soviet aid, there may be other irritants in their relations. Opposing evaluations of revolutionary situations in Latin America, Soviet ties to orthodox communist parties, and Castro's links to more radical groups always lurk as possible sources of altercation. Differences were evident in Soviet and Cuban media treatments of events in Grenada in 1983, and periodic meetings are held to negotiate the two countries' division of labor in Africa. The current or a subsequent Soviet leadership may not be so adroit in handling Cuba, especially when Castro leaves the scene. At the present time, however, all indications are that the mutual benefit each partner derives will be decisive for some time to come in the relationship between Moscow and Havana.

NICARAGUA: THE NEXT POTENTIAL BASE

Soviet spokesmen hailed the Sandinista victory in Nicaragua as an historic watershed reversing the 1973 overthrow of Allende, providing a powerful impulse to revolutionary movements elsewhere in the region, and adding to Cuba another breach in the doctrine of "geographic fatalism" which Moscow once thought would bar U.S. acceptance of a radical pro-Soviet regime in Latin America. While Castro has claimed that the Soviet regime had no personal ties with the Sandinistas before their victory, there has been no denying the Sandinistas' long and close relationship with Cuba.

The USSR moved even more rapidly than it had with Castro to establish diplomatic, economic, and other relations with the Sandinista regime. Since March 1980, when four top members of the Sandinista leadership made their first important visit to the Soviet bloc, an extraordinary stream of Nicaraguan junta members has come to Moscow, most notably Daniel Ortega, who has made the trip a number of times, beginning in March.

There has been a steady strengthening of ideological affinities between Moscow and Managua. Among the agreements signed during the visit of the first major Sandinista delegation to Moscow, in March 1980, was a party-to-party agreement which reflected Soviet expectations that the Sandinista National Liberation Front (FSLN) would eventually become a Soviet-style ruling party. A Soviet article in July 1986 took the position that the FSLN was moving steadily in this direction.[12]

The Sandinistas have increasingly aligned themselves with Moscow's foreign policy positions; their delegate to the twenty-seventh Soviet Party Congress, Bayardo Arce, stressed that "the Sandinista people's revolution" is "part of the world revolution."[13] Nicaragua is a member of every important international communist organization, and frequently participates in international communist symposia. An impressive array of political ties has developed between Nicaragua and various communist states. Nicaragua has cultural, educational, radio, and other agreements with the USSR, and annually sends a substantial number of students to the Soviet bloc. In July 1986 it was hooked into the Soviet space satellite network.

Although both Moscow and Havana have urged the Sandinistas to accept economic aid from whatever sources are available, an increasing share of Nicaragua's economic relations is directed toward the Soviet sphere. While only thirteen percent of Nicaraguan trade in 1983 was with the USSR and its allies, by 1985 it had risen to twenty percent. The USSR in 1980 and 1982 granted at least $150 million in credits to Nicaragua, supplementing $164 million from Libya, Cuba, and Eastern Europe. In September 1983, Nicaragua was given observer status in CMEA.

Since the advent of the Reagan administration, Moscow has issued frequent warnings about the danger of US military intervention against Nicaragua, citing US regional maneuvers, the US invasion of Grenada and, for the past few years, US support for the Contras. At the same time, Moscow has also paid close attention to factors inhibiting the US from drastic actions against Nicaragua, such as Congressional and popular opposition in the

US, the political costs that the US would incur, especially in Latin America, and the military difficulties of an invasion.

The Gorbachev regime has stepped up both economic and military assistance to the Sandinistas. Shortly after the U.S. House of Representatives voted against aid to the contras, Daniel Ortega made another of his visits to Moscow where he signed an agreement on the establishment of an inter-governmental commission on economic, commercial and scientific-technical cooperation. Ortega told foreign newsmen that Nicaragua was to receive $200 million in further Soviet aid. Upon his return home, he revealed that the Soviet Union would supply 80 to 90 percent of Nicaragua's oil needs in 1985, replacing Mexico and Venezuela as suppliers of oil to Nicaragua and dramatically escalating the USSR's economic commitment to Managua.[14]

Anticipating further US aid to the Contras, the Soviet Union stepped up deliveries of troop-carrying and assault helicopters to Nicaragua. According to Pentagon sources, Soviet military shipments to Nicaragua in 1986 doubled the total amount sent during all of 1985, with four shiploads coming directly to Nicaragua from the Soviet Union rather than by way of Cuba.[15] Parts of the 1986 shipments may have constituted replacements of weapons lost in the war against the Contras. Deliveries in 1987 approached 1986 levels.

Despite its military aid, Moscow has exercised considerable caution in its commitments to Nicaragua. MiG planes said to be earmarked for Nicaragua remain in Cuba, although Nicaragua is constructing a large new military airport and top Sandinista officials are cited from time to time by Moscow on Nicaragua's sovereign right to get military aid from any source. Moscow has never publicly acknowledged its military aid to Nicaragua and there are, according to the Pentagon, at most fifty to seventy Soviet military advisers in Nicaragua compared to more than 500 from Cuba.

With few exceptions, Soviet writers have avoided granting

Nicaragua ideological status implying the kind of commitment made to Cuba and Afghanistan. Soviet spokesmen have consistently sidestepped inquiries about what the USSR would do if Nicaragua were invaded, and frequently express confidence that the Sandinistas will survive all threats to their existence.

THE REST OF CENTRAL AMERICA

Moscow interpreted the Sandinista victory as producing a domino effect in the rest of Central America, especially in El Salvador. Within months after the Sandinista accession to power, the Soviet journal *Latinskaia Amerika* (January-March 1980) reversed previous negative views of Che Guevara's emphasis on the importance of armed struggle. This reversal was reaffirmed during international communist discussions summarized in the Prague-based *World Marxist Review* in June 1981, October 1982, and May 1984, which also stressed seizure of power as the prime objective of communist policies, and the importance of unity with other radical groups.

This change in doctrine and party line indicated Soviet determination not to have its followers caught off base as they had been in Cuba and Nicaragua when groups more militant and radical than the pro-Soviet communist parties led the insurgencies that ultimately seized power. Under Cuba's aegis, broad coalition organizations of Salvadoran groups were formed in 1980. Similar processes were carried out in Guatemala and Honduras in 1982. Unlike Nicaragua, a key role was assigned to the El Salvador Communist Party, whose leader Shafik Jorge Handal served as guerrilla representative in a 1980 arms shopping trip to the Soviet bloc.

Even more than in the case of Nicaragua, Moscow has acted with extreme circumspection about direct involvement in El Salvador. During the Handal shopping trip, it was evident that the USSR would arrange deals with third parties. Soviet spokesmen have denied any intention of shipping arms to the guerrillas of El Salvador. The Soviets have taken the position that the Salvadoran conflict stems completely from domestic causes and should not be considered an East-West issue.

Soviet commentaries about rebel prospects in El Salvador have gone through a variety of phases, depending on the actual course of military activities "on the ground" and perceptions on possible US intervention. Since the failure of the guerrilla "final offensive" in early 1981, when Soviet hopes of a complete guerrilla victory were all but explicit, Moscow has in general appeared to prepare for a long protracted struggle combining both military and political means. Soviet analyses since the advent of Gorbachev have described a continuing "revolutionary situation" in El Salvador.

To ease pressures on Cuba, Nicaragua and the Salvadoran left, Moscow has repeatedly issued warnings about the dangers of US intervention and extolled the virtues of a political settlement. Soviet delegations to Latin America and Soviet statements during the visits of Latin American leaders to the USSR never fail to bring up these themes.

Moscow, however, has appeared ambivalent about both the Contadora process and government-rebel negotiations in El Salvador. Soviet expressions of approval aim to forestall US military action and foster cleavages between the US and Latin America. However, as an authoritative Soviet article commented in June 1986:

> In coming out for a political solution of the conflict in the subregion, the Contadora group at the same time is striving to limit the revolutionary processes in Central America within a bourgeois-democratic framework. This, in particular, is manifested in attempts to impose an obligation on Nicaragua to begin a political dialogue with the counterrevolutionary opposition, taking as an example the talks between President Duarte and Salvadoran patriots, though the basic differences in the domestic situation in these two states are obvious.[16]

Moscow has similarly been dubious about government-rebel talks in El Salvador. The lead article of the April 1984 issue of *Latinskaia Amerika* emphasized that "civil wars do not end in compromise."[17] Moscow denounced elections in El Salvador and Duarte's motivation in holding talks with Salvadoran guerrillas as tricks and emphasized the need for the guerrillas not to budge from demands to share power and meanwhile to continue military operations.

NON-MARXIST LATIN AMERICA

From the perspective of many Soviet observers, events in Central America are part of a broader process of growing Latin American assertiveness, independence, and anti-US feeling. Soviet analysts for a number of years have perceived an overall weakening of the US political position in the hemisphere encompassing noncommunist and even right-wing regimes. The OAS is seen as in decline and the Monroe Doctrine long since dead. Soviet commentaries sought to use the Falklands crisis to discredit the 1947 Rio Treaty and frequently made the point to Latin American audiences that US support for the United Kingdom shows the low priority given Latin America in US calculations.

At the same time, Soviet journals have carried varying assessments of the degree of capitalist development in Latin America and the dependence of the region on the US economic presence. A note of pessimism was introduced at an authoritative level in an article in *Pravda* on January 10, 1986. The writer, Central Committee functionary Karen Brutents, emphasized the growing solidarity of capitalism in the Third World and noted that "countries have emerged in Latin America, Asia, and the Pacific where solid industrial structures, and in some cases even monopolistic forms of capitalist ownership, have developed."

Assessments of this sort suggest that the Soviet Union is under no illusions about the likelihood of revolutionary change in most of Latin America in the near future. However, it has long been developing a wide panoply of political, economic and cultural interactions with Latin American states quite independently of the changing fortunes of radical forces in the area. These policies have been designed to establish a permanent Soviet presence in Latin America and encourage peaceful trends of political separation from the United States that already are apparent throughout the region. Indeed, one Soviet scholar has identified the emergence of a new international subsystem of socialist-Latin American relations. As he explained:

> For the two decades which have passed since the victory of the Cuban revolution, when for the first time world socialism became a direct actor in the international relations in the Western hemisphere, there has unfolded a stable and constant subsystem of 'socialist states-Latin America' ties. It already has a very well developed legal base through a variety of treaties (the number of agreements concluded between the two groups has reached 80) and includes economic, political, scientific-technical, and cultural ties." [18]

Whereas at the end of the 1950s, the Soviet Union had diplomatic and trade relations with only four Latin American countries, by 1982 it had diplomatic relations with 19, and trade relations with more than 20. A succession of Supreme Soviet delegations has gone to Latin America in recent years, most notably two headed by then Party Secretaries Zimianin and Kapitonov to Brazil and Mexico in 1984.

According to Soviet statistics, trade turnover between the USSR and Latin America (excluding Cuba) rose from 116.5 million rubles in 1969 to over 3 billion rubles per year in the 1980s. Most of this trade has been with Argentina and Brazil, with substantial imbalances in favor of the Latin Americans and fluctuations from year to year. Although only a small percentage of Latin American trade as a whole (Cuba excepted), the USSR's trade with Argentina, for example, attained considerable importance for both countries in 1980 when

Argentina (along with Brazil) refused to take part in a U.S.-sponsored agricultural boycott of the Soviet Union. Argentina, in turn, found the Soviet Union eager to become the largest purchaser of its grain and meat exports.

Soviet information activity in Latin America has grown substantially. By the end of 1984, the USSR and its allies were broadcasting almost 800 hours of radio per week to Latin America, 135 by the USSR itself, 234.5 by Cuba, and 63 by Nicaragua. From 1959 to 1980, the Soviet output of Spanish-language publications rose from about a half million copies per year to 10.6 million copies.

The USSR has long been making a determined effort to strengthen its intellectual ties with Latin America. A State Department publication reported that 6,800 students from the region were being trained in the USSR and Eastern Europe as of 1982.[19] The cumulative effect of this effort is considerable. Thus, Peru's Ambassador to the USSR pointed out in 1985 that more than 10,000 Peruvian students had received stipends for study in the Soviet Union since 1969.[20] Following the Sandinistas' accession to power, the total number of Soviet and Cuban scholarships to Central American youths increased rapidly, so that by 1983 there reportedly were 7,500 recipients.[21]

The Soviet Institute of Latin America is also steadily increasing its ties with university and research institutes in the region. It reported with pride in 1986 that it already had formal ties with counterparts in Argentina, Bolivia, the Dominican Republic, Colombia, and Mexico, and was projecting future ones in Brazil, Venezuela, Ecuador, Guyana, and Jamaica. It also exchanges publications with 400 libraries and institutions throughout the world and its journal *Latinskaia Amerika*, issued in Russian and Spanish, is distributed in fifty-four countries.[22]

One element of the Soviet bloc-Latin American subsystem not mentioned by the Institute is the large number of Latin American Communist Parties, which are a major source of Soviet support in the international communist movement as well as an important source of information for the Soviet Union about Latin America. Thus, in addition to Cuba and Nicaragua, Communist or extreme leftist representatives from twenty-two Latin American countries (all but El Salvador) attended the twenty-sixth Soviet Communist Party Congress in February 1981; representatives from the same number of countries (this time including El Salvador but not Puerto Rico) attended the twenty-seventh Party Congress in March 1986.

Although the USSR had shown no compunction about dealing with authoritarian military regimes, it has seen new opportunities in the changeover of several countries—notably Argentina, Brazil, and Uruguay—to democratic civilian governments. Moscow has particularly welcomed foreign policy changes such as the establishment of relations by the latter two with Cuba and domestic changes such as the legalization of the communist parties. As if to justify this heightened Soviet optimism, the Foreign Ministers of Brazil, Argentina, and Uruguay, in December 1985, January, and July 1986, respectively, paid the first official visits at this level to the USSR in the history of Soviet relations with these countries.

The visits provided significant improvement in the USSR's political ties with the countries concerned. In all three cases agreements were concluded on bilateral consultations by foreign ministry officials, thereby codifying recent practices that have included annual visits to Latin America by Soviet officials to discuss forthcoming issues at the UN General Assembly.

Agreements on cultural cooperation were also signed during these visits, which the previous military leaders avoided. These, together with a cultural accord signed with Peru in May 1985, mean that the Gorbachev regime has filled the major gaps in the network of cultural agreements between the USSR and Latin America. In another bid for improved relations with Latin American intellectuals, agreements were also signed during the visits of the three Foreign Ministers on the preparation of joint anthologies on the history of relations between the USSR and each of their countries.

A comparison of the three visits underscores the special place of Argentina in Soviet relations with the principal countries of Latin America. Soviet Foreign Minister Shevardnadze especially praised Argentina's "responsible and mature approach" on matters of international peace, particularly its joint nuclear test ban proposals with five other nonaligned countries which have been given a prominent role in Gorbachev's nuclear disarmament campaign.[23]

In another bid clearly directed at Argentina, Soviet spokesmen used the visits of the Foreign Ministers to express concern at "steps for the militarization of the south Atlantic."[24] While the Uruguayan joint communique avoided specifics, the document concluding Argentine Foreign Minister Caputo's visit defined the danger as coming from "Britain's creation of a large military base on the Falkland Islands (Malvinas), which is leading to the militarization of the south Atlantic and the intensification of the threat to peace and security."[25]

Moscow sought during the Foreign Ministerial visits to reduce the deficit in its trade with Latin America, which reached a high point of 2.9 billion rubles (about $4.4 billion) in 1981. In the case of Argentina, an agreement was signed calling for Soviet purchase of at least 4.5 million tons of grain annually and Argentine purchase of $500 million worth of Soviet industrial goods over a five-year period. An agreement signed during the visit of the Brazilian Foreign Minister also called for increased Soviet exports.

CONCLUSIONS AND PROSPECTS

The Gorbachev regime has demonstrated by its increased military and economic aid to Cuba and Nicaragua its intention to strengthen the assets it already has in Latin America. Indeed, current policy on Cuba and Nicaragua reflects a determination on Moscow's part to pursue its role both as a world power in competition with the United States and as self-appointed leader of the world revolutionary process. Within Latin America, this policy is designed to show the Soviet Union's value as a source of support and to raise the costs of any US plans for intervention.

Although Moscow is no longer as optimistic as it was in the early 1980s about the spread of revolution in Central America, the presence at the twenty-seventh Soviet Party Congress of the Salvadoran Communist Party and Farabundo Marti National Liberation Front (FMLN) representatives indicated continued Soviet determination to support the rebel cause in El Salvador. As long as this support does not jeopardize Cuba or Nicaragua, the Kremlin is not averse to seeing the US divert military resources from areas of greater importance to the USSR and become involved in conflicts which could jeopardize US positions in more important countries on the continent.

Soviet military aid (after some hesitation) to the regime of Maurice Bishop of Grenada suggested Soviet optimism that the island could serve Soviet interests in the Caribbean. While the US invasion spelled the loss of an ally, the most important consequences of the Grenadian events for Moscow were their unsettling impact on Cuba and Nicaragua and the clear indication of US willingness to use force to reassert influence.[26]

With Grenada possibly in mind, Carlos Rafael Rodriguez, at a March 1986 conference in Moscow, expressed doubts about short-term prospects for socialism in Latin America and cited Castro as saying that "securing Latin American unity as a counterweight to the US has greater significance than a chance revolutionary outburst in one or another country, even if it will bring it to socialism."[27] In carrying this speech in *Latinskaia Amerika*, Moscow implied approval for its sentiments.

The Gorbachev regime can be expected to intensify efforts to strengthen its ties especially with the larger states of Latin America. The visit to Moscow in October 1986 of Argentine

President Alfonsin may have given new impetus to this policy, as would visits by Brazilian President Sarney and Uruguayan President Sanguinetti, both of whom were proffered invitations during the visits of their Foreign Ministers.

Far more dramatic, however, would be a visit by General Secretary Gorbachev to Latin America. Such a journey would underline the importance the USSR attaches to relations with the region. The only previous trip to Latin America by the top Soviet leader was one by the late Leonid Brezhnev, who attended a congress of the Cuban Communist Party in 1975. Soviet Foreign Minister Shevardnadze sought to lay the groundwork for a Gorbachev visit to Mexico during a diplomatic call in Mexico City in October 1986.

The shift from military to civilian regimes in a number of countries and the overthrow of Duvalier in Haiti have encouraged Soviet speculation about comparable changes in Chile and Paraguay. The replacement of the Pinochet regime would be a source of particular satisfaction for Moscow and may explain why the Chilean Communist Party supported armed violence, whereas the other Latin American parties under military rule participated in coalitions that pressed for the peaceful transfer from military to civilian officials.

In an unprecedented show of direct Soviet support, Moscow has loaned its official radio station to the Chilean Communist Party since 1981 for broadcasts to Chile advocating its militant party line. The Chilean Communist delegate to the twenty-seventh Soviet Party Congress reaffirmed this line, but several months later the Chilean party appeared to be modifying its position in order to make possible agreement with more moderate opposition groups.

In its efforts to encourage anti-US tendencies, Soviet analyses are devoting increasing attention to the potential political consequences of the Latin American debt problem. At a minimum, the USSR is seeking to define the issue as one of Latin America and other Third World countries against the West, especially the

US. Soviet spokesmen brought up the debt issue during the visit of all three Foreign Ministers in 1985 and 1986. While Castro sought to unite Latin America behind his demand in 1985 that all debts be canceled, the USSR in January 1986 proposed that the UN act to alleviate the problem.

While its positions in Cuba and Nicaragua and, to a certain extent, the network of its ties with the rest of Latin America have transformed the USSR from a complete outsider to a factor of significance in the affairs of the continent, and its perception of long-term anti-American trends and unresolved development problems have given its efforts special impetus, the Gorbachev regime (like its predecessors) will operate under a variety of constraints.

First, Moscow can be expected to retain considerable respect for US military, political, and economic advantages in the region. This will include continued observance of limits on the types of military aid it gives to Cuba and Nicaragua, as well as circumspect handling of outside aid to insurgencies, in order to avoid direct confrontations with the United States. The strategic importance attached to Central America by the Reagan administration and the 1983 US invasion of Grenada have undoubtedly increased Soviet caution. Moreover, too forward a posture would lend credence to US policy justifications and might drive the rest of Latin America back more closely into the US fold.

A second major constraint will continue to be limitations on Soviet resources, especially when confronted by competing domestic and international demands. In 1986 the USSR failed to live up to its January commitment to purchase 4.5 million tons of Argentine grain, because of Argentina's failure to buy more Soviet goods. Latin American reluctance to purchase Soviet products, despite agreements to do so, has been a perennial problem in their economic relations. Although the sharp decline in Argentine exports to the USSR in 1986 was partly reversed in 1987 and the grain purchase agreement was reconfirmed during President Alfonsin's visit to Moscow in October 1986,[28] it appears that the Gorbachev regime is taking a tougher position on this question than its predecessors.

Unlike the rest of the Third World, Moscow has no military aid program in South America except for Peru. Although there has been a fairly extensive exchange of military delegations between the USSR and Argentina, this has not resulted in Soviet military aid, even after the Falklands debacle. About 160 Soviet military advisers are said to be in Peru, about 90 with the Peruvian army. Although Soviet military aid was contracted during Peruvian military rule, the continued Sendero Luminoso (Shining Path) insurgency leaves open the possibility that the Peruvian government will seek further Soviet military aid. In April 1985, the USSR agreed to payment of Peru's debt for Soviet weaponry through delivery of Peruvian goods to the USSR and Eastern Europe.

Finally, distance remains an important limiting factor on Soviet activities, as do the comparatively modest leverage the USSR has accumulated except in Cuba and Nicaragua, and continuing Soviet uncertainty about the nature of the region. Given Soviet views of Latin America as the "strategic rear" of the United States, Moscow will feel impelled to take action as targets of opportunity present themselves. At the same time, Soviet ideology also allows for ebbs and flows, and Gorbachev's emphasis on the need for "realism" would seem to dictate continued caution in Latin America.

NOTES

1. Leon Goure and Morris Rothenberg, *Soviet Penetration of Latin America* (Miami: University of Miami, 1975), p. 54; Castro speech to Third Party Congress, Havana Domestic Service, February 4, 1986, in Foreign Broadcast Information Service Daily Report (hereafter *FBIS*) *Latin America*, Vol. VI, February 7, 1986, p. Q 42.
2. Jose Ramon Machado Ventura article in *Pravda*, September 19, 1984 in *FBIS Soviet Union*, Vol. 1, October 4, 1984, pp. K 3-6.
3. Department of State and Department of Defense, *The Soviet-Cuban Connection in Central America and the Caribbean* (Washington: March 1985), p. 3.
4. Congressional Research Service, *The Soviet Union in the Third World, 1980-85: An Imperial Burden or Political Asset?* (Washington: Government Printing Office, 1985), p. 300.
5. V. Burmistrov, "The First Soviet-Cuban Long-Term Trade Agreement (1976-80): Its Results," *Foreign Trade* (Moscow), January 1982, p. 9.
6. TASS, March 2, 1986 in *FBIS Soviet Union*, Vol. III, March 3, 1986, pp. Q 28-29.
7. Ibid.
8. *FBIS Latin America*, Vol. VI, February 7, 1986, p. Q 21.
9. *New York Times*, June 5, 1985.
10. CANA (Bridgetown), April 11, 1986 in *FBIS Latin America*, Vol. VI, April 14, 1986, p. Q 1.
11. EFE (Madrid), May 19, 1986 in *FBIS Latin America*, Vol. VI, May 21, 1986, pp. Q 1-2.
12. I. M. Bulychev, "The FSLN—The Ideological-Political Vanguard of the Popular Revolution," *Latinskaia Amerika*, July 1986, pp. 60-68.
13. *Pravda*, March 4, 1986, in *FBIS Soviet Union*, Vol. III, Supplement, March 19, 1986, p. 0 10.

14. *New York Times*, May 21, 1985.
15. *Washington Times*, June 27, 1986.
16. V. P. Sudarev, "Central America: Dangerous Development of Events," *Latinskaia Amerika*, June 1986, p. 12.
17. M. F. Gornov, Yu. N. Korolev, "The Revolutionary Process in the Countries of Central America: Historical Continuities and Peculiarities," *Latinskaia Amerika*, April 1984, p. 7.
18. A. N. Glinkin, "A Systems Approach—Basis for a Deep Analysis of the Foreign Policy Activities of Latin American States," *Latinskaia Amerika*, p. 50; cited in Morris Rothenberg, "Latin America in Soviet Eyes," *Problems of Communism*, Vol. XXXII, No. 5 (September-October 1983), p. 16.
19. United States Department of State, *Soviet and East European Aid to the Third World, 1981* (Washington: February 1983), Table 12, p. 23.
20. Interview in *Latinskaia Amerika*, October 1985, p. 72.
21. Congressional Research Service, *The Soviet Union in the Third World*, p. 303.
22. K. A. Torkova, "Cooperation Expands," *Latinskaia Amerika*, April 1986, pp. 127-130.
23. TASS, January 29, 1986, in *FBIS Soviet Union*, Vol. III, January 30, 1986, pp. Q 1-2.
24. TASS, January 28, 1986, *FBIS Soviet Union*, Vol. III, January 29, 1986, p. K 1.
25. TASS, January 29, 1986, *FBIS Soviet Union*, Vol. III, January 30, 1986, pp. Q 1, 2.
26. See Jiri and Virginia Valenta, "Leninism in Grenada," *Problems of Communism*, Vol. XXXIII, Nov. 4 (July-August 1984), pp. 1-23.
27. Carlos Rafael Rodriguez, "The Struggle for Unity—An Important Direction of Our Policy," *Latinskaia Amerika*, July 1986, p. 8.

28. AFP (Paris), October 15, 1986 in *FBIS Soviet Union*, Vol. III, October 16, 1986, p. K 2.

SUGGESTED READINGS

Blasier, Cole. *The Giant's Rival: The USSR and Latin America*. Rev. ed. Pittsburgh: University of Pittsburgh Press, 1987.

Duncan, W. Raymond. "Soviet Power in Latin America: Success or Failure?" in Robert H. Donaldson, ed. *The Soviet Union in the Third World*. Boulder: Westview Press, 1981.

Evanson, Robert K. "Soviet Political Uses of Trade with Latin America," *Journal of InterAmerican Studies and World Affairs*, 27, 2 (Summer 1985).

MacFarlane, S. N. *Superpower Rivalry and Soviet Policy in the Caribbean Basin*. Ottawa: Canadian Institute for International Peace and Security, 1986.

Varas, Augusto. "Ideology and Politics in Latin American-Soviet Relations," *Problems of Communism*, XXXIII, 1 (Jan.-Feb. 1984).

TWELVE

SOVIET MILITARY STRATEGY
POWER PROJECTION AND FOREIGN INTELLIGENCE EFFORTS *

James Hansen

A paramount concern of the new Soviet leadership is the peacetime direction of its military and intelligence forces. These forces are particularly significant, as they underwrite Moscow's claim to superpower status.

Within the parameters of this chapter the following topics are discussed in this order: an overview of Soviet strategy; the global focus of this strategy; arms sales and military aid; forces for power projection (naval assets, merchant fleet, and airlift units); Soviet "vanguard" forces (*spetsnaz* special forces, airborne

*This chapter has been reviewed by US Government authorities to assist in eliminating any possible classified information. That review does not constitute endorsement of the views expressed here, which are mine alone and do not necessarily represent the official government position.

divisions, and naval infantry units); the KGB, the GRU military intelligence service, and the East European/Cuban intelligence services; a survey of Soviet extension of military forces outward over the past two decades; shortcomings in the Soviet effort to project power and influence abroad; and a summary assessment of these topics.

This discussion does not concern the throw-weight of ICBMs, nor space defense programs, nor even the buildup of Soviet/Warsaw Pact theater forces in Europe. Instead, it focuses on various dimensions of distant operations and indirect conflict, on forces which are now in use. The Soviets have developed these assets because they recognize the payoff of a war of manipulation (as currently practiced) as opposed to a war of annihilation (which neither side wishes to try). The Soviets have gained distinct advantages in the international arena from these factors: an unwavering belief in the use of force—whether direct or indirect; a coherent and thoroughly calculated approach to international relations; and the will and ability to manipulate opinions and governments.

Space limitations permit only a brief survey of the topics to be covered here, but this discussion may illustrate the many diverse components of Moscow's foreign policy and security strategy. One distinguishing characteristic of this strategy is the willingness to mobilize all relevant resources—both military and nonmilitary—to defend the Soviet state and advance its interests abroad.

MILITARY STRATEGY

According to the Soviet definition, military strategy is concerned with defining the strategic tasks of the armed forces; preparing the military, the economy, and the population for war; assessing potential enemies; and determining the size and composition of forces necessary to wage war.[1] Military strategy is developed by the High Command, the General Staff, and associated military and staff institutions.

According to the Soviets, military strategy and politics are closely interrelated. Military strategy is a direct instrument of politics, a reflection of the Communist Party's political strategy. The Soviet armed forces are charged with devising military strategy subject to overall Party guidance. This guidance comes primarily from the Defense Council, the top strategic decision-making body whose membership includes about ten of the highest Party and government officials. The proper fulfillment of political tasks by military strategy creates the "objective capabilities of achieving victory." Put another way, it is the duty of military strategy to devise the means for winning wars.[2]

Moscow's military strategy is underwritten by the sheer size of the Soviet armed forces. The USSR has always had a large standing force of conventional units, but in the 1960s and 1970s it made great strides in strategic missiles, giving it parity with the United States in strategic nuclear forces. The Soviets maintain a force of about 1,400 ICBMs, 62 modern nuclear submarines carrying strategic submarine-launched ballistic missiles (SLBMs), and about 180 heavy bombers with intercontinental missiles. The Soviets are now committed to a new generation of mobile ICBMs as well as new missile submarines and intercontinental bombers. The USSR has also flight tested different types of cruise missiles, which will eventually bring a new dimension to its strategic nuclear capability. In recent years, US and Soviet negotiators have been meeting at the START talks in Geneva to discuss limitations on these weapons and their US equivalents.

Soviet military strategy recognizes the requirement for coalition warfare against NATO in Europe should deterrence fail. As such, Moscow has devoted considerable energy toward building the Warsaw Treaty Organization (WTO) or Warsaw Pact into a strong military alliance as well as implementing a single strategic policy for the combined Warsaw Pact forces. As one illustration, Marshal Kulikov, Commander-in-Chief of the Warsaw Pact, has referred to his command as a unified combat formation. Since its inception in 1955, the Warsaw Pact has been headed by a Soviet marshal, has relied almost exclusively on Soviet-built weaponry, has adopted Soviet military doctrine, and has conducted a series of joint maneuvers designed to test military concepts in the field. The mainline Warsaw Pact nations include East Germany, Poland, Czechoslovakia, Hungary, and Bulgaria. Romania still belongs, but does not commit its units to Warsaw Pact field training exercises. With such forces as a backdrop, US and Soviet negotiators have been meeting in Vienna since 1973 to discuss troop reductions in Central Europe, without visible progress in the talks. Arms control negotiators have also been meeting at the INF (intermediate nuclear force) talks in Geneva to discuss possible reductions in the size of missile forces such as the Soviet SS-20 or the US Pershing II and ground-launched cruise missile. Agreement was reached in 1987.

The USSR's military strategy has had a rich historical development, and Soviet military thought has progressed through several distinct stages. These stages include the period of early development (1917-1941), the Great Patriotic War and the last years of Stalin's rule (1941-1953), the period which the Soviets term the "Revolution in Military Affairs," when the armed forces were equipped with nuclear weapons (1953-1959), the period of the strategic nuclear buildup (1960-1968), the years of development of a controlled conflict capability—with emphasis on conventional weapons and local wars (1969-1973), and the opening era of power projection (1974-1980). According to Harriet and William Scott, who defined these stages for Western students, there is ample continuity of Soviet military thought despite many changes since 1917. The political input has changed little since Lenin's time, and Soviet writers almost always invoke his name in discussing military topics. Even now, Soviet military textbooks emphasize the lessons of the Civil War and the Great Patriotic War, pointing out the applicability of such lessons today. Accordingly, Soviet strategy has usually evolved gradually—in degrees rather than in dramatic lurches.

The fundamental tenet of military strategy—preparing the USSR for the possibility of nuclear war—remains intact, although this strategy has been modified. Soviet writings on military strategy have responded to changes that have occurred during the late 1960s and 1970s. Specifically, strategy now recognizes that Soviet units must be prepared to fight with or without nuclear weapons, and also that the USSR must be prepared to "resist aggression" no matter "from where and from whom" it comes.[3] Accordingly, Soviet planners perceive a requirement to meet and outflank all potential enemies.

These modifications recognize a world which has changed radically over the past few decades. This is clear in the writing of Marshal Nikolai Ogarkov, former chief of the General Staff of the armed forces. He notes that a world war might start and be waged for a certain period of time with only conventional weapons, although widening military actions could lead to use of strategic nuclear weapons. He also notes that Soviet military strategy takes into account the possibility of local wars arising, the political nature of which is determined according to Leninist theses on just and unjust wars. "While supporting national-liberation wars, the Soviet Union decisively opposes the unleashing by imperialists of local wars...".[4] The 1983 *Military Encyclopedic Dictionary*, prepared under Marshal Ogarkov's general editorship, notes that Soviet military strategy is concerned with "protecting the revolutionary gains" of the Soviet people as well as the people of friendly socialist nations.[5] This definition suggests a broad requirement for the global role of Soviet forces. To judge from these military writings and from Soviet actions, it is clear that the Defense Council and General Staff have focused far beyond Soviet state frontiers as well as on a style of conflict that is indirect and oblique, yet carefully crafted and methodical, and bold and innovative, as well.

Western observers sometimes question the degree to which Soviet military policy is coherent and rational. In fact, the more one examines the correlation between Soviet leadership initiatives, doctrinal writings, field training exercises, and weapons deployed, the more evidence accumulates of a strong thread of coherence and rationality running though Soviet military policy and security planning. A number of topics can be forwarded to support this argument. The USSR is a nation of planners, and everything of importance in Soviet society is planned at the central levels. The military is governed by the Five Year Plans as well as its own long-term strategic guidelines drawn up by the General Staff, which has directorates to plan and project far into the future. A number of military institutes and research facilities assist Soviet military policy-makers in their planning. Moreover, there is a fusion of military and political leadership at the highest levels—in the Defense Council, for example, and in the Military-Industrial Commission (VPK), the coordinating body for the entire defense industry. As such, the Soviet Union's military planning is coordinated with the long-term directions of the Communist Party and government. Finally, the top figures in the Soviet defense establishment stay on the job for long periods of time, a factor which ensures continuity from one period to the next. In sum, although the USSR is forced to react to unexpected developments abroad and occasionally blunders, the weight of the evidence indicates that Soviet military policy is developed in a well thought-out manner. The general directions of Soviet strategy and force improvement are products of cumulative decisions taken at the all-Union level.

GLOBAL FOCUS

The USSR's armed forces have not always had a global focus. Until the 1960s, the Soviet military was unable to operate beyond its immediate peripheral areas. Khrushchev and his contemporaries recognized the importance of the Third World, but they were also acutely aware of Soviet weaknesses. During the late 1950s and 1960s, Soviet strategists began to design forces with a global orientation.

Soviet military thought recognizes the watershed period of the early 1970s, when the USSR attained strategic parity with the United States. The twenty-fourth Party Congress of 1971 focused on development of an assertive Soviet policy abroad. In 1972, a prominent military strategist, Colonel V. M. Kulish, along with other members of the Institute of World Economy and International Relations, noted that "greater importance is being attached to Soviet military presence in various regions of the world..." This presence would be "reinforced by an adequate level of strategic mobility for its armed forces."[6] In 1974, Marshal Grechko, Minister of Defense, noted that the historic function of the Soviet armed forces "is not restricted merely to their function in defending the Motherland and other socialist countries." He declared that the USSR supports national liberation struggles, and "resolutely resists imperialist aggression in whatever distant region of our planet it may appear."[7]

The 1970s were characterized by steady Soviet military growth as well as new challenges to the West—including the use of Cuban troops twice in Africa. The USSR augmented and finetuned its support of friendly governments as well as pro-Soviet insurgent groups struggling for power. Boris Ponomarev, then chief of the Central Committee's International Department, noted that "fighters for true freedom... have the right to depend on our solidarity and support." The decade was also noted by American defeat, impotence, doubt, and indecision. Taken together, these factors strongly suggested that the "correlation of forces" (a broadbased Soviet method for calculating the distribution of power) was tilting in Moscow's direction. Soviet commentators reminded America, "Sooner or later... (America) will be forced to accept the world as it is becoming," and concluded that "In general, it's time that the United States learned to behave more modestly," for "this would be better for America itself and for the whole world."[8]

This discussion now turns to the means to carry out Soviet policy in the international arena. These include: weapons sales and associated military aid; means for long-distance projection of military force; Soviet "vanguard" units for use in crisis situations; and the Soviet intelligence services. It concludes with a review of specific Soviet gains, some constraints in carrying out this policy, and an assessment of this overall effort.

ARMS SALES AND MILITARY AID

Military assistance is an integral part of the Soviet concept for expanding influence abroad, for it complements the USSR's projection of its own forces. Moscow has extended military aid to more than fifty less developed countries, with the most costly and sophisticated weapons going to the top recipients. The Soviets have become the world's leading supplier of weapons to developing nations, many of which have a revolutionary or anti-Western orientation.

The post-Brezhnev regimes have sharply increased this effort, and weapons sales and advisers abroad have reached new record levels. During 1982-1984, the USSR contracted for $24 billion worth of weapons to the Third World, about half this amount earmarked for Middle East countries. Significantly, this figure for three years outstrips the amount for the entire period of 1954-1975, $22 billion worth of arms.[9] Beginning in the late 1970s, the USSR exported new sophisticated weapons, apparently to obtain hard currency and to keep pace with Western arms suppliers. Specific weapons now available for export include the Su-25 FROGFOOT and MiG-29 FULCRUM combat aircraft, the Il-76 CANDID heavy transport, the SA-5 long-range SAM, the SS-21 tactical SSM, plus late-model artillery and armor.

The list of customers is growing, as some nations have recently received Soviet weaponry for the first time. Countries which have no ideological affinity with the USSR are attracted by low prices of Soviet equipment, concessional interest rates, lengthy repayment periods, and rapid delivery. In comparison with US arms sales, the Soviets deliver more fighter and bomber aircraft, tanks, antiaircraft guns, surface-to-air missiles, and artillery pieces—in short, those weapons with immediate combat potential.

Traditionally, the USSR has been a major supplier of the Mideast nations governed by regimes which are generally in line with Moscow's foreign policy. Libya and Syria are two key examples. The USSR has supplied these nations with the most advanced weapons, some not even available to members of the Warsaw Pact. In the late 1970s, the USSR sharply stepped up aid to sub-Saharan African countries: during 1979-1981, military aid to these nations outstripped aid to Mideast recipients. The leading clients have been Ethiopia, Angola, and Mozambique. Arms sales to this region emphasize quantity over sophistication, as many of the older weapons available have been taken from operational Soviet/Warsaw Pact units and refurbished.

The advisory program is a fundamental link in Soviet arms sales to developing nations, and the steady growth in Soviet military advisors abroad reflects ever-greater attention to the developing world. Starting from only several hundred advisors in the mid-1950s (mostly in the Mideast), the USSR had 3,600 in 16 countries by the mid-1960s. This figure doubled to 7,200 in the mid-1970s, and doubled again to about 16,000 by 1979. As of 1985, 24,000 Soviet military advisors were stationed in 30 nations.[10] This advisory program is conducted by the Tenth Chief Directorate of the General Staff.

Such an effort requires a correspondingly large training program based in the Warsaw Pact nations. Over the past 30 years, about 63,000 and 12,000 military men from developing nations have gone to the USSR and East European countries, respectively, for training. In recent years those countries sending the most trainees to the USSR and East Europe have been Mozambique, Nicaragua, Iraq, Afghanistan, Nigeria, Ethiopia, and Angola.[11]

FORCES FOR POWER PROJECTION

During the late 1970s, it became fashionable for US analysts to talk of Soviet "projection" capabilities. The term "power projection" is not defined in authoritative works such as the Joint Chiefs of Staff publication, *Dictionary of Military and Associated Terms*, the *NATO Glossary of Terms and Definitions*, nor in the Soviets' own reference book, *The Dictionary of Basic Military Terms*. US writers describing the Soviets generally use the term to mean the use of naval surface units, sealift and airlift forces, allied forces (such as the Cubans) to do the fighting, and overall Soviet control of the operation. The discussion now turns to specific equipment which the USSR has developed for this role.

The Soviets have enhanced these capabilities at a sure and steady pace, in evolutionary stages. Even now, these projection means are only at an intermediate stage. The USSR has made great strides recently, but there are areas where improvements are called for and anticipated. Within a decade, the USSR will have more capital ships and heavy transport aircraft and will be much better equipped to carry out distant operations than it is now.

The enhancement of the Soviet Navy into an ocean-going fleet has fulfilled many doctrinal requirements laid down by strategists. Between 1964 and 1976, the scale of Soviet out-of-area forward naval operations expanded by a factor of almost 14, from fewer than 4,000 ship-days annually to nearly 48,000.[12] Up to 1964, this fleet's only operations away from home waters were in the Norwegian Sea. By 1964, it had units in the Mediterranean, and by 1968 in the Indian Ocean. Soviet ships were seen in the Caribbean and off the West African coast in 1969, and the fleet expanded operations off West Africa in 1970. In 1979, Soviet ships began to operate in the South China Sea with regularity.

The new surface ships are ideally suited for operations in distant waters. They are larger than previous models, with better armament, and far greater endurance. These are listed below, along with the year of their commissioning:

- ROPUCHA-class landing ship (1975)
- KIEV-class V/STOL carrier (1976)
- BEREZINA-class fleet replenishment ship (1977)
- IVAN ROGOV-class landing dock (1978)
- KIROV-class cruiser (1980)
- OB'-class hospital ship (1980)
- SOVREMENNYY-class destroyer (1982)
- UDALOY-class destroyer (1982)
- SLAVA-class cruiser (1982)

Most of these models continue in production today. Some are optimized for ASW missions, but can also be used to project power in distant areas. Taken together, this fleet offers Moscow what one Western authority calls "an important new instrument of policy in peacetime."[13]

The Soviet merchant fleet (Morflot) has grown dramatically from an insignificant, coastal-oriented fleet in the 1950s to first in the world in ocean-going cargo ships. This fleet has made port calls in over 125 countries, a sure sign of its global reach. Today, it has over 1,700 ships, of which 350-400 are believed to be equipped and suitable for long-range military sealift. Morflot has developed ships with direct military applications: roll-on/roll-off (RO/RO), roll-on/float-off (RO/FLO), and lighter aboard ship (LASH) designs. The new ones have been built to military standards, with such features as chemical protection, increased endurance and service speeds, as well as advanced communications, navigation, and electronics. Several times the Soviets have rapidly adjusted Morflot assets from programmed commercial schedules to military support missions. Merchant ships could readily provide heavy-lift backup to Soviet/allied amphibious operations or arms-supply missions. In local combat in Africa during the 1970s, merchant ships delivered the overwhelming percentage of heavy weapons.[14]

The USSR also has the means for quick-response military aid, in the form of Military Transport Aviation (VTA). This fleet includes 55 An-22 COCK and nearly 300 Il-76 CANDID heavy transports (the current backbone of the airlift forces), as well as An-12 medium transports. These are being joined by the new An-124 CONDOR, with triple the payload of the Il-76.[15] On several recent occasions, the USSR has mounted "surge" airlifts to assist a client: in 1973 during the Yom Kippur War; in 1975-1976 during the Angolan conflict; in Ethiopia in 1977-1978; and Afghanistan in 1979-1980. Indeed, to a Soviet-backed client regime or movement fighting for its existence, the sight of an incoming Soviet transport aircraft is most reassuring, a tangible symbol of support.

The civilian airline, Aeroflot, can augment the military in any crisis. Aeroflot has about 1,400 medium- and long-range aircraft which could be pressed into service. This "civilian" airline—headed by a chief marshal of aviation—regularly supports Soviet forces twice a year during troop rotations to and from East Europe; it has also ferried Cuban troops to wars in Angola and Ethiopia.

"VANGUARD" FORCES

We now turn to *spetsnaz* (special forces), airborne, and naval infantry units. These are called "vanguard" forces, in view of their high degree of combat readiness, their role as leading elements of Soviet deployments abroad, and their qualitative superiority over other units. Moscow evidently sees these forces as trump cards to be played in local wars and crises around the Soviet periphery. Accordingly, they have been used to "show the flag," to demonstrate Soviet concern and involvement in regional conflicts, and to intervene in combat situations.

The USSR maintains the largest body of special forces in the world. Controlled by the GRU, they are apparently the best-trained troops in all the Soviet armed forces. Each of the 16 military districts (MDs) in the USSR, the four groups of forces in the forward area, and the four fleets reportedly has a *spetsnaz* ("special designations") brigade. Each brigade could field about 100 teams, each of which would comprise five to twelve men. In addition, every Soviet army has an independent *spetsnaz* company. As such, several thousand *spetsnaz* troops are ready for action in each theater of military operations (TVD) around the USSR.

These forces have demonstrated their punch in recent crises, both of which involved Soviet-sponsored changes of government and massive intervention of ground forces. During August 1968, *spetsnaz* forces ensured the success of the invasion of Czechoslovakia. The seizure of the Prague airport and other vital points was carried out by *spetsnaz* units acting under KGB orders. *Spetsnaz* troops arrested Alexander Dubcek and other liberals, who were dispatched to Moscow. These elite troops were instrumental in the overall success of the invasion which crushed the "Prague Spring" movement.

Spetsnaz troops played a similarly critical role in the invasion of Afghanistan. Working under the KGB's guidance, they provided the muscle to get rid of President Hafizullah Amin. In December 1979, they went to Amin's palace in Kabul; during a wild firefight, he was killed along with at least forty family members, friends, and staff. Other *spetsnaz* units had been placed throughout critical areas of the country long before the invasion. After Amin's death, Moscow replaced him with a more pliant puppet, Babrak Karmal, who had been waiting in the wings. According to Edward Luttwak, this spectacular operation proved that Moscow not only had "sledgehammers" in its tool kit, but "sharp knives" as well.[16]

Airborne units form the working core of Moscow's own rapid deployment forces. They are among the most competent and trusted troops, along with their *spetsnaz* cousins. The USSR maintains seven line airborne divisions, each with about 6,500 men. As such, the Soviets maintain about 45,500 airborne troops.

Airborne units have been tested repeatedly in combat in Afghanistan, and are highly visible actors during crises. As these units have sharpened their combat potential, Moscow has relied on them increasingly in tense situations. In October 1973, they nearly intervened in the Middle East in order to deter further Israeli advances. All seven line divisions were alerted; three were on the highest alert, with troops waiting at airfields with their weapons, ready to take off. The airborne divisions were alerted again during the Cyprus crisis of July 1974.[17]

Soviet Naval Infantry (SNI) makes up the third component of the "vanguard forces." This is a relatively small force, but it has raised its profile in recent years through gradual expansion and wide-ranging exercises. It has 16,000 troops, with about half this number stationed with the Pacific Ocean Fleet, and is continuing to grow. SNI is supported by amphibious ships, merchant ships, and—in recent years—large high-speed hovercraft.

SNI has also participated in local crises in the Third World. Typically, it has been used when Soviet policy makers have opted for showing the flag—a choice between doing nothing and sending in airborne divisions. Soviet amphibious units have appeared near the Middle East in 1973, off Africa in 1976 and 1978, in the South China Sea during the Vietnam-China border war in 1979, and in the Seychelles in the 1980s, when the local socialist government was beset by crises.[18]

SOVIET INTELLIGENCE SERVICES

The KGB and GRU are critical components of Moscow's foreign and security policy. Together they make up a giant intelligence establishment responsible for all facets of human-source collection, technical collection, and support for indirect warfare.

The KGB, or Committee for State Security, is the dominant service. Since 1982 it has been headed by Viktor Chebrikov, a Politburo member; its responsibilities include espionage, domestic counter-intelligence, border protection, and population control, as well as "active measures." The KGB has no counterpart in the West; the centralization of these diverse functions under a single body would not be possible in a democracy. The KGB's role and stature derive not only from its size and status, but also from the way Soviet leaders have used it as a political weapon and have given it unwavering support. Because of these factors, it is different from—and more potent than—intelligence and security services in other nations. It is the largest and arguably the most powerful intelligence system in the world.[19]

The KGB is represented abroad by its First Chief Directorate. This body has components which specialize in clandestine human-source networks, scientific and technical collection, counterintelligence abroad, the use of "illegal" agents (those posing as Westerners, not covered by overt, official Soviet status), as well as dissemination of the intelligence product.

The First Chief Directorate also conducts "active measures" (*aktivniye meropriyatiya*), a unique Russian term for a wide range of political and psychological actions designed to advance Soviet goals by distorting, manipulating, inflaming, and in some cases controlling Western public opinion. This term also includes overt or covert propaganda, subsidies to fronts, blackmail, forgeries, support for terrorists and insurgents, and sabotage in various forms. Active measures are intended to demoralize and erode power internally in the target countries, thereby helping to advance Soviet goals. In this area the KGB works harder, more consistently, and with greater resource commitment than does any other intelligence service anywhere. The Soviets perceive no sharp distinction between propaganda and action, political operations and military actions, or overt and covert actions.[20] This enhances the role of active measures as an adjunct to traditional methods of statecraft.

The First Chief Directorate's manpower is only a fraction of the total size of the KGB. The First Chief Directorate consists of about 20,000 officers.[21] Of this number, up to 5,000 are posted abroad, in virtually every official installation. This last number is only an estimate, but between 30-40 percent of all

Soviet officials stationed abroad are career intelligence officers.

A military intelligence service known as the GRU (Chief Intelligence Directorate) of the General Staff also operates abroad with a high profile. Headed by Army General Petr Ivashutin since 1963, this is a professional and generally effective service, staffed largely by military career officers who have completed postgraduate training. The GRU collects and evaluates mainly military information, but also scientific and technical information with military applications, as well as political and economic data which may influence foreign military perceptions and decisions. As such, there is substantial overlap with the KGB's collection operations.

The GRU's charter is much broader than that of other military intelligence services. It is much larger than any other MI service, with about 10,000 officers.[22] It is plausible that up to 2,500 GRU officers are posted abroad. The GRU maintains its own separate schools in and around Moscow for training "illegals", this program is comparable to the KGB's, but has no connection with the other service. The GRU oversees training of revolutionary, insurgent, and terrorist movements from Third World nations. The GRU also oversees operations of the intelligence directorates of the sixteen military districts (MDs) in the USSR, groups of forces in the forward area, and fleets; thus, it supervises the operations of 24 smaller intelligence bodies. Moreover, the GRU maintains its own technical collection directorates for signals intelligence and for space-based reconnaissance. Like the KGB, the GRU forwards its analytical product to the top leadership levels. As such, one could argue that the USSR maintains not only the world's most powerful intelligence organization (the KGB), but also the second most powerful as well—the GRU.

The several intelligence services of the East European countries and Cuba must also be considered as adjuncts to the KGB and GRU. Although these services are formally subordinated to their governments, they are directed and exploited by the Soviets.

Moscow is informed about every major aspect of their activities, and Russian advisers participate in planning their operations and assessing the results. No important decision is made without these advisers, and they also help to develop long-term collection directives which affect these services' operations. East European and Cuban intelligence officers attend training courses in Moscow, ensuring another form of Soviet control.[23]

These services can help the Soviets in intelligence collection, with operational leads, and through participation in active measures. As of 1980, the estimated manpower of the services of the Warsaw Pact countries (including Romania) and Cuba totaled 11,300 officers.[24] Of this total, perhaps one-fourth, or about 2,800, would be posted abroad.

OUTWARD REACH—A REVIEW OF THE PAST TWO DECADES

If one measures the number of troops stationed outside Soviet borders, one sees that the USSR has moved out from its traditional frontiers. Stemming from a treaty of friendship and cooperation with Mongolia in January 1966, the USSR has placed 75,000 troops there. Based on the Soviet/Warsaw Pact invasion of Czechoslovakia and the resulting status-of-forces agreement in October 1968, the USSR maintains 80,000 troops there. The USSR's 1978 treaty of friendship and cooperation with Afghanistan, the invasion a year later, and subsequent augmentation have resulted in at least 115,000 troops in that country. Thus the Defense Council has succeeded in putting 270,000 troops across Soviet frontiers. (This figure includes neither the buildup in the Soviet Kurile Islands, involving up to 14,000 troops, nor military advisory contingents stationed abroad; nor does it take into account the withdrawal of Soviet troops from Afghanistan, which began in May 1988.)[25]

These are backed up by diplomatic accomplishments. Since the early 1970s, the USSR has entered into treaties of friendship and cooperation with many developing nations. In recent years, signatory nations have included: Angola (1976), Mozambique (1977), Vietnam (1978), Ethiopia (1978), Afghanistan (1978), South Yemen (1979), Syria (1980), the Congo (1981), and Yemen (1984). These treaties formalize the "brotherly" relations of these nations with the USSR, and some contain provisions for security consultations and related assistance.

Some people—especially those with a benign view of recent events—would not find such facts alarming. Why should they? The military contingents may be explained away as "defensive" or for "occupation duties." Accordingly, this reasoning follows, they do not pose a credible threat to the United States. Likewise, some "experts" are quick to point out that the Soviets have been expelled from other developing countries. This semantical discussion illustrates that in international relations, perceptions are often at least as important as reality, and that the Soviets are well versed in shaping the perceptions which others have of them. The novice specialist in the field of Soviet studies must often choose between two differing interpretations of events. For example, was the Afghanistan invasion for "defensive" or "offensive" purposes? Is the blue-water Soviet Navy a "defensive" force (designed to counter the US fleet) or an "offensive" force (for power projection)? According to one Canadian expert, we are in an era of "psycho-strategy," in which the use of information, its dissemination, and its careful structuring to a variety of publics now becomes an extraordinarily important vehicle for a state.[26]

CONSTRAINTS AND SHORTCOMINGS

This review should not conclude with such a deterministic picture: a massive and growing army of elite troops, advisors, spies, and their accomplices and stooges on the march everywhere, bound to succeed in all revolutionary situations, and backed up by a supportive and bovine Soviet population. This picture screens out real constraints on Moscow's efforts abroad.

One should not take for granted that the Soviets, even with their formidable assets, will automatically achieve the results they desire. Recent history is replete with efforts by the super-powers to impose their influence on Third World nations, only later to discover the difficulty of the task or to have the result turn out to be the opposite of the original intention. It is even possible that both superpowers now wield less clout in the developing world than was earlier the case.

The USSR is discovering the difficulties of keeping a coalition of states working together in pursuit of a common goal. It is apparent that the Cuban population has become "war-weary" from Havana's long combat involvement in Africa. Moreover, important Soviet client states occasionally forge a semi-autonomous foreign policy; this has occurred with Iraq, for example—a major recipient of Soviet arms but one which has increasingly emphasized its own interests.

Some observers have concluded that the Soviets have often supplied poor, second-generation hardware, outmatched by that of the West, subject to maintenance problems and degraded combat performance. The Israeli walkover of the Syrian air force in 1982 stands as one dramatic example. The presence of Soviet advisors has not helped, and they are often quick to blame the recipient's armed forces for incompetence.

The Soviets are handicapped in efforts to extend influence abroad by their condescending attitude toward foreigners in general and toward blacks and Moslems in particular. Military training programs in the USSR have produced countless stories by trainees of outright racism and hostility as well as heavy-handed political indoctrination. In many areas of Africa and the Mideast where Soviet officials are present, this cultural fac-tor makes it hard for them to mount any effective "hearts and minds" program to accompany their other initiatives.

It remains a fair question whether Moscow has overextended itself abroad. The USSR and its allies are engaged in numerous counterinsurgency and pacification roles abroad: Afghanistan,

Ethiopia, Angola, Cambodia, and Nicaragua. Frequently on the wrong side of the "self-determination" issue, they are opposed by guerrilla groups which will not accept subjugation. Even Soviet defense planners must compete for resources, and there are other critical military tasks which have a more direct bearing on the security of the heartland. This dilemma will pose difficult choices for Moscow in the years ahead.

One must also wonder whether these efforts might someday "overload" Soviet society. Does the introspective Muscovite, for example, like what he hears about Afghanistan or South Yemen? Does the Politburo really trust the "jeans culture" generation to thrill in the glorification of "proletarian internationalism"? As we know, the opinion of the average Soviet citizen counts for nothing in foreign policy planning. But what about the long-term social effects of the Afghanistan war, after all the casualty reports are in and thousands of men may be hooked on drugs? And what about the long-term economic effects on the consumer sector of the economy? This is an unhealthy economy, demanding that Gorbachev devote the next several years to long-term systemic reform.

On the purely military side of the equation, Soviet projection forces need to be enhanced in some areas. The VTA air transport fleet still has a long way to go (figuratively) in its ability to generate a sustained, high-volume airlift to distant areas. It has no comparable experience in maintaining such an effort, such as the US did to and from Vietnam. Also, Soviet amphibious forces remain unimpressive by US standards. SNI is one of the smallest components of the armed forces, and still lacks high-performance airpower and heavy landing ships in significant numbers. Other Western experts have testified to problems in the rest of the Soviet Navy.

A major constraint is the ever-present possibility of a vigorous Western response to a Soviet-backed initiative. President Reagan has made this an article of faith, a policy which probably has complicated Soviet planning. Even during the late 1970s, other countries occasionally stepped forward when the US did not. The example of France's activist role in Africa comes to mind. In effect, Soviet strategists must always integrate the "response factor" in their assessments of the correlation of forces.

SUMMARY

At the risk of stating the obvious, maintenance of these military and intelligence ties to Soviet allies and to the Third World is demanding, and development of a potent intervention force can be expensive. Why might the new leadership in Moscow continue to emphasize forces for distant operations and low-intensity combat?

One possible reason is the standing requirement for Soviet forces to be prepared to conduct operations along any area of the USSR's periphery, at any level of hostilities. Moscow's global military strategy calls for units deployed along—and occasionally beyond—the USSR's borders, all the better to respond to "threats" from US and Chinese forces. Also, Soviet military thought places great emphasis on thorough preparations before hostilities begin. Seen in this manner only, Soviet forces based abroad are a hedge against the possibility of a two-front war and are intended to help buy the USSR added "security." Unfortunately, this "security" comes at the expense of neighboring nations, who see far more sinister designs or are victims of aggression.

Another plausible reason is Moscow's effort to develop and retain foreign markets against pessimistic forecasts for the Soviet domestic economy. The earlier forecast of Soviet oil shortages in the late 1980s comes to mind as one example. The Soviet economy is integrated with the fortunes of many noncommunist nations, and it is arguable that Moscow has shaped its military as a kind of long-term "insurance" to safeguard these ties to the outside world. Also, the possibility of disrupting the West's mineral supply (oil and precious metals) cannot be ignored. In this regard, the sustained Soviet effort to develop access to facilities along the African coastline and throughout the East warrants a close look. To an increasing degree, economic planning and strategic planning are intertwined.

Another reason is perhaps more obvious: attainment of an option to "swing" local conflicts in favor of the Soviet-backed client. The USSR's military might and means for indirect warfare have already "given history a push" by establishing friendly regimes. From Moscow's viewpoint, it is considered a "victory" when the client state begins to serve Soviet interests—whether political, economic, or strategic in nature. The Soviet means discussed have brought tangible results at a relatively modest cost, compared with strategic military programs.

Soviet foreign policy has not changed fundamentally in the recent past, and no such change is anticipated even during the early Gorbachev years. The two major goals remain: (1) defend the state, and (2) promote Moscow-style communism abroad. The spatial scale of Soviet pursuit of these objectives has expanded to cover most areas of the developing world that can aid the USSR in the future. Accordingly, the new leadership views its means of power projection and low-intensity warfare as essential supporting mechanisms for the Soviet state in the years to come.

As the USSR moves through the late 1980s, Gorbachev and his colleagues face several key dilemmas regarding the larger issues of Soviet military power and strategic policy. To what degree will the Soviets choose to continue the momentum of their improvements to conventional and long-range mobility forces? To what degree will they dare to reduce their formidable contingents along the Sino-Soviet border? To what degree will they commit themselves to largescale restructuring of the economic system while ensuring that the military gets what it says it needs? These questions will continue to pose hard choices for the Gorbachev leadership, and American students of this leadership will be challenged to discern the most plausible Soviet responses.

NOTES

1. US Department of Defense, *Soviet Military Power*, 1985 edition, p. 11.
2. John J. Dziak, *Soviet Perceptions of Military Doctrine and Military Power*, (New York: Crane Russak & Co., Inc., 1981), p. 30.
3. Harriet F. and William F. Scott, *The Armed Forces of the USSR* (Boulder, CO: Westview Press, 1979), p. 80.
4. Marshal N. V. Ogarkov, "Military Strategy," in Harriet F. and William F. Scott, *The Soviet Art of War* (Boulder, CO: Westview Press, 1982), p. 247. Marshal Ogarkov's article here is excerpted from his contribution to *Sovetskaya Voyennaya Entsiklopediya* (Soviet Military Encyclopedia), Volume 7 (Moscow: Voyenizdat, 1979).
5. *Voyenno-Entsiklopedicheskiy Slovar* (Military-Encyclopedic Dictionary) (Moscow: Voyenizdat, 1983), p. 712.
6. Cited in William F. Scott, "The USSR's Growing Global Mobility," *Air Force*, March 1977, p. 57.
7. Ibid., p. 57.
8. "Political Commentator's Opinion," *Izvestia*, January 13, 1980. Cited in *Current Digest of the Soviet Press*, February 13, 1980, p. 6.
9. Central Intelligence Agency, *Handbook of Economic Statistics, 1985*. CPAS 85-10001, September 1985, p. 15.
10. Department of Defense, op. cit., p. 114. Earlier numbers are taken from unclassified US Government studies and hearings, and are presented in James Hansen, *Correlation of Forces. Four Decades of Soviet Military Development* (New York: Praeger, 1987).
11. CIA (see note 9), pp 120-121.
12. James M. McConnell and Bradford Dismukes, "Soviet Diplomacy of Force in the Third World," *Problems of Communism*, Volume XXVIII, January-February 1979, p.

17. The 48,000 ship-days annually mean an average daily figure of over 130 ships operating out of Soviet waters.

13. Quote by Michael MccGwire in James Hansen, "Soviet Projection Forces—Their Status and Outlook," *Armed Forces Journal*, October 1981, p. 78.

14. Hansen, p. 81.

15. International Institute for Strategic Studies, *The Military Balance 1985-1986* (London: IISS, 1985), p. 24. See US Department of Defense, (see note 1), p. 80, for the reference to triple the payload of the I1-76.

16. See James Hansen, "Soviet Vanguard Forces—Spetsnaz," *National Defense*, March 1986. Luttwak's quote is from *The Pentagon and the Art of War* (New York: Simon and Schuster, 1985), p. 113.

17. See James Hansen, "Soviet Vanguard Forces—Airborne," *National Defense*, April 1986.

18. See James Hansen, "Soviet Vanguard Forces—Naval Infantry," *National Defense*, May 1986. This article was the third and last of the "Vanguard" series.

19. See Ladislav Bittman, *The KGB and Soviet Disinformation. An Insider's View* (McLean, VA: Pergammon-Brassey's, 1985). This is a thorough and well-documented look at the KGB. See also Thomas Polgar, *The KGB: An Instrument of Soviet Power* (McLean, VA: Association of Former Intelligence Officers, undated).

20. Bittman, p. 43.

21. Bittman, p. 18.

22. Bittman, p. 18. Better open-source information is available about the GRU than was the case just a few years ago. This service warrants serious study, in the same way that the KGB has drawn the attention of Western specialists.

23. Bittman, pp. 29-30.

24. Bittman, p. 33.

25. These figures of troop strength for units outside the

USSR are from US Department of Defense, (see note 1).

26. Brian Macdonald, ed., *The Grand Strategy of the Soviet Union* (Toronto: The Canadian Institute of Strategic Studies, 1984) p. 2. This original thesis was presented by John Starnes, former director-general of RCMP Security. This book is a compilation of papers presented at the Institute in late 1983. The high quality of these papers suggests that many American specialists on the USSR stand to learn a great deal from their Canadian counterparts.

SUGGESTED READINGS

Barron, John. *KGB Today: The Hidden Hand*. New York: Reader's Digest Press, 1983.

Hansen, James. *Correlation of Forces. Four Decades of Soviet Military Development*. New York: Praeger, 1987.

Jones, David R., ed. *Soviet Armed Forces Review Annual*. Volumes 4-8. Gulf Breeze, FL: Academic International Press, 1980-1985.

Kaplan, Stephen S. *Diplomacy of Power: Soviet Armed Forces as a Political Instrument*. Washington, D.C.: Brookings Institution, 1981.

Lee, William T. and Richard F. Starr. *Soviet Military Policy Since World War II*. Stanford, CA: Hoover Institution Press, 1986.

Luttwak, Edward N. *The Grand Strategy of the Soviet Union*. New York: St. Martin's Press, 1983.

Scott, Harriet Fast and William F. *The Armed Forces of the USSR*. Boulder, CO: Westview Press, 1979.

Starr, Richard F. *USSR Foreign Policies After Detente*. Stanford, CA: Hoover Institution Press, 1985.

US Department of Defense. *Soviet Military Power*. Washington, D.C.: USGPO, 1986.

CONTRIBUTORS

ROBERT K. EVANSON is Associate Professor of Political Science, University of Missouri, Kansas City. He is the author of a number of articles on Czechoslovakia and on Soviet foreign policy. Dr. Evanson holds a Ph.D from the University of Wisconsin, Madison.

ŠUMIT GANGULY is Assistant Professor of Political Science, Hunter College, City University of New York. He has published a number of articles on selected aspects of international affairs. Dr. Ganguly holds a Ph.D from the University of Illinois, Urbana, and was a postdoctoral fellow at Columbia University.

TROND GILBERG is Professor and Head of the Political Science Department, Pennsylvania State University, and Associate Director of the Penn State Slavic Center. He is the author of *The Soviet Communist Party and Scandinavian Communism* (1973), *Modernization in Romania since World War II* (1975), and a forthcoming volume on coalition strategies and tactics of Marxist parties. He has contributed chapters to numerous volumes on Soviet and East European politics and has published a number of related journal articles. Dr. Gilberg holds a Ph.D. from the University of Wisconsin, Madison.

JAMES HANSEN is a senior analyst at the Defense Intelligence Agency, US Department of Defense. He is the author of *Correlation of Forces* (1987) and has published a number of articles on military and intelligence matters. Mr. Hansen holds an MA from the University of Michigan.

ROGER E. KANET is Professor and Head of the Political Science Department, University of Illinois, Urbana. He is the editor or co-editor of *Soviet Foreign Policy in the 1980s* (1982), *Soviet Foreign Policy and East-West Relations* (1982), *Background to Crisis: Policy and Politics in Gierek's Poland* (1981), and *The Soviet Union and the Developing Nations* (1975), among others. He has also published more than eighty journal articles on various aspects of Soviet and East European foreign and domestic policies. Dr. Kanet holds a Ph.D. from Princeton University.

JOHN J. KARCH was a senior Foreign Service Officer, US Information Agency (USIA) until his retirement in February 1986. His last assignment was as public affairs adviser to the US delegation and western spokesman at the Mutual and Balanced Force Reduction Negotiations in Vienna. He also served with USIA in the USSR and several East European states. He is the author of a number of articles and book chapters. Dr. Karch holds a Ph.D. from American University.

DANIEL R. KEMPTON is Assistant Professor of Political Science at Northern Illinois University. He is completing doctoral studies in the Department of Political Science, University of Illinois, Urbana, where his doctoral dissertation focuses on Soviet policy toward national liberation movements in southern Africa.

ILPYONG J. KIM is Professor of Political Science, University of Connecticut. He is the author of *Communist Politics in North Korea* (1975) and *The Politics of Chinese Communism: Kiangsi under the Soviets* (1973) as well as a number of articles on China and North Korea in journals and books. Dr. Kim holds a Ph.D. from Columbia University.

DONALD W. KLEIN is Professor of Political Science, Tufts University. He is co-author of the two-volume *Biographic Directory of Chinese Communism, 1921-1965* (1971) and *Rebels and Bureaucrats: China's December 9ers* (1976), as well as numerous articles on Chinese domestic and foreign policies in journals and newspapers. He has also contributed chapters to several volumes on China. Dr. Klein holds a Ph.D. from Columbia University.

THOMAS W. ROBINSON is Director of the China Policy Project at the American Enterprise Institute and Adjunct Professor of National Security Studies, Georgetown University. He is the editor of *Forecasting in International Relations* (1978) and *The Cultural Revolution in China* (1971), to which he also contributed several chapters. He has also published many articles on China, the USSR, and international relations, and chapters to edited volumes and in scholarly journals. Dr. Robinson holds a Ph.D. from Columbia University.

MORRIS ROTHENBERG was Director of the Advanced International Studies Institute (New Hampshire). He served with the US Department of State from 1948-1974. He is the author of *Whither China: The View from the Kremlin* (1977), *The USSR and Africa* (1980), and co-author of *Soviet Penetration of Latin America* (1975), as well as a number of articles on Soviet foreign policy.

ALVIN Z. RUBINSTEIN is Professor of Political Science at the University of Pennsylvania and Senior Fellow, Foreign Policy Research Institute. He is the author of numerous books, including *Soviet Foreign Policy since World War II: Imperial and Global* (1985), *Soviet Policy Toward Turkey, Iran, and Afghanistan: The Dynamics of Influence* (1982), and *Red Star on the Nile: The Soviet-Egyptian Influence Relationship since the June War* (1977). He has edited or co-edited volumes on Soviet foreign policy, Sino-Soviet competition, and the Middle East. He has also contributed chapters to many edited collections and published a large number of articles in scholarly journals. Dr. Rubinstein holds a Ph.D. from the University of Pennsylvania.

ROLF H. W. THEEN is Professor of Political Science, Purdue University. He is the author of *Lenin: Genesis and Development of a Revolutionary* (1973), translator/editor of Nilolai Valentinov, *The Early Years of Lenin* (1969), and co-author of *Comparative*

Politics: An Introduction (1987). He has also published numerous journal articles on various aspects of Soviet politics. Dr. Theen holds a Ph.D. from Indiana University.

IVAN VOLGYES is Professor of Political Science and Special Projects Manager for the Institute for International Studies, University of Nebraska, Lincoln. He is the author of numerous books, including *Politics in Eastern Europe* (1986), *Hungary: A Nation of Contradictions* (1985), and *Political Socialization in the Soviet Navy* (1984). He has co-authored and co-edited a number of volumes on Soviet, East European, and comparative politics. Dr. Volgyes holds a Ph.D. from American University.

JANE SHAPIRO ZACEK is Director, Management Resources Project, jointly sponsored by the New York State Governor's Office of Employee Relations and the Rockefeller Institute of Government, State University of New York. She has co-edited several volumes on Soviet and East European politics, including *Politics and Participation under Communist Rule* (1983), *From the Cold War to Detente* (1976), and *Change and Adaptation in Soviet and East European Politics* (1976). She has also published a number of journal articles on these general topics. Dr. Zacek holds a Ph.D. from Columbia University.

INDEX